For Reference

Not to be taken from this room

Voting Rights in America

Books in the **Contemporary World Issues** series address vital issues in today's society such as genetic engineering, pollution, and biodiversity. Written by professional writers, scholars, and nonacademic experts, these books are authoritative, clearly written, up to date, and objective. They provide a good starting point for research by high school and college students, scholars, and general readers as well as by legislators, businesspeople, activists, and others.

Each book, carefully organized and easy to use, contains an overview of the subject, a detailed chronology, biographical sketches, facts and data and/or documents and other primary source material, a forum of authoritative perspective essays, annotated lists of print and nonprint resources, and an index.

Readers of books in the Contemporary World Issues series will find the information they need in order to have a better understanding of the social, political, environmental, and economic issues facing the world today.

Voting Rights in America

A REFERENCE HANDBOOK

Richard A. Glenn and Kyle L. Kreider

ABC-CLIO®

An Imprint of ABC-CLIO, LLC
Santa Barbara, California • Denver, Colorado

Library of Congress Cataloging-in-Publication Data

Names: Glenn, Richard A., author. | Kreider, Kyle L., author.
Title: Voting rights in America : a reference handbook / Richard A. Glenn and Kyle L. Kreider.
Description: Santa Barbara : ABC-CLIO, [2020] | Series: Contemporary world issues | Includes bibliographical references and index.
Identifiers: LCCN 2020020765 (print) | LCCN 2020020766 (ebook) | ISBN 9781440870927 (hardcover) | ISBN 9781440870934 (ebook)
Subjects: LCSH: Suffrage—United States—History.
Classification: LCC JF831 .G54 2020 (print) | LCC JF831 (ebook) | DDC 324.6/20973—dc23
LC record available at https://lccn.loc.gov/2020020765
LC ebook record available at https://lccn.loc.gov/2020020766

ISBN: 978-1-4408-7092-7 (print)
    978-1-4408-7093-4 (ebook)

24 23 22 21 20   1 2 3 4 5

This book is also available as an eBook.

ABC-CLIO
An Imprint of ABC-CLIO, LLC

ABC-CLIO, LLC
147 Castilian Drive
Santa Barbara, California 93117
www.abc-clio.com

This book is printed on acid-free paper ∞

Manufactured in the United States of America

Contents

Representative government is a fundamental principle of the American political system. Without free, fair, and regularly scheduled elections—in which people select those who govern them—representative government is not possible. The right to vote is the ability to confer, withhold, or withdraw consent by casting votes in elections where representatives are chosen and to have those votes properly counted; it is essential to democratic governance.

The principles of representative government and popular consent have deep roots in the American experience. In the 1760s, "no taxation without representation" was the political cry of the thirteen colonies in expressing their grievances against the Crown and English Parliament. A decade later, the Declaration of Independence famously declared, "Governments are instituted among Men, deriving their just powers from the consent of the governed." In the Gettysburg Address, President Abraham Lincoln talked about "government of the people, by the people, and for the people." In 1873, Susan B. Anthony, criticizing laws that prohibited women from voting, noted, "To [women], this government has no just powers derived from the consent of the governed." Representative government was the motivation for Martin Luther King Jr.'s "Give us the Ballot" speech in 1957. These principles have even been offered as justification for war, numerous presidents having sent soldiers to foreign countries to rid those countries of autocratic leaders and restore control to the people.

All government is in the free consent of the people is a powerful idea. And it is not achievable without elections and the right to vote, the crucial mechanisms by which the people determine who will govern. Elections thus bestow upon government a legitimacy that is otherwise unattainable.

Elections in the United States are seemingly ever-present, the sheer number and frequency often mindboggling to all but the most active political participants. Because the United States employs a federal structure, elections occur at three separate levels—national, state, and local. No year passes without some election, and most years have elections at all levels.

Congressional elections occur on the Tuesday following the first Monday in November in even-numbered years. Terms in the House of Representatives are only two years in length; as such, there are 435 House elections alone every other year. In the Senate, terms are six years in length, so roughly thirty-three Senate elections happen every other year. Presidential elections are conducted every four years, but always on the same day as congressional elections.

Elections for state and local offices are even more numerous. Every year, voters cast ballots for governors, state legislators, state judges, and a host of local candidates—county commissioners, mayors, city councilmembers, district attorneys, sheriffs, fire wardens, coroners, prothonotaries, registers of wills, judges, court clerks, justices of the peace, and so forth. (Even the modern-day political insult, "You could not be elected dogcatcher," rings somewhat hollow. At least up until the middle of the twentieth century, dogcatcher was an elected position in many small jurisdictions. As recently as 2018, voters in Duxbury, Vermont, reelected Zeb Towne dogcatcher, the only remaining elected dogcatcher in the country. Later that year, however, a lawyer for the Vermont League of Cities and Towns informed Duxbury that dogcatcher was not an official elected position under Vermont law. Towne was then appointed to the post; the vote was unanimous.)

Moreover, these are just the standard elections; they do not include primaries and special elections, which are just as common at the national, state, and local levels. Nor does this list include direct-democracy elections—ballot measures that permit voters to enact laws, approve or reject laws proposed by legislative bodies, or remove state officials from office.

Elections are the hallmark of democracy because they are the primary means by which political power is acquired, retained, and lost. The exercise of citizens' voting rights in elections is thus crucial for the success of representative government. Even the appearance of the right to vote is important: Witness the authoritarian regimes that often hold elections—sham, though they may be—in an attempt to convey the appearance upon their exercise of political power. Dictators, too, crave political legitimacy.

It may seem remarkable then that, even in the United States, the right to vote—called suffrage or the franchise—does not, and has never, applied universally across the population. Unlike freedom of speech and the free exercise of religion, for example, which are civil *liberties* and extend to all persons, voting is a civil *right*, a privilege conferred selectively upon citizens by governments. One perceptive commentator writes:

> That is why access to the ballot . . . was not always discussed in terms of a "right" at all. Rather, people spoke of suffrage or the franchise in terms of the *privilege* of voting. Voting was not seen as concomitant with one's humanity or even with citizenship, as was true with many other rights. Instead, access to the ballot was conferred on, or given to, an individual by those who already possessed it. The Declaration of Independence spoke of individuals as having been "endowed by their Creator with certain unalienable Rights, that among these are Life, Liberty, and the pursuit of Happiness." It did not mention voting. Being able to vote was instead a sign of a special kind of

citizenship. Having the franchise was like flying first class or holding membership in an exclusive club. (Stephenson 2004, xx–xxi)

For most of U.S. history, that privilege of voting has been denied to certain people for a variety of reasons. Those who did not own property were excluded because they had no legitimate stake in society. Individuals under a certain age were prevented because they were too young to formulate opinions. Blacks were disallowed because they were not citizens; immigrants because of their divided loyalties; women because they were too delicate and too busy caring for their husbands, children, and homes; felons because they had broken the social contract and forfeited their right to participate in civil society; and so forth.

In chapter 1, we trace the history of voting rights in the American experience, from the colonial period through the twentieth century. We identify the cultural changes, political movements, and legal activities that defined the expansion of the electorate. It is the story of the journey, arguably yet completed, from property to democracy.

Chapter 2 examines more recent problems and controversies related to voting rights, including felon disenfranchisement laws, voter ID requirements, voter registration reform, voter roll purging, voting reforms, partisan and racial gerrymandering, and the Electoral College. This chapter discusses proposed solutions, where appropriate.

Chapter 3 is a collection of ten original essays on various topics related to voting rights, written by scholars and other invested individuals.

The next four chapters are supplementary. Chapter 4 contains profiles on key individuals and organizations in the voting rights story. Chapter 5 provides data on voting and voting rights and excerpts from documents related to voting rights that are discussed in the first three chapters. Chapter 6 includes an annotated bibliography of all noncase sources; a table of cases, with full citations, of those judicial decisions mentioned in the preceding chapters; and a guide to voting and voting rights sources available on the Internet. And chapter 7 is a chronology of important voting rights events. The book concludes with a glossary, containing definitions of keywords that can be found in the text and other terms that the reader may come across when researching this topic.

A Note on Sources

Of the many works we consulted, particularly in chapter 1, several proved invaluable. Kirk Porter's *A History of Suffrage in the United States* (1918) and Chilton Williamson's *American Suffrage from Property to Democracy, 1760–1860* (1960) were essential reading for understanding voting rights in the colonial and early national periods. Alexander Keyssar's *The Right to Vote: The Contested History of Democracy in the United States* (2000) is the modern-day standard for scholarship on voting rights. No single volume is more thorough. The sixty-three-page appendix assembles twenty tables that provide a factual skeleton of the evolution of the franchise in the United States; we profited greatly from this compilation of state suffrage laws. And *The Right to Vote: Rights and Liberties under the Law* (2004) by Donald Grier Stephenson Jr. does a marvelous job of explaining the interplay of the elements, forces, and factors that directed the development of voting rights in the United States. If we drew from these wells too often, the reason is their exceptional scholarship.

This book was made possible only through the assistance of a number of people. To each, we offer sincere thanks.

Millersville University and Wilkes University supported this work by granting us sabbaticals, and colleagues took on additional responsibilities during our absences. At Millersville University, Adam B. Lawrence, associate professor of government, assumed department chair duties. At Wilkes University, Paul Riggs, dean of the College of Arts, Humanities, and Social Sciences, encouraged the project, and Robert Tuttle, professor of sociology, fulfilled division chair obligations.

Lianna Souza, secretary in the Department of Government and Political Affairs at Millersville University, and Andrea Rizzo, office assistant in the Division of Behavioral and Social Sciences at Wilkes University, provided clerical support.

D. Grier Stephenson, professor of government emeritus at Franklin and Marshall College, offered sound advice and welcomed encouragement.

Ruth Baltozer read parts of the work and proposed editorial suggestions.

Catherine M. Lafuente, ABC-CLIO's acquisitions editor, and Robin Tutt, ABC-CLIO's development editor, provided insightful comments and prompt responses to our inquiries.

Of course, even with all this help, we alone are responsible for errors of fact and interpretation.

Our families merit the most thanks.

RAG: My wife, Lorena, has far more patience and grace and understanding than I deserve. My sons, Ryan and Andrew, make fatherhood a joy.

KLK: My wife, Susanne, has been a beacon of support, love, and comfort during the writing process. My daughter, Kathryn, and son, Benjamin, are the best children anyone can ask for and provide endless love and laughter. My wife and children ground me and are constant reminders of what is important in life.

Voting Rights in America

Introduction

In a free country, no right is more precious than that of having a voice in the election of those who make the law. This chapter traces the history of voting rights in America. That history has not been characterized "by a smooth and inexorable progress toward universal political participation. It has instead been much messier, littered with periods of both expansion and retraction of the franchise with respect to many groups of potential voters" (Hayden 2002, 819).

We begin with an overview of voting rights in England and its American colonies through the revolutionary period. We then discuss the suffrage debates at the constitutional convention and during the ratification period. Next, we turn to voting rights in the United States, between the birth of the Republic and the mid-eighteenth century, emphasizing the forces of expansion that lead to near-universal adult white male suffrage by the outset of the Civil War. We then examine the struggles of specific groups—blacks and women primarily but also others—to earn and enjoy the franchise between the Civil War and World War I. Finally, we consider the long, slow march to near-universal adult suffrage that defined the twentieth century.

A suffragette campaign for the right to vote for women at a parade in 1914. What began in upstate New York in 1848 morphed into the largest mass movement for suffrage in the nation's history. In 1860, women could not vote in any state or territory; by 1920, the Constitution prohibited states from denying the right to vote based on sex. (Library of Congress)

Voting Rights in England and the American Colonies through the Revolutionary Period

While the idea that government's legitimacy is predicated upon popular consent has antecedents that reach back to ancient times, disagreements about the identity of those entitled to participate in the compact have long existed.

The "Forty-Shilling Freeholders"

In England, prior to the fifteenth century, it is probable that all free inhabitant householders voted and that the only parliamentary qualification was residency. But in 1430, Parliament, believing that elections had been crowded "by persons of low estate, and that confusion had thereby resulted," limited its electors to "forty-shilling freeholders," those who owned property worth forty shillings a year in rental value or income, or the lawful or customary equivalents. Implicit in English suffrage was the belief that so long as property owners directly paid the bulk of public taxes it was not unequitable or unjust to confine parliamentary elections to them (Williamson 1960, 5–6).

Limiting the franchise to freeholders, however, may have been broader in practice than it appeared, the term "freehold" apparently applicable to many types of property, including annuities, rents, dowers of wives, and pews in churches (Seymour 2017, 10–11). Regardless, the Act of 1430 clearly marked the beginning of a property requirement for voting that had not previously existed in English law. Of special interest, this limitation was irrespective of the sex of the property owner, thus permitting—though it occurred rarely—unmarried women or widows to vote in parliamentary elections.

The Debates at Putney: Property and Politics

In 1646, England's first civil war concluded with the Parliamentarians (supporters of Parliament) victorious over the Royalists (backers of King Charles I). The following year, Parliament attempted to disband the parliamentary army without making satisfactory provisions for the troops or for the political rights of the English people. The army mutinied. Some within the army, a moderate faction of officers from the landed gentry known as the "Grandees," drafted a "Declaration of the Army," which insisted on modest demands for parliamentary reform prior to the "restoration of the troops to obedience." This declaration did not satisfy the more radical elements of the army, rank-and-file soldiers known as the "Levelers" or "Agitators," who countered with the egalitarian "Agreement of the People," which demanded that all men be made politically "level." These conflicting positions led to a grand debate within the General Council of the Parliamentary Army, held at Putney in the fall of 1647. Much of the debate centered around whether suffrage should be limited to property holders, and evidenced a clash between economic and political self-interest and revolutionary principles (Mason and Leach 1959, 4–7; Mason 1965, 22–24; Stephenson 2004, 34–40).

While both sides agreed that civil government had to be based on consent, they disagreed over the identity of those entitled to consent. The Grandees, led by Oliver Cromwell and Henry Ireton, favored a narrow franchise, insisting that only property owners—those with a permanent interest or stake in society—be permitted to vote. In early English usage, the word "franchise" meant an entitlement that government could withhold, grant, or withdraw at its pleasure. To permit the unpropertied to vote, they argued, would enthrone the power to legislate property out of existence. By contrast, the Levelers favored a broad franchise, believing that the right to vote did not derive from property but was inherent in all freeborn Englishmen. Thomas Rainboro summarized the Leveler's position simply: "[E]very man that is to live under a Government ought first by his own consent to put himself under that Government" (Mason 1965, 23).

Neither side succeeded in convincing the other. The debates did not lead to an immediate expansion of the franchise. Nevertheless, "[t]o one extent or another, every voting rights debate for more than 200 years afterwards echoed the debates at Putney" (Stephenson 2004, 35). The debate in the American colonies was no exception.

The Case for Property Restrictions

Limiting the franchise to property owners has been justified on multiple grounds (Williamson 1960, 5–6; Keyssar 2000, 5–13; Stephenson 2004, 39–40). First, those who possessed property had a common interest and personal attachment in the policies of the state, particularly taxation. Landownership fostered stability, good character, and respect for the personal and property rights of others.

Second, property holders possessed sufficient independence, whereas those dependent upon others for their domicile or livelihood were subject to undue electoral pressures. As William Blackstone (1872, 170) wrote: "The true reason of requiring any qualification with regard to property in voters is to exclude such persons as are in so mean a situation as to be esteemed to have no will of their own." If tenants had votes, they would be tempted to dispose of them under the undue influence of their landlords. Urban working people would be susceptible to the blandishments and threats of their employers and so forth.

Third, those without property were incapable of appreciating the utility of it; allowing them to vote would thus threaten property interests. Because it was likely that in future times the landless would outnumber the landed, the propertied feared that if the propertyless were permitted to vote they might unite under the influence of their common situation and elect lawmakers hostile to property rights. This argument—men without property will have too much influence—is, of course, wholly contradictory to the "no will of their own" argument (Keyssar 2000, 10–11).

Fourth, property ownership conveyed competence. In a world where economic opportunities were believed to abound, the inability of a person to acquire property was perceived as an indication of incompetence.

The Colonial Experience

Given that the staple of English suffrage was the restriction on voting to adult property-owning males, it is not surprising that suffrage in America followed suit. Colonial assemblies mirrored that with which they were familiar and for the same reasons. The first representative assembly in America convened in Jamestown, Virginia, on July 30, 1619. Membership in its lower house was composed of twenty-two burgesses elected by the free, white, male, *property-owning* inhabitants of the towns and boroughs of the colony. (Colonists typically did not vote for their governors or members of the upper houses of their colonial assemblies, both of whom were appointed by the Crown.)

By the American Revolution, each of the thirteen colonies had a property requirement. But aside from this imperial expectation that the franchise be limited to freeholders, each colony decided the specifics of the property requirement. Some colonies extended suffrage based on the amount of property (measured in acres); others did so on the value of the property; and still others on the income the property produced or taxes paid. Table 1.1 (adapted from Porter 1918, 12, and Stephenson 2004, 43) offers a general summary of property qualifications just before the Revolutionary War.

Georgia, North Carolina, and Virginia demanded a certain acreage. New Hampshire, New York, and Rhode Island insisted on property worth a specified monetary value, or in Rhode Island's situation, yielding a specific annual income. The remaining seven colonies—Pennsylvania, Delaware, Maryland, New Jersey, Connecticut, Massachusetts, and South Carolina—required acreage, land income, other property, or tax payments. Table 1.1 makes clear that the colonies were expanding on the concept of "stake in society" that had

Table 1.1   Property Qualifications for Voting Just before the Revolutionary War

Colony	Real Estate Required	Alternative
Acreage		
Georgia	50 acres	None
North Carolina	50 acres	None
Virginia	50 acres vacant, or 25 acres cultivated, and a house 12 x 12, or a town lot and house 12 x 12	None
Value		
New Hampshire	Worth 50 pounds	None
New York	Worth 40 pounds	None
Rhode Island	Worth 40 pounds, or yielding 40 shillings annual income	None
Other Than Acreage or Value		
Connecticut	Yielding 40 shillings annual income	Other property worth 40 pounds
Delaware	50 acres (12 cleared)	Other property worth 40 pounds
Maryland	50 acres	Other property worth 40 pounds
Massachusetts	Yielding 40 shillings annual income	Other property worth 40 pounds
New Jersey	100 acres	Some real estate and personal property worth 50 pounds
Pennsylvania	50 acres	Other property worth 50 pounds
South Carolina	100 acres on which taxes are paid, or town house or lot worth 60 pounds on which taxes are paid	Payment of 10 shillings in taxes

for centuries limited the franchise to landowners. By the mid-1770s, that "stake" could be something other than land, most notably personal property or payment of taxes.

Though property remained the most important qualification for voting, it was not the only one.

Six colonies limited the franchise to those who had reached the age of twenty-one. Some made English citizenship a pre-condition; others instituted residency requirements; still others assessed a poll tax. Many colonies expressly denied suffrage to servants, paupers, women, nonnaturalized aliens, mulattoes, and Native Americans. Slaves could not vote in any colony. In several Southern colonies, even free blacks were prohibited from casting a ballot. In New England, moral qualifications were prominent, and voters were sometimes compelled to show proof of "good character." Disenfranchisement on religious grounds was also common: Catholics could not vote in five colonies, and Jews were barred in four. South Carolina insisted that voters acknowledge the being of God and believe in a future state of rewards and punishments. In many instances, no reasons were provided for why so many people could not vote, the reasons presumably obvious.

A continuing debate among historians is the extent of the franchise. The property-of-some-sort requirement clearly limited the pool of voters, though historians disagree on the breadth of that limitation. Some maintain that property requirements prevented most white males from voting (Beard 1913, 71). Others believe that "the diffusion of real and personal property was so great as to render the property tests for voting much less restrictive than they appear to be" (Williamson 1960, 22). More recent scholarship suggests that by the mid-1770s less than 60 percent of the adult white male population was eligible to vote. Even so, "[o]n the whole, the franchise was far more widespread than it was in England" (Keyssar 2000, 7).

A brief note about voting procedures: It was not uncommon in colonial America for elections to be held viva voce—by public voice votes. "As each freeholder came before the sheriff, his name was called out in a loud voice, and the sheriff inquired how he would vote. The freeholder replied by giving the name of his preference. The appropriate clerk then wrote down the voter's name, the sheriff announced it as enrolled, and often the candidate for whom he had voted arose, bowed, and publicly thanked him" (Sydnor 1962, 29). A tally sheet indicated who was ahead and who was trailing; in close elections, each side feverishly sought to round up additional voters to poll on the "right" side. Viva voce differs greatly from the modern experience of voting, in which a voter's choice is anonymous, but it seemingly fit well with the theory of the freehold, which assumed an electorate made up of voters independent of electoral pressures. Yet, on another level, viva voce and the principle of the freehold are at odds. "It takes barely a moment's reflection to realize that few individuals, then or now, are truly independent and not subject to another's influence, whether that influence be familial, social, economic, political, or intellectual" (Stephenson 2004, 49).

The years between 1763 and 1783 marked "the turning point in the conscious democratization of ideas about the suffrage" and in the "actual liberalization" of suffrage laws (Williamson 1960, 76). The revolutionary fervor of that period was sparked by Britain's insistence that it could levy taxes upon the colonists though denying to them representation in Parliament. The colonists objected to "taxation without representation," challenging Parliament's right to rule the colonies. But the American Revolution was far more than a generic dissatisfaction with taxes; it was really about the only legitimate source of governmental authority. As Thomas Jefferson noted in the Declaration of Independence: "Governments are instituted among Men, deriving their just Powers from the Consent of the Governed." Of course, if government may exercise power only with the consent of the governed—and voting is the means by which individuals confer, withhold, or withdraw consent—then even a franchise limited to adult white male freeholders is difficult to justify. By giving voice to a new set of arguments for extending the franchise beyond the propertied, the American Revolution marked the beginning of a new era in the history of voting.

The Declaration of Independence transferred sovereignty from the Crown to the states (the former colonies). The formation of legally constituted state governments was a strategic move in the revolutionary process. Between 1776 and 1780, all states except two adopted new written constitutions. (In Rhode Island and Connecticut, the old charters, save for the royal connections, were regarded as acceptable frames of government; they continued to serve well into the nineteenth century.) In creating these new governments, states were compelled to rethink suffrage requirements.

The Case against Property Restrictions

Some of the arguments for extending the franchise to the propertyless had been suggested centuries prior; others were unique to the revolutionary period. First, it made little sense to prate about "consent of the governed" if your own governments were not so constituted. Many of the state constitutions drafted during these years emphasized this link between popular consent and governmental legitimacy.

Second, voting was a "natural right" inherent in individuals rather than property. Benjamin Franklin thought that any other conclusion was ridiculous:

> Today a man owns a jackass worth fifty dollars and he is entitled to vote; but before the next election the jackass dies. The man in the meantime has become more experienced, his knowledge of the principles of government, and his acquaintance with mankind, are more extensive, and he is therefore better qualified to make a proper selection of rulers—but the jackass is dead and the man cannot vote. Now gentlemen, pray inform me, in whom is the right of suffrage? In the man or in the jackass? (Waldman 2016, 15)

This rhetorically powerful idea—voting as a natural right—had at least three advantages in late–eighteenth-century America: (1) it "fit" with the Lockean political theory that had become popular among the Americans; (2) it had a clear antimonarchial thrust, at a time when monarchies were being questioned; and

(3) it was "resonant and fresh . . . welcome as well as liberating" (Keyssar 2000, 12). Support for this idea was not universal, even during the revolutionary period. "No taxation without representation" was a far more valuable rallying cry than a public policy pronouncement, and many prominent political leaders feared that if voting were acknowledged to be a "natural right," it would be difficult to deny the vote to women, blacks, children, aliens, and others historically deemed unworthy of the ballot.

Third, expanding the franchise had the potential to generate more support for the Revolution and attract more soldiers for the Revolutionary War. If the Revolution were perceived simply as a grievance by freeholders over voting rights, those without voting rights would be less likely to support it. Moreover, if the Revolution were to be successful, men were going to be needed to do the fighting. On the shoulders of these soldiers and militiamen, disproportionately young and unlikely to meet the property qualification for voting, would rest the burden of combat. Just as Cromwell's men had demanded the right to vote, colonials of military age demanded "the same right for the same reason" (Williamson 1960, 80). Though occurring after the Revolutionary War, an incident in Pennsylvania illustrates this connection between military service and suffrage. In a 1783 election, supervisors attempted to turn away a group of soldiers because they had "no will of their own." One soldier replied that the state had not objected to their fighting and "now you have to our voting. This is not just; we have fought for the right of voting & we will now exercise it." The reporter of this incident concluded, "It was not possible to reply to such an argument" (Williamson 1960, 133).

The Revolution's Effect

The Revolution had only a slight immediate effect on suffrage. Table 1.2 (adapted from Porter 1918, 13, and Stephenson 2004, 52) offers a general summary of property qualifications just after the Revolutionary War. Only two states, North

Table 1.2   Property Qualifications for Voting Just after the Revolutionary War

State	Real Estate Required	Alternative
Acreage		
North Carolina	50 acres	None
Virginia	50 acres vacant, or 25 acres cultivated, and a house 12 x 12, or a town lot and house 12 x 12	None
Value		
Rhode Island	Worth 40 pounds, or yielding 40 shillings annual income	None
New York	Worth 20 pounds, or yielding 40 shillings annual income, and payment of state tax	None
Other Than Acreage or Value		
Connecticut	Yielding 40 shillings annual income	Other property worth 40 pounds
Delaware	50 acres (12 cleared)	Other property worth 40 pounds
Maryland	50 acres	30 pounds in money
Massachusetts	Yielding 30 pounds annual income	Other property worth 60 pounds
South Carolina	50 acres, or a town lot	Payment of a tax equal to a tax on 50 acres
No Real Estate Required		
Georgia	Property valued at 10 pounds	None
New Hampshire	Payment of poll tax	None
New Jersey	50 pounds proclamation money	None
Pennsylvania	Payment of public taxes	None

Carolina and Virginia, insisted upon a certain acreage. Two others, Rhode Island and New York, demanded real estate worth or yielding a specific amount. The remaining nine allowed voting based on acreage, land income, other property, or tax payments. So, while "property" was still important, land ownership was less so. By the late 1780s, the real accomplishment was the breakdown of the old English principle that suffrage should only go with ownership of real estate. This breakdown took place in two steps: first, the substitution of personal property for real estate; and second, the substitution of taxpaying for property of any kind (Porter 1918, 11). The result was a minimally broader electorate.

But what of other suffrage limitations? Remarkably, aside from age—twenty-one was universally proscribed—the revolutionary constitutions were relatively free of restrictions on voting other than those concerning property. In practice, a property or taxpaying test was itself sufficiently strict to render other limitations unnecessary.

> When a man owned property or paid state taxes it was frequently considered quite unnecessary even to limit the term of residence. There was practically no race problem to deal with, for the northern states did not concern themselves greatly about the few free negroes who might dwell in the state, and in the South it was not necessary specifically to exclude negroes. The foreigner was not yet a problem. . . .
>
> Where sex was not mentioned, and it seldom was except incidentally, the presumption of course was that only men could vote. . . . Such undesirable persons as paupers, idiots, the insane, etc., were practically excluded by the property test, and the need for specifically disqualifying them did not appear until the property test was gone. Exclusion for a crime was not a general practice until somewhat later and possibly for the same reason. Relatively few criminals would be found among the property owners and taxpayers. (Porter 1918, 20–21)

The Suffrage Debates at the Constitutional Convention: 1787

Between the end of the Revolution and 1787, no state separated property from voting. (The Articles of Confederation was silent on voting rights. Just as suffrage in colonial America had been determined by each colony, suffrage under the Articles remained exclusively a state prerogative. The one exception to that was voting rights in the Northwest Territory, federal land north and west of the Ohio River to the Mississippi River that today includes Ohio, Indiana, Illinois, Michigan, and Wisconsin. In 1787, the confederal Congress passed the Northwest Ordinance, which limited the franchise in the Northwest Territory to citizens and aliens who own fifty acres of land. The U.S. Congress reaffirmed the Ordinance in 1789.) By the Constitutional Convention, four states mandated that voters be landowners, while nine linked suffrage to financial circumstances, by limiting the franchise to those who owned personal property, possessed suitable income, or paid taxes. The diversity among the states underscored the centuries-old debate about the relationship between property and politics. Like the states they represented, the delegates to the Constitutional Convention were divided.

The Constitutional Convention

The delegates were not divided on the importance of property rights. Virtually all belonging to the propertied class, they believed that the chief end, the "first object," of government was the protection of property. James Madison, who set the agenda for the Convention, did not think "life, liberty, and the pursuit of happiness" were possible without property. In 1789, after ratification, he suggested that the following declaration be prefixed to the Constitution: "[G]overnment is instituted and ought to be exercised for the benefit of the people; which consists in the enjoyment of life and liberty, with the right of acquiring and using property and generally of pursuing and obtaining happiness" (U.S. Congress, *Annals*, 1834, I, 451).

After determining most of the structural and procedural contours of the new government, the delegates could not avoid the issue of suffrage. The link between property and voting rights was at the fore of that discussion (Bowen 1966, 69–79; Beeman 2009, 279–281). In late July 1787, the Convention referred the issue to the Committee of Detail, to hammer out the details of a tentative agreement reached by the delegates that endorsed a property and citizenship requirement for voting. The committee ultimately proposed that the qualifications for voting for members of the House of Representatives be the same as the qualifications for voting for members of the legislature in each of the respective states. (Under the unamended Constitution, members of the House were the only national officers elected by the people. Senators were appointed by state legislatures. Presidents were chosen by presidential "Electors" appointed by the state legislatures. And federal judges were nominated by the president and appointed by and with the "Advice and Consent" of the Senate.)

The return of the committee's proposal to the full Convention prompted a broader discussion on whether suffrage would be too broad. Gouverneur Morris proposed that the right to vote for members of the House be limited to freeholders. John Dickinson defended the property requirement as protection against "the dangerous influence of those multitudes without property, and without principle" (Padover 1962, 239). The delegates who opposed Morris's proposal suggested that a freehold requirement would make the House resemble an aristocracy. Morris was having none of it. What the delegates should really fear, he maintained, was the danger of a lawmaking body elected by people without property (Elliot 1859, V, 335). Madison, who was particularly alert to the political consequences of anticipated demographic changes that would result in a great majority of people without property, concurred: "The rights of liberty and property will not be secure in their hands" (Padover 1962, 239).

The views of Morris, Dickinson, Madison, and others did not go unanswered. Invoking the "leveling spirit" of the seventeenth century, delegates objected to vesting voting rights exclusively in property owners. George Mason expressed that "every man having evidence of attachment to, and permanent common interest with the society, ought to share in all its rights and privileges." Oliver Ellsworth argued that the people would not subscribe to the Constitution if it subjected them to disenfranchisement. Benjamin Franklin's justification for decoupling property and suffrage was particularly simple and sincere: It was important to honor the loyalty and sacrifice of the militiamen and soldiers who had prosecuted the War for Independence (Farrand 1966, II, 202–205).

Neither side succeeded in convincing the other. In the end, the delegates agreed that suffrage was a "tender point" jealously guarded by most state constitutions. They therefore accepted Ellsworth's assessment that "[t]he states are the best judges of the circumstances and temper of their people" (Padover 1962, 240). The Convention ultimately agreed on the following: "The House of Representatives shall be composed of Members chosen by the People of the several States, and the Electors in each State shall have the Qualifications requisite for Electors of the most numerous Branch of the State Legislature."

By its neutrality on suffrage, the Convention disarmed some who might otherwise have opposed the proposed constitution, for in the hands of the states alone *remained* the critical question of who could vote. Any national suffrage requirement would generate fierce opposition and had the potential to derail ratification. As Madison observed, "To have reduced the different qualifications in the different States to one uniform rule would probably have been as dissatisfactory to some of the States as it would have been difficult to the convention" (Hamilton, Madison, and Jay 1961, 294).

In each state, popularly elected conventions debated the proposed constitution. The attendees argued about great political issues and principles—federalism, the powers of the central government, separation of powers, majority rule, the desirability of a bill of rights, and so forth. But because the proposed constitution proffered no uniform rule on the franchise, the state ratifying debates were largely silent on that topic.

The Motives of the Framers

Political scientists and historians have long debated the motives of the framers. In the early twentieth century, Charles Beard (1913, 188) concluded that the Constitution represented "an economic document drawn with superb skill by men whose property interests were immediately at stake." By the middle of the century, that view had fallen into disfavor among some scholars, who criticized Beard for using specious statistics and for failing to consider fully the effect of political ideology, religion, social divisions, and other economic factors on the attendees in Philadelphia. Nevertheless, one thing is clear: The delegates to the Constitutional Convention—most of whom came from higher social strata, owned property, and had greater concern for preserving order and stability—were far less committed to the principles of individual rights and true representative government than textbooks portray. The very thought that an unpropertied majority might democratically take away the property rights of landowners frightened and motivated many of them.

By linking the franchise in national elections to state suffrage laws—all the states at that time having some form of property requirement—the framers effectively limited the electorate. In doing so, they held together a fragile and fractious coalition of delegates, avoided a potentially explosive political problem, prevented far more contentious debates at state ratifying conventions, and increased prospects for constitutional ratification. That compromise, though, was not without cost. The decision to divorce citizenship in the new nation from the right to vote "was to have significant repercussions for almost two centuries" (Keyssar 2000, 24).

The Democratization of the Electorate: 1789–1860

The first seven decades of the Republic witnessed remarkable changes. The country extended from the eastern seaboard to the Pacific Ocean; it stretched from sea to shining sea. The population swelled from four to thirty-one million. The number of states tripled from eleven to thirty-three. Cities grew. Settlers went westward. Commerce, to include manufacturing, developed. The country's transformation brought about political change as well. In the immediate years following the adoption of the Constitution, the people exhibited a renewed interest in the management of their political institutions; these years were characterized by "considerable constitution-making" (Williamson 1960, 131). Between 1790 and 1860, *every* state convened at least one constitutional convention; most convened multiple. These conventions naturally came to focus on the issue of suffrage and led to near-universal adult white male suffrage by the Civil War. Property tests vanished. Taxpaying requirements were minimized. Religious tests disappeared. Even noncitizens (in a few states) were welcomed into the franchise.

The Demise of Property Restrictions

It is beyond the scope of this section to examine in detail the suffrage debates in state constitutional conventions and legislative chambers. Others (Porter 1918, 20–134; Mason and Leach 1959, 228–257; Williamson 1960, 138–299; Peterson 1966; Keyssar 2000, 26–52) have done so well beyond our ability to add or detract. Nevertheless, a brief look at the progression and the general debate is instructive. While the property requirements in state constitutions and state law began to lose their grip after 1789, it would take more than a half century to eliminate them. For much of that time, it remained a man's property—"not his character, his nationality, beliefs, or residence"—that entitled him to vote (Porter 1918, 3). The property requirements rarely gave way altogether or easily. More commonly, states progressed from property to tax payment to near-universal adult white male suffrage.

In 1789, eleven of the thirteen former colonies had a property requirement for voting. Pennsylvania and New Hampshire had eliminated the property requirement in their constitutions of 1776 and 1784, respectively. Between 1789 and 1800, two others states did so: Georgia in 1789 and Delaware in 1792. No state admitted to the union after the original thirteen required an exclusive property test for voting. Vermont, which joined in 1791, permitted all free adult white males to vote; no property or taxpaying requirement ever prevailed in Vermont, even prior to statehood. Kentucky entered in 1792 without a property requirement. (Presaging problems to come, the Kentucky Constitution of 1799 excluded blacks, mulattoes, and Native Americans.) Tennessee, which affiliated in 1796, had a freehold requirement, though it did not stipulate size or value, but made an exception for free men who had been inhabitants of any county in the state for six months.

By 1800, then, only nine of the sixteen states retained a property qualification. Between 1800 and 1860, however, all of those states eliminated the requirement or provided taxpaying, residency, or militia alternatives. Maryland dropped the freehold requirement by statute in 1801 and by constitution in 1810. South Carolina adopted a freehold requirement by constitution in 1810, but allowed a residency alternative. Connecticut statutorily abandoned the freehold requirement in 1817, only to reinsert it by constitution with taxpaying and militia alternatives the following year.

Connecticut let go the requirement altogether in 1845. Massachusetts and New York discontinued the property requirement in their 1821 constitutions, the latter doing so only for white persons. Rhode Island ratified a new constitution in 1842 that exempted native-born males and two-year state residents from its centuries-old property requirement. By constitution, New Jersey jettisoned its property requirement in 1844; Virginia did so in 1850; and North Carolina followed in 1856.

The debates on suffrage that took place in the first half of the nineteenth century were every bit as intense and charged with political meaning as the debates of centuries past, from Parliament to Putney to Philadelphia. Likely at no other time in American history were the debates on suffrage so exhaustive.

Witness the speech of Chancellor James Kent at New York's constitutional convention of 1821 in opposition to broadening the electorate:

> The tendency of universal suffrage, is to jeopardize the rights of property, and the principles of liberty. . . . [T]here is a tendency in the poor to covet and to share the plunder of the rich; in the debtor to relax or avoid the obligation of contracts; in the majority to tyrannize over the minority, and trample down their rights; in the indolent and the profligate, to cast the whole burdens of society upon the industrious and the virtuous.

Property must be protected from democracy: "Universal suffrage once granted is granted forever, and never can be recalled. There is no retrograde step in the rear of democracy. However mischievous the precedent may be in its consequences, or however fatal in its effects, universal suffrage never can be recalled or checked but by the strength of the bayonet" (Mason and Leach 1959, 233–235).

Others, equally luminous to Kent, countered. In Virginia, John Marshall, chief justice of the United States and most assuredly a freeholder, delivered the "Memorial of the Non-Freeholders of the City of Richmond" to the Virginia constitutional convention of 1829: "To deny to the great body of the people all share in the Government; on suspicion that they may deprive others of their property, to rob them in advance of their rights; to look to a privileged order as the fountain and depository of all power; is to depart from the fundamental maxims, to destroy the chief beauty, the characteristic feature, indeed, of Republican Government" (Mason and Leach 1959, 250–251).

These debates waged all across the country. It is possible, even today, to sense the resolve with which men argued and the firmness and sincerity with which they held their views.

Between 1800 and 1860, seventeen states joined the nation, more than doubling—from sixteen to thirty-three—

the number of states at the turn of the century. None linked property to voting rights. Accordingly, by 1860, no state made property ownership a condition for voting. (New York, Rhode Island, and South Carolina had property requirements, but they fell only on certain groups of people: New York's applied to blacks; Rhode Island's to the foreign-born; and South Carolina's to those who had not been residents for at least six months.)

The Rise and Fall of Taxpayer Requirements

The repeal of property requirements did not eliminate economic barriers to voting. Taxpaying requirements, common in the late eighteenth and early nineteenth centuries, typically took one of three forms: (1) that one pay all state or local taxes owed; (2) that one owe (and pay) taxes; or (3) that one pay a poll tax (a uniform tax on each voter). By 1800, five states had taxpaying requirements, either standing alone or as an alternative to property ownership. In 1789 and 1790, respectively, Georgia and Pennsylvania compelled voters to have paid all taxes for a specified period of time preceding the election. South Carolina, also in 1790, mandated that voters who did not own property pay a tax in the year preceding the election. Delaware adopted a taxpaying requirement in 1792. Additionally, North Carolina conferred a partial franchise suffrage upon taxpayers: A freehold of land was necessary to vote for the Senate, but only a tax payment to vote for the House of Commons. New Hampshire abandoned its poll tax in 1792. Maryland, Vermont, Kentucky, and Tennessee never had taxpaying requirements.

In the first half of the nineteenth century, every remaining former colony—New Jersey (1807), Connecticut (1818), Massachusetts (1821), New York (1821), Virginia (1830), and Rhode Island (1842)—and several other states—Ohio (1803), Louisiana (1812), and Mississippi (1817)—implemented taxpaying requirements. Interestingly, the rise of taxpaying requirements often tracked the expiration of property qualifications. Georgia (1789), Pennsylvania (1790), Delaware (1792), Massachusetts (1821), and New York (1821) instituted taxpaying requirements in the very constitutions that discarded property qualifications.

After Mississippi's admission in 1817, no state entered the union with a taxpaying (or property) requirement. That, of course, did not end these requirements; for many decades thereafter, the remaining restrictions precluded substantial numbers from voting. South Carolina became the first state in the nineteenth century to end taxpayer qualifications in 1810. Between 1826 and 1851, six other states did so. By 1860, only six states insisted that voters pay taxes. Table 1.3 (adapted from Stephenson 2004, 71) summarizes the demise of property and taxpaying requirements between 1789 and 1860.

Table 1.3 The Demise of Property and Taxpaying Requirements, 1789–1860

State	Entered Union	Property Qualifica- tion Ended	Taxpayer Qualifi- cation Ended
Delaware	1789	1792	Continuing
Pennsylvania	1789	1790	Continuing
New Jersey	1789	1844	1844
Georgia	1789	1789	Continuing
Connecticut	1789	1818	1845
Massachusetts	1789	1821	Continuing
Maryland	1789	1801	n/a
South Carolina	1789	1810 (for residents)	1810
New Hampshire	1789	n/a	1792
Virginia	1789	1850	1850
New York	1789	1821 (for white men)	1826 (for white men)
North Carolina	1789	1856	Continuing
Rhode Island	1790	1842 (for native- born males)	Continuing
Vermont	1791	n/a	n/a

(Continued)

Table 1.3   (Continued)

State	Entered Union	Property Qualifica-tion Ended	Taxpayer Qualifi-cation Ended
Kentucky	1792	n/a	n/a
Tennessee	1796	1834	n/a
Ohio	1803	n/a	1851
Louisiana	1812	n/a	1845
Indiana	1816	n/a	n/a
Mississippi	1817	n/a	1832
Illinois	1818	n/a	n/a
Alabama	1819	n/a	n/a
Maine	1820	n/a	n/a
Missouri	1821	n/a	n/a
Arkansas	1836	n/a	n/a
Michigan	1837	n/a	n/a
Florida	1845	n/a	n/a
Texas	1845	n/a	n/a
Iowa	1846	n/a	n/a
Wisconsin	1848	n/a	n/a
California	1850	n/a	n/a
Minnesota	1858	n/a	n/a
Oregon	1859	n/a	n/a

Forces of Expansion

The abandonment of property and taxpaying requirements in the early nineteenth century—and the resulting growth of the franchise—was the result of a number of ideas, forces, and factors. These include the power of democratic ideals and ideas, war, westward expansion, the rise of political parties, and socioeconomic changes (Keyssar 2000, 33–52; Stephenson 2004, 62–70).

Democratic principles conspired against property and taxpaying requirements. The first step in this process was the substitution of personal property for real estate; the second permitted a taxpaying alternative to land ownership. These early concessions were significant, for they demonstrated that some colonies were expanding on the concept of "stake in society." Additionally, these concessions were consistent with the principles of the American Revolution. The homegrown revolutionary cry of "no taxation without representation," so effectively used in the 1770s, was appropriated decades later by those who inveighed against property and taxpaying requirements. Equally important was the concept, now widely accepted, that government should be by consent of the governed. Those who were "governed" were not exclusively, or even primarily, property owners and taxpayers, and they "more or less blindly demanded the ballot," relying for support in the "natural-right philosophy and government by the consent-of-the-governed doctrine" (Porter 1918, 32).

War accelerated the demise of property and taxpaying requirements. Soldiers, whether volunteers or conscripts, asked to defend the liberties of others should not themselves be denied those same liberties. The previously mentioned "Memorial of the Non-Freeholders of the City of Richmond," after ridiculing that popular notion that "virtue" and "intelligence" were byproducts of landownership, pointed out that states had no problem calling upon the "depraved" and "ignorant" for military service.

> In the hour of danger, they have drawn no invidious distinctions between the sons of Virginia. The muster rolls have undergone no scrutiny, no comparison with the land books, with a view to expunge those who have been struck from the ranks of freemen. If the landless citizens have been ignominiously driven from the polls, in time of peace, they have at least been generously summoned, in war, to the battle-field. (Keyssar 2000, 36)

Eliminating these requirements was more than a matter of simple fairness for soldiers, however. Military preparedness and the nation's security also weighed heavily. During the War of 1812, the national government had tremendous difficulty in coaxing men to enlist. The ranks were so thin that Congress eventually had to call up state militia to assist. Similar hurdles to soldier recruitment emerged during the Mexican-American War between 1846 and 1848. Removing property or taxpaying qualifications would have the added benefit of making soldiers and militiamen, many of whom were young, poor, and unpropertied, more enthusiastic about enlisting and defending their country. Connecticut (1817), Mississippi (1817), New York (1821), and Rhode Island (1842) provided militia alternatives to property or taxpaying qualifications. Additionally, some southern states—South Carolina (1810) and Virginia (1850)—eliminated these requirements at least in part to entice poor whites to join militias that might be summoned to put down slave rebellions. Though less celebrated than other forces of expansion, war mattered. In nearly every debate over the franchise after 1812, the soldier was invoked. (As will be seen later, nearly every major suffrage extension in American history occurred during or shortly after wars.)

In 1893, historian Frederick Jackson Turner suggested that American democracy was formed not out of the British or revolutionary experiences but by the American frontier (Turner 1920). This "frontier thesis" cannot alone account for the democratization of the republic, however. After all, many states along the eastern seaboard broadened the franchise well before their westward counterparts did. But westward expansion certainly contributed to the demise of property and taxpaying requirements. Frontier states "took the democratic rhetoric seriously and incorporated provisions protecting individual rights (including voting) into state constitutions" (Crotty 1977, 11). Between 1803 and 1860, seventeen states joined the union; fourteen of them fell west of the Mississippi River. And only three of the seventeen—Ohio (1803), Louisiana (1812), and Mississippi (1817)—adopted property or taxpaying requirements. These "frontier" states viewed suffrage as a means to recruit residents, which would increase property value, spur economic development, and grow tax revenues. By the mid-1800s, Indiana, Wisconsin, Michigan, Oregon, and the Kansas Territory even permitted alien declarants (noncitizens who had formally declared their intent to seek U.S. citizenship) to vote.

The rise of national political parties in the 1830s contributed to the broadening of the franchise. Scholars tend to think of the history of political parties in the United States as a succession of five two-party systems. The first party system, between 1800 and 1828, organized around the conflict between the Federalist and Democratic-Republican parties. Generally speaking, the Federalists, who were mostly from the Northeast, opposed a broader electorate, while the Democratic-Republicans, primarily from the South, favored one. Andrew Jackson's election as president in 1828 ushered in the second party system, which featured competition between the Democratic (formerly Democratic-Republican) and Whig parties. Until this time, political parties had been more aristocratic than democratic. The new Democratic Party moved aggressively to organize state and local party organizations that could get out the vote during elections and invented party conventions to give members of state and local parties a say in the nomination of candidates and the writing of the party platform. The Democrats also demanded for the people greater participation in government. By contrast, the Whigs, intellectual successors to the Federalists, were less eager to embrace a broader franchise.

Ideological differences aside, the competitive party environment during the second party system created strong incentive to reform the electorate. To win elections, parties needed votes. It was therefore natural for parties to try to broaden (or narrow) the franchise, if doing so increased the likelihood of electoral success. The Democrats opposed property qualifications (and citizenship requirements) because they believed those without property (and aliens) would vote Democratic. The Whigs, at least initially, wanted to retain property qualifications (and citizenship requirements) for the same reason: They feared the propertyless (and aliens) would vote Democratic.

Parties unsurprisingly sought to swell their ranks by enfranchising their supporters.

Finally, various socioeconomic factors contributed to electoral democratization. Most notable among these were the development of manufacturing, the rise of a large industrial working class, and the growth of cities, leading to changes in the American population and a more complex social order. In the early part of the century, protective tariffs, technological innovations, and proximity to raw materials moved manufacturing from the home workshop to the urban factory or mill. Cities grew and were populated with artisans, canal operators, craftsmen, factory workers, laborers, lawyers, mechanics, newspaper editors, shopkeepers, small merchants, and railroad operators, many of whom "owed little or nothing to the old ideal of a landed freeholder citizenry" (Wilentz 1992, 35–36). Alongside these "new men of the market revolution" was the free peasantry—planters, small farmers, and tenant farmers—most of whom were men of no or little property who had never been part of early political arrangements of power. No longer was the nation divided neatly between those with and without property, between those with and without a stake in its future. Together, these "real people," as Jackson called them, citizens and immigrants alike, played critical roles in mobilizing support for enlarging the electorate and brokering reforms in state conventions and legislatures.

Suffrage Limited in Other Ways

By the middle of the nineteenth century, suffrage reforms had advanced democratic principles and increased political participation considerably. During the 1830s and 1840s, turnout in some jurisdictions reached 80 percent of adult white male citizens (Keyssar 2000, 52). But suffrage reforms are rarely unidirectional. While the franchise notably broadened during this critical period, states maintained or erected barriers to voting that were unrelated to property and taxes. The most common of these were restrictions on aliens, the young, paupers, criminals, illiterates, Native Americans, blacks, and women.

In the first decades of the Republic, little consensus, in law or practice, existed with respect to citizenship. Colonial charters and early state constitutions most often used the term "inhabitant" to define the electorate; the designation "citizen" was not yet in common use. Some states made alienage a disqualifying factor for voting; others welcomed all white male "inhabitants." Once Congress established a uniform rule for naturalization in 1802, numerous states revised their constitutions to limit the franchise in a way that would negatively affect the foreign-born. By the 1830s, aliens were barred in almost every state, and this held true for more than a quarter century. The only exceptions were North Carolina, which never had a citizenship requirement, and the four states that between 1848 and 1857 enfranchised alien declarants.

The extension of the franchise to aliens in those states, coupled with an uptick in Irish and German immigration, kindled American nativism. The Native American Party (later the American Party) was hostile to immigration, suspicious of the foreign-born (and Catholics), and fearful of the demise of the American way. The party that emerged from a clandestine fraternal order in New York was known more commonly as the "Know-Nothings." (When asked by outsiders about their "secret" society, the members replied, "I know nothing.") The Know-Nothings supported long residency requirements, tough voter registration laws, and stringent literacy tests. By 1854, they boasted a million members. By 1856, they claimed mayoralties in Boston, Philadelphia, and Chicago; control of six state legislatures; eight governorships; and at least fifty members of Congress, including a speaker of the House of Representatives. Acknowledging that it is nearly impossible to count membership in a secret organization, one historian suggests that as many as 124 House members were, or had been, affiliated with the Know-Nothings (Annbinder 1992, ix–xiv; 197, n.8). No one could have predicted that a party "burrowing in secret like a mole in the dark" and "proscribing men on account of their birth and peculiar religious faiths" would have had so much success so quickly, wrote the nineteenth-century journalist William Lloyd Garrison (Mayer 1998, 451). The Know-Nothings' departure from the national scene was just as sudden. By 1857, the party was no more, having succumbed to divisions over slavery. Nevertheless, its brief run stands as evidence that many Americans were unnerved by expanding suffrage to foreigners perceived to be ignorant, immoral, prone to liquor, susceptible to money, and dangerously un-American. (Following the Civil War, the practice of alien voting spread to other states in the South and the West where it continued for more than a half century.)

English law and colonial practice limited the franchise to those twenty-one years of age and older. That did not change in the decades preceding the Civil War.

Believing pauperism a moral failure, nine states denied suffrage to those who received public aid or lived in poorhouses, poor asylums, or charitable institutions. "To be stuck in the poorhouse" was, among other things, to be voteless.

In at least two dozen states, constitutions or laws excluded those convicted of certain criminal offenses. (Felon disenfranchisement would become even more widespread after the Civil War.)

In 1855, Connecticut became the first state to adopt a literacy test, believing that limiting the franchise to the educated would improve the quality of electoral decision-making. Massachusetts did so two years later. As the tests were in English, an additional benefit was that voters would be required to learn the language, which would promote greater cultural assimilation. Though class-neutral on its face, the tests disproportionately affected the economically disadvantaged and foreign-born. For that reason, Democrats opposed literacy tests. (Literacy tests proved to be a significant restriction on the franchise for the next century, during which they were used to legitimize ethnic and racial marginalization.)

Three other groups disenfranchised in the first half of the nineteenth century—Native Americans, blacks, and women—are worthy of brief remarks here. The latter two will receive greater attention later in this chapter.

Native Americans were largely denied the right to vote because they were not citizens, but members of a quasi-sovereign "domestic dependent nation" within the United States. A few states, however, permitted Native Americans to vote if assimilated into the general population. Wisconsin (1848) and Michigan (1850) included "civilized" persons of Indian descent who were not "members of any tribe." Minnesota (1857) was more specific, insisting that persons of Indian blood adopt the "language, customs, and habits of civilization," as determined by a state court. (It would not be until 1924 that Congress conferred citizenship upon Native Americans.)

Disqualification by race was common. In 1790, only three states excluded voters based on race; all were southern—Virginia, Georgia, and South Carolina. By 1820, fourteen states, spread across the Republic, either explicitly excluded blacks or specifically limited the franchise to whites; twenty years later, twenty states were on board. And in 1860, prohibitions could be found in twenty-eight of the thirty-three states. Every state that entered the union after 1819 denied suffrage to blacks, and all of the states where (free) blacks could vote were clustered in New England—Massachusetts, New Hampshire, Rhode Island, Vermont, and Maine. Even in those states, however, blacks may have been denied from voting by other restrictions.

Between 1789 and 1860, no state allowed women to vote. Abigail Adams's pleas to her husband in the 1780s notwithstanding, no state or territory seriously entertained the notion until after the Civil War.

Electoral Reforms

A few other matters related to voting during this period merit brief mention. First, states adopted residency requirements.

These varied from state to state, with some asking for a relatively short three months and a few demanding a full two years. Presumably, the length of residence demonstrated a greater commitment to the community. While several states lengthened residency requirements to keep vagrants and transients from voting, others shortened them to attract new residents. Second, states compelled voter registration. This practice obligated voters to register (join the official list of eligible voters) in advance of elections, ostensibly to prevent voter fraud. The stated justifications for these electoral procedures aside, some voters were undoubtedly denied suffrage because of them.

Other changes altered the physical act of voting. To recall, it was common in colonial America for votes to be cast viva voce—publicly and by voice. (A variant of this process involved voters writing their names in a pool book under the name of their preferred candidate.) Early nineteenth-century reforms required voters to hand-write the name of the recipient of their vote on a scrap of paper, then place that paper in a ballot box or hand it to an election official. As a result of the increase in the number of elected offices, parties began printing their own ballots. The "party ballot" listed only its own candidates for each office. (As this list of candidates grew, the "party ballot" did also, eventually resembling a timetable on a railroad ticket, hence the term "party ticket.") Voters had to choose which party's ballot to use; thus, it was nearly impossible for a voter to cast anything other than a straight-ticket ballot. Moreover, given that the party ballots often used distinctive graphics and colors, it was easy for party enforcers to monitor the allegiances of voters. By midcentury, states were experimenting with ballots sealed in envelopes.

Near-Universal Adult White Male Suffrage

Between 1789 and 1860, property and taxpaying qualifications all but disappeared. The franchise expanded. One historian refers to this period as "Democracy Ascendant" (Keyssar 2000, 26). That is inarguable. The expansion of suffrage was a "reform of considerable magnitude in the context of the history of the United States and also of the world" (Williamson 1960, vii). But universal adult white male suffrage had not arrived. Perhaps "near-universal" adult white male suffrage had. Even in 1860, plenty of people, including some adult white men, remained disenfranchised by restrictions unrelated to property and taxation.

Suffrage and Disenfranchisement: 1860–1920

The "buoyant optimism about political participation" that had culminated by midcentury surrendered to fear less than a generation later (Keyssar 2000, 79). The decades between the Civil War and 1920 were marked not by a steady expansion of the franchise but rather by deep and protracted political and legal struggles resulting in a selective narrowing of it.

Arguments about the denial of suffrage to specific individuals during this period tend to focus on blacks and women, two large groups effectively denied the right to vote throughout most of American history. Slaves, of course, had never been able to vote; and in 1860, free black suffrage was limited to five states in New England. Women were disallowed in every state. By 1920, blacks and women had been formally enfranchised by constitutional amendment. The Fifteenth Amendment, ratified in 1870, prohibited states from denying the right to vote based on "race, color, or previous condition of servitude." This guarantee, however, proved more mirage than substance, especially in the South after Reconstruction, where by violence or fraud blacks were denied the ballot. ("Reconstruction" is the general term used to describe the years between 1863 and 1877 when the nation's central political theme was the "reconstruction"— the putting back together—of the Union that had been torn apart by Civil War.) Female suffrage earned constitutional assent a half century later. The Nineteenth Amendment, ratified in 1920, barred states from abridging the right to vote on account of sex. Though arriving much later, female suffrage, once granted, was immediate and far more permanent than black suffrage.

Given the ineffectiveness of the Fifteenth Amendment in protecting the right of blacks to vote and the Nineteenth Amendment's late appearance, the franchise did not expand between the Civil War and World War I. In fact, when other groups are considered, the trend reveals a contraction.

The Civil War and the Reconstruction Amendments

No issue in U.S. history so deeply divided its people as that of slavery. By 1830, the nation was split—half slave and half free. The Republic stood simultaneously (and remarkably) as among the "freest" in the world and the "greatest" slaveholding power of the nineteenth-century world (Levine 1992, 4–5). The Civil War resulted from that contradiction born of the American Revolution. No event in U.S. history was more consequential than the Civil War. The cost was enormous: In human capital alone, it claimed the lives of more than six hundred thousand soldiers and countless civilians (out of a population that numbered about thirty-one million). The Confederate surrender at Appomattox settled the matters of secession and union. Left unanswered, however, was the political status of the former slave population, and left undetermined was the nation's commitment to, in Abraham Lincoln's memorable words, a "new birth of freedom." The Reconstruction Amendments answered the former. With these amendments came renewed hope among blacks (and even women) that they would be afforded full citizenship—and voting rights—in the "new" nation. Those hopes were soon dashed. The nation was not yet committed to the principle of equality nor would it be for some time.

The Thirteenth Amendment, ratified in 1865, banned slavery and "involuntary servitude." For the first time, the Constitution imposed a significant limitation on the power of states to define the status of their residents.

In the years immediately after the Civil War, Southern states passed "black codes" relegating the former slaves to a subservient status by limiting their economic, legal, and political opportunities. All but the most racist Northerners agreed that federal guarantees were needed to prevent a return to a functional equivalent of slavery. Ratified in 1868, the Fourteenth Amendment is an amalgam of numerous promises, prohibitions, and punishments. Section 1 defined political membership: "All persons born or naturalized in the United States and subject to the jurisdiction thereof, are citizens of the United States and of the state wherein they reside." This single sentence erased the effects of one of the worst decisions in Supreme Court history, *Dred Scott* v. *Sandford* (1857), which declared that persons of African descent were not intended by the framers to be included within the meaning of the word "citizens." Section 1 also limited state power: "No State shall make or enforce any law which shall abridge the privileges or immunities of citizens of the United States; nor shall any State deprive any person of life, liberty, or property, without due process of law; nor deny to any person the equal protection of the laws."

Section 2 indirectly referenced voting rights by reducing a state's representation in Congress and in the Electoral College in proportion to the number of male inhabitants of the state, also being twenty-one years of age and citizens of the United States, denied "the right to vote." (An exception was made for "participation in rebellion, or other crime.") The amendment thus seemed to recognize the principle of adult male suffrage. It did not, however, insist upon black suffrage. Rather, it exacted a punishment on those states that denied voting rights to adult male citizens. The punishment was significantly steep for Southern states, though: Denying black suffrage would diminish the electoral prospects of a Democratic resurgence. (Following the Civil War, the Republican Party became the party of the North, while the Democratic Party was solidly entrenched in the South.)

Section 3 disqualified from holding federal office those who had once sworn to uphold the Constitution and then engaged in rebellion. Section 4 protected the federal war debt and prohibited the United States from assuming the war debt of the rebellious states. And Section 5 gave Congress the authority to enforce the amendment.

Neither the Thirteenth nor Fourteenth Amendment addressed directly voting rights for the former slaves. Prior to the Civil War, though the political parties differed on slavery, neither supported black suffrage. Not even Lincoln, who in his debates with Stephen Douglas in 1858 remarked, "I am not nor ever have been in favor of making voters . . . of negroes" (Oakes 2007, 120). But parties and people evolve. The Republicans needed to win elections nationwide to prevent the Southern-based Democratic Party from retaking control of the federal government. That was not doable unless blacks—a large and natural constituency—were allowed to vote. Lincoln, too, warmed to the idea of making voters of some blacks, privately endorsing suffrage to "the very intelligent, and on those who serve our cause as soldiers" (Donald 1995, 585).

But the Thirteenth and Fourteenth Amendments further pressed the issue by turning four million former slaves into free citizens who promptly petitioned for the exercise of their political rights. They insisted upon the ballot as an acknowledgment of their new status as free citizens and to protect themselves against a Southern populace bitter over its defeat. Northern blacks also demanded suffrage. They had supported the Union cause: More than 180,000 had fought and plenty had died. Just as militiamen during the American Revolution had demanded the franchise, so too did black regiments returning from the Civil War.

Most white Americans opposed black suffrage. Southern whites were afraid that black suffrage would disrupt centuries of norms and threaten their efforts to reassert control over the black population. In many locales, blacks outnumbered whites. Simple arithmetic led them to conclude that enfranchisement would produce "Negro domination." Moreover, it was a mistake to enfranchise people who were seen as naturally inferior in mental capacity and, by habit and practice, "wholly unprepared" for democracy. Northern whites, while less antagonistic, feared the political, social, and economic effects of free enfranchised blacks migrating north.

Congressional enactments in 1867—known as the Reconstruction Acts—authorized federal military rule in the South and insisted that former Confederate states ratify the Fourteenth Amendment and adopt adult black male suffrage as a condition for readmission to the Union. The governor of South Carolina objected to throwing control of the South into the hands of "ignorant, stupid, demi-savage paupers." Citizens in Alabama begged Congress not to subject them to "negroes . . . ignorant generally, wholly unacquainted with the principles of free Governments, improvident, disinclined to work, credulous yet suspicious, dishonest, untruthful, incapable of self-restraint, and easily impelled . . . into folly and crime" (Foner 2014, 294). Despite protestations, all former states of the Confederacy complied, even if unenthusiastically, by 1870.

Most northern states were reluctant to embrace black suffrage. Between 1863 and 1870, seventeen northern states or territories considered black male enfranchisement. In only two states—Iowa and Minnesota, both with small black populations—was black suffrage adopted (Keyssar 2000, 89). Curiously, then, black male suffrage was the "law of the land" in former states of the Confederacy, but not in most northern states. One historian explained this double standard: "In the North, the man of African descent is as secure as his white neighbor in the possession of the rights to life, liberty, and the pursuit of happiness guaranteed to every citizen by the Constitution of the United States." By contrast, "in the South the ballot is necessary to protect the colored man's life liberty, and property from assault by men in whom the feelings and opinions engendered by slavery are not yet extinct" (Hill 1868, 175).

Republican disappointment in the election of 1868 motivated the party to rethink its passivity toward black voting in the North. Support for black suffrage brought political risk, most notably the loss of white votes. But whatever risks inhered in advocating black enfranchisement, the greater hazard was in failing to assure it. Additionally, any lost white votes could be offset by appreciative black ones. A constitutional amendment was needed to make black suffrage permanent.

The Fifteenth Amendment was the crown jewel of Reconstruction. Congress considered and rejected a proposal that banned voting restrictions based on "race, color, nativity, property, education, or religious beliefs." Various versions would have eliminated property qualifications, poll taxes, and literacy tests and guaranteed the right of blacks to hold public office. The final draft was silent on all of those matters. Instead, the amendment merely precluded race as a formal criterion for voting: "The right of citizens of the United States to vote shall not be denied or abridged by the United States or by any State on account of race, color, or previous condition of servitude."

Following congressional approval, the proposed amendment was sent to the states for ratification. The new president, Ulysses S. Grant, who had united the Republican Party after four years of discord under Johnson, supported ratification. Likely to benefit from the votes of enfranchised blacks, Republican-dominated state legislatures ratified. On March 30, 1870, the amendment was certified. Every northern state that had rejected black suffrage in the 1860s ratified the amendment by 1870. Northern white voters, either out of principle or self-interest or party interest, welcomed something heretofore largely unseen in U.S. history—black suffrage.

The Reconstruction Amendments defined duties incumbent on the states. The states were prohibited from protecting slavery, defining citizenship, depriving persons of due process of law, denying to persons the equal protection of the laws, and disenfranchising voters on the basis of race. Considered together, they reinvented the United States on the basis of a new set of principles. While the unamended Constitution placed few limits on the legislative competence of the states, the "second constitution" insisted that states treat those within their jurisdiction decently and with respect. Or so was the hope.

With respect to the Fifteenth Amendment, however, hope and reality diverged. "Never has so specific a constitutional directive been so plainly disregard for so long" (Stephenson 1988, 47). Indeed, it would take almost a century to fulfill the promise of the Fifteenth Amendment.

Reconstruction

Reconstruction was unwelcomed in the South. The Ku Klux Klan's reign of violence in the late 1860s—usually ignored, though sometimes supported, by police and other local officials—finally persuaded Congress to exercise the authority granted it in each of the Reconstruction Amendments, namely, to enforce them "by appropriate legislation." The Enforcement Act of 1870 made it a federal crime for state officials to discriminate among voters on account of race; and for private citizens to conspire together with intent to prevent or hinder any citizen from the exercise and enjoyment of rights and privileges granted by the Constitution. On its face, the Act appeared to be an "appropriate" exercise of Congress's authority to guarantee that elections and other constitutional privileges remain free from racial discrimination.

Under the Constitution, however, Congress does not determine the constitutionality of its acts. That is the prerogative of federal courts in suits properly before them. Prior to Reconstruction, federal courts had few opportunities to decide voting rights cases as the franchise had largely been a state function. But federal legislation intended to augment the Fourteenth and Fifteenth Amendments provided opportunities. Two 1876 decisions—*United States* v. *Reese* and *United States* v. *Cruikshank*—are critically important.

Reese involved two Kentucky election officials who were indicted under the Act for refusing to receive and count the vote of a black citizen. When the case reached the Supreme Court, the primary issue was the meaning of the Fifteenth Amendment. *Reese* held that the amendment did not "confer the right of suffrage upon anyone." The justices conceded that the amendment invested citizens with a new constitutional right. That right, however, was not the right to vote, but rather the right to vote free from racial discrimination. As such, states were not precluded from denying suffrage, but just from denying suffrage on account of race. The Court then turned its attention to the Act. To be "appropriate legislation" under the amendment, the Act could criminalize only that which the amendment prohibited—denials of suffrage based on race. Yet, the two sections of the Act under which the officials had been indicted did not mention race. The Court, therefore, deemed them unconstitutional.

The second case resulted from the Colfax Massacre of 1873, an armed white rebellion over a disputed gubernatorial election in Louisiana, in which at least sixty blacks were killed. The Department of Justice (DOJ) indicted William Cruikshank and seven others under the Enforcement Act for conspiring to deny constitutional rights to black citizens. In *Cruikshank*, a unanimous Supreme Court found the indictments deficient because they failed to specify that race was the rioter's motivation. "We suspect that race was the cause of the hostility," said the Court, "but it is not so averred." As such, whatever occurred in Colfax did not interfere with a federal civil right. Rather it was an "ordinary" state crime beyond the authority of congressional power to suppress under the guise of civil rights enforcement.

Perhaps more importantly, the Court noted that the Fourteenth Amendment only prohibited *states*, not private individuals, from denying civil rights. As such, Congress's options to protect civil rights were severely limited. If a state actor, on account of race, violated a citizen's civil rights, federal authorities could intervene. But if it were a private individual who interfered with the exercise of a citizen's constitutional right, federal authorities were without remedy. *Cruikshank* thus had the effect of rendering federal prosecutions for crimes against blacks nearly impossible. To be sure, states possessed the power to prosecute private individuals for such crimes; failure of political will, especially in the South, however, resulted in very few of them. One author offered this sobering conclusion: The decision in *Cruikshank* marked "the day freedom died" (Lane 2008).

In invalidating two sections of the Enforcement Act and dismissing indictments under another, *Reese* and *Cruikshank* sharply narrowed congressional power to enforce the Fourteenth and Fifteenth Amendments, thereby limiting federal authority to protect the civil rights of American citizens. Congress could have amended the unconstitutional sections of the Enforcement Act to clarify that they applied to race, the absence of which had been dispositive in *Reese*. But Republicans no longer possessed an interest in civil rights or the power to do something about it, having ceded control of the House of Representatives in 1875 to the Democrats. Critics called it a betrayal of Reconstruction.

Judicial decisions alone did not bring Reconstruction to an end. Resolution of the most contentious, bitter, and protracted presidential election in American history also played a role. In the months following the contested election of 1876, Republican and Democratic leaders resolved the impasse by awarding Republican Rutherford B. Hayes the presidency in exchange for his promise to remove federal troops from the South. The "Compromise of 1877" resulted in "a decisive retreat from the idea, born during the Civil War, of a powerful [federal government] protecting the fundamental rights of American citizens" (Foner 2014, 582). Southern blacks were now at the mercy of state governments hostile to freedom, citizenship, and constitutional equality for blacks, and free from federal supervision. Congress would not pass another civil rights bill until 1957.

The South Redeemed

While blacks in the South did not stop voting when Reconstruction ended, their ability to influence elections greatly diminished. The removal of federal troops from the South quietly gave Southern whites opportunity to reassert political control by pursuing strategies to prevent blacks from voting. These strategies typically fell into four broad categories: physical violence, economic intimidation, ballot fraud, and discriminatory-in-effect election laws. The specter of Reconstruction demanded nothing less than "the total disenfranchisement of the Negro" (Woodward 1957, 66).

Voting meant trouble for blacks, many of whom understood well the meaning of democracy when defined by white Southerners: "Man from Georgia said, 'we dont [sic] stop colored from voting if he want to vote, but a bullet would follow him out the door'" (Litwack 1998, 228). Well-financed "White Line" private militias employed violent tactics that left thousands of blacks dead and kept hundreds of thousands of others from voting out of fear. State officials usually stood by, but some joined in.

Black economic dependence also worked to reduce the black vote. Farm tenancy and sharecropping demonstrated the extraordinary economic power that whites wielded over black livelihood. Vote, or vote the wrong way, and whatever limited economic security blacks possessed was at risk.

Physical violence and economic intimidation were effective, but less so than fraud conducted by election officials. Though there were few documented cases of electoral fraud, talk of ballot-box stuffing, lost ballots, miscounts, and repeat voters was commonplace. Some election officials even admitted to the corruption. A Virginia Democrat in the late nineteenth century noted that elections in his state were "crimes against popular government and treason against liberty" (Kousser 1984, III, 1245).

By far the most effective and permanent mechanism to disenfranchise blacks, however, was the passage of race-neutral laws that had the effect of preventing blacks from voting. The South's mean-spiritedness was only limited by its imagination. By the early twentieth century, Southern states had used a variety of methods—a veritable roll-call of devices—to preserve the traditional "whites only" voting. Democratic-controlled state conventions and legislatures drew blatantly gerrymandered congressional and state legislative districts, authorized "white primaries," made voter registration more difficult, revived property qualifications, lengthened residency requirements, barred men convicted of minor crimes, mandated literacy tests and tests of "understanding," assessed poll and cumulative poll taxes, moved or closed polling places, and complicated ballot configurations.

Because these election changes and voting restrictions were race-neutral—that is, they did not single out blacks for disfavorable treatment—some whites were also adversely affected. To prevent inadvertent white disenfranchisement, nine Southern states approved "grandfather" or "good character" clauses. Grandfather clauses, adopted in six Southern states, excused individuals from certain voting requirements if they, or their ancestors, had been eligible to vote prior to a certain date. The date chosen was always a year in which most blacks had not been eligible to vote. "Good character" clauses, employed in three Southern states, exempted individuals from voting requirements if they could get a local official to certify their good character.

Though none of these methods was discriminatory on its face—and all were justified by some nebulous and seemingly noble "integrity of the electoral process" or "producing a more qualified electorate" argument—each had a disproportionate effect on blacks. Moreover, to protect whites, these measures were often administered with barefaced partisan and racial bias. An error on a registration form might or might not be disqualifying, the choice dependent on the caprice of the election official (and no doubt the reputation of the voter). An election supervisor might demand the production of tax receipts from some voters, but make no similar request from others. Discrimination was also inherent in literacy and "understanding" tests, the official having to judge the adequacy of the response. "Discrimination! Why, that is precisely what we propose," said a delegate to Virginia's constitutional convention in 1901–1902. "That, exactly, is what this Convention was elected for—to discriminate to the very extremity of permissible action under the limitations of the Federal Constitution, with a view to the elimination of every negro voter who can be gotten rid of, legally, without materially impairing the numerical strength of the white electorate" (Keyssar 2000, 112).

The Supreme Court, for the most part, favored nonintervention in cases of voting rights. *Williams* v. *Mississippi* (1898) is illustrative of this. Henry Williams, a black citizen, claimed that the Mississippi Constitution violated the Fifteenth Amendment by effectively disenfranchising all blacks through literacy tests, taxpaying requirements, and criminal exclusion. He further argued that state law vested in election officers too much discretion to register and reject voters. Yet, because neither the state constitution nor laws explicitly discriminated on race, a unanimous Court found no constitutional violation.

In *Giles* v. *Harris* (1903), the Supreme Court upheld a provision of the Alabama Constitution that granted lifetime registration to voters who registered before a specific date, but required strict property, literacy, and employment qualifications for all others. The complaint arose because the state constitution permitted only certain groups of people to register before the specific date, and had the effect of disenfranchising nearly all blacks. After acknowledging the racial motivation at work— "the whole registration scheme of the Alabama constitution is a fraud upon the Constitution of the United States"—the Court still refused to provide relief. The opinion concluded with an admission of judicial weakness, admitting that the federal judiciary was incapable of supervising registration procedures in Alabama. Relief would have to come, if at all, from the state or Congress.

The most notable exception to the Court's nonintervention between 1860 and 1920 was *Guinn* v. *United States* (1915). Here, the Court invalidated Oklahoma's grandfather clause, which allowed almost everyone but blacks to avoid a literacy test.

Though racially neutral on its face, the clause was clearly intended to interfere with voting rights protected by the Fifteenth Amendment. This decision, however, was more symbolic than substantive for three reasons. First, almost all states with grandfather clauses had allowed them to lapse. Second, the clauses were so blatantly discriminatory as to be an embarrassment. And third, southern states had other methods to disenfranchise blacks.

It would not be until the middle of the twentieth century that the Supreme Court began to alter the voting landscape in any meaningful way for blacks.

That the Southern stratagems were effective is inarguable. The statistics are staggering. In Mississippi, after 1890, fewer than 9,000 out of nearly 147,000 voting-age blacks were registered to vote. In Louisiana, which kept meticulous statistics on registration by race, the 130,000 blacks registered to vote in 1896 reduced to 1,342 by 1904. By 1910, Virginia showed only 15 percent of black men on voter registration lists; in Georgia, 4 percent; and in Alabama, 2 percent.

As a whole, Southern states, which had seen post-Reconstruction turnout levels of 60 to 85 percent, witnessed a drop to 50 percent for whites and single digits for blacks. "The enlargement of the suffrage that was one of the signal achievements of Reconstruction had been reversed, and the rollback had restored the southern electorate to—at best—pre-Civil War proportions" (Keyssar 2000, 114–115).

The narrowness of the Fifteenth Amendment allowed the South to circumvent its intent. Political machinations led to the withdrawal of federal troops from the South. And the failure of political will resulted in the abandonment of the nation's brief post–Civil War commitment to constitutional equality and democracy. Long after the Civil War concluded, the nation remained deeply divided. Well into the twentieth century, the South remained anti-black, anti-Republican, and governed by one-party rule. From 1880 to 1916, no Republican presidential candidate won even one of the eleven former states of the Confederacy.

Narrowing in the North

A similar, though less drastic, pattern of disenfranchisement emerged in the North. The motive, however, was not race. This is not to suggest that racial inequality was nonexistent above the Mason-Dixon line. To the contrary, Northern blacks lived as second-class citizens, trapped by political, legal, and economic realities. Though the discrimination and segregation were less brazen than that which occurred in the South, it was no less real. Most Northern blacks lived in declining neighborhoods, attended racially segregated and inferior public schools, and were excluded from public accommodations by Jim Crow laws that received the stamp of imprimatur from the Supreme Court in the late nineteenth century. Additionally, blacks were disproportionately unemployed and impoverished as private behavior and market forces denied to them economic security. But unlike blacks in the South, black voters in the North were *never* systematically disenfranchised. Instead, pressures to "clean up" government, ethnic, and class prejudices and self-interest gave rise to voting restrictions on immigrants, the uneducated, transients, the poor, and the criminally convicted.

Between the Civil War and World War I, the United States witnessed the rapid growth of three related phenomena: industry, cities, and immigrants. The United States became the world leader in manufacturing, boasted eight cities of more than a half-million residents, and welcomed nearly twenty-five million immigrants. With these economic and social changes came tremendous political corruption at state and local levels. By the mid-1870s, a group of middle- to upper-class intellectuals, lawyers, politicians, journalists, Protestant ministers, and other "old stock Americans"—Republicans and Democrats—frustrated by the "machines" that horded political power in Northeastern cities and in fear of what an immigrant class manipulated by those machines might be able to accomplish at the ballot box, began to question the nation's embrace of near-universal adult male suffrage.

To these early Progressives, this mass of immigrant workers—poor and uneducated, ignorant of American traditions, not committed to American values, inclined toward radicalism, easily duped by the political machines that ruled urban areas, prone to voting illegally and irresponsibly, and a threat to property rights—was "an unwelcomed addition to the electorate" (Keyssar 2000, 121). To Francis Parkman (1878, 7), a leading Progressive intellectual writing in 1878, this mass should be feared:

A New England village of the olden time—that is to say, of some forty years ago—would have been safely and well governed by the votes of every man in it; but, now that the village has grown into a populous city, with its factories and workshops, its acres of tenement-houses, and thousands and ten thousands of restless workmen, foreigners for the most part, to whom liberty means license and politics means plunder, to whom the public good is nothing and their own trivial interests everything, who love the country for what they can get out of it, and whose ears are open to the promptings of every rascally agitator, the case is completely changed, and universal suffrage became a questionable blessing.

Some challenged this thinking, pointing out that corporations, capitalists, and property owners were also predisposed to using politics for their own private benefit. Nevertheless, in a recurring theme in American history, citizens doubted the value of broad suffrage.

Progressive reformers sought to reduce the effects of industrialization, urbanization, immigration, and the resulting political corruption by imposing burdensome registration procedures, adopting property or taxpaying qualifications, barring noncitizen voting, requiring literacy tests, lengthening residency requirements, and excluding paupers. These restrictive measures were justified as necessary to produce a more competent electorate and prevent electoral fraud. But most had as their target the Democratic Party urban political machines and as their objective the disenfranchisement of the immigrant urban working class.

To prevent fraud, cut down on election-day conflicts, and gain an electoral advantage, Progressives pressed for voter registration, especially in large cities. The majority of states, in the North and nationwide, required voters to certify their eligibility, often prior to election day. The laws varied widely from state to state—"the length of the registration period, its proximity to the election, the size of registration districts, the frequency of reregistration, the necessity of documentary evidence of eligibility, the location of the burden of proof," all subject to partisan jockeying. Though quantifying the effect of these laws is difficult, voter turnout "dropped steadily" during these years, with some historians estimating that the implementation of registration schemes was responsible for one-third of that drop (Keyssar 2000, 158).

At least six Northern states (and three Western states) adopted property or taxpaying requirements. In *Myers* v. *Anderson* (1915), the Supreme Court declared that property and tax-paying qualifications were presumptively constitutional.

If immigrants were to be feared, immigrant suffrage was more so. The first step was to repeal alien declarant laws that had become popular on the frontier by the mid-nineteenth century. By 1920, every Northern state that had permitted the practice had ceased doing so; by 1926, no state allowed alien declarants to vote. The next step was to make it difficult for foreign-born U.S. citizens to vote. Some jurisdictions insisted that naturalized citizens produce documentation prior to registration; others imposed lengthy waiting periods between naturalization and voter eligibility. Congressional intervention in the early twentieth century made citizenship more difficult to obtain and thus reduced the number of immigrants who could vote.

The literacy test, so devastatingly effective when used against Southern blacks, was ostensibly an ethnic- and class-neutral way to improve the quality of the electorate. In practice, how-ever, it tended to operate along both lines. At least six Northern states (and nine Western states) made literacy or educational achievement a precondition for voting. The justification for doing so was threefold. First, illiterate men lacked intelligence and were dangerous. Second, literacy was necessary to under-stand American values. And third, restricting the franchise to the literate would encourage education and cultural assimila-tion. Voting by the ignorant, wrote two Yale law professors in 1918, would lead to "anarchy to-day and . . . despotism to-morrow" (Seymour and Frary 1918, II, 321). Most states demanded that voters be able to read (in English) a passage from the U.S. Constitution and be able to write his (or her, in some Western states) name.

Residency requirements returned. By 1920, all forty-eight states had residency requirements, the shortest being forty days. Most insisted upon six months to a year, though for a brief period Rhode Island (like five Southern states) demanded a full two years.

Finally, by 1920, paupers were excluded from the franchise in five northern states, two of which exempted Civil War vet-erans. And individuals convicted of various infamous crimes—bribery, electoral fraud, or, in few cases, "betting on the results of an election," for example—were denied the ballot is all but a few Northern states. Maine, Massachusetts, and Michigan were the exceptions.

Industrialization and the influx of immigrants led to a siz-able and influential portion of the population doubting the merits of universal adult male suffrage. As in the South, the result was the winnowing of the franchise, disproportionately excluding the lower classes. In Philadelphia, Chicago, and Boston, for example, only 60–70 percent of voting-age males were registered to vote between 1910 and 1920. The parallels between South and North, however, should not be overdrawn: "What transpired in the southern states was far more draco-nian, sweeping, and violent. The disfranchisement was massive rather than segmented, the laws were enforced brutally, and they were always administered with overtly discriminatory intent" (Keyssar 2000, 170).

The Special Case of Native Americans

A few states conferred voting rights on "civilized" Native Americans prior to the Civil War; most did not because of the citizenship issue. In stipulating that citizenship derived to "[a]ll persons born or naturalized in the United States and subject to the jurisdiction thereof," the Fourteenth Amendment raised the possibility of citizenship for Native Americans.

The Supreme Court addressed the issue in *Elk* v. *Watkins* (1884). John Elk, an Indian born on a reservation, had renounced his tribal allegiance, moved off the reservation, and claimed citizenship under the Fourteenth Amendment. After being denied suffrage by the registrar of voters, Elk asserted a Fifteenth Amendment violation. To recall, that amendment prohibited states from denying to *citizens* the right to vote on account of race, color, or previous condition of servitude. The issue thus became whether Elk was a citizen under the Fourteenth Amendment. The Court held that because Elk was not "subject to the jurisdiction" of the United States at birth, the Fourteenth Amendment did not confer citizenship upon him. His right to vote, therefore, was not protected by the Fifteenth Amendment.

Congress later reversed the effect of this decision. In 1887, the General Allotment Act provided citizenship to those Native Americans born in the United States who had voluntarily taken up residence "separate and apart from any tribe . . . and adopted the habits of civilized life." (And in 1924, Congress granted citizenship to all Native Americans born in the United States.)

Women's Suffrage

The one notable exception to the systematic retrenchment of voting rights during this period was women's suffrage. In 1860, women could not vote in any state or territory; by 1920, the Constitution prohibited states from denying the right to vote based on sex. While blacks and women were simultaneously advocating for the franchise, their experiences were much different. First, the discriminations against women were, by comparison, mild. Most adult women relied for physical safety upon their husbands, men who also had an interest in promoting the economic and social wellbeing of their wives (and daughters). By contrast, blacks had fewer effective protectors and advocates. Second, full political equality for women took much longer. Black men went from slavery to freedom to citizenship to the polls in five years. It took more than seven decades for women to earn the right to vote. And third, once granted, women's suffrage was accepted instantaneously and proved far more stable than black suffrage. Blacks may have won the franchise in 1870, but the story of black suffrage was written in the century that followed. Women earned the franchise in 1920; that story, however, came in the century before.

The women's rights movement, the largest mass movement for suffrage in the nation's history, began in upstate New York in 1848, when five women—including Lucretia Mott and Elizabeth Cady Stanton, both of whom had been active in the antislavery movement—announced "A Convention to discuss the social, civil, and religious condition and rights of women," to be held in Seneca Falls. The product of that convention was a "Declaration of Sentiments." Invoking arguments and phraseology from the Declaration of Independence, this statement asserted as self-evident the political equality of men and women; offered evidence of injuries and usurpations on the part of men toward women, including denial of the right to vote; and insisted that women have "immediate admission" to all the rights and privileges of citizenship. (Women had enjoyed limited suffrage before 1848. Parliament's "forty-shilling freehold" requirement of 1430 was not confined to males. New Jersey permitted property-owning women to vote prior to 1807. And in 1838, Kentucky let some women to vote in school elections.)

The Civil War diverted attention from the issue of suffrage. Reconstruction revived it. Women's-rights advocates were initially optimistic that Republicans would simultaneously embrace black and female civil rights. That never happened. "One question at a time," said Wendell Phillips. "This hour belongs to the Negro" (Keyssar 2000, 177).

The first serious, though unsuccessful, effort to secure voting rights for women took place at the New York Constitutional Convention of 1867, which marked the earliest occasion on which the proposition "had occupied the attention of a constituent assembly for any considerable length of time and had required the deliberative thought of able statesmen on both sides" (Porter 1918, 233). Pro-suffrage arguments were familiar, having been previously offered by the propertyless, free blacks, and aliens, merely adjusted to the new situation. Government was not deriving its powers from the consent of the governed. Women were taxed without representation. Civil rights were an empty promise without political power. And, the most common argument, women possessed an inherent right to share in self-government through voting.

Those opposed to women's suffrage countered with history, the glorification of womanly virtues and distinctly womanly functions, and religion. Voting was not a natural right. It was instead a privilege that government could withhold, grant, or withdraw at its pleasure, as governments had done for centuries. Moreover, there were few reasons to grant the privilege to those who were already adequately represented and protected by men, emotional rather than rational, focused on the home and family, and too fragile to participate in the rough-and-tumble world of politics. As one delegate remarked at a New York Constitutional Convention, "I love to look upon the sweet face of a virtuous woman. I love to see her standing at her place in the family circle, with a new, clean, gingham dress on, baking warm biscuits for tea. I love [*ad nauseam* about gentle, tender, loving woman; sweet, charming influence; bright star in the sanctuary of the home, angel voices, etc.]" (Porter 1918,

237). Finally, scripture made clear God's intended design for women. In 1873, when upholding a state law that denied women the right to practice law, the Supreme Court noted, "The paramount destiny and mission of woman are to fulfill the noble and benign offices of wife and mother. This is the law of the Creator" (*Bradwell* v. *Illinois*). The arguments for and against women's suffrage would evolve over the next half century, but the basic outlines remained the same.

When the nation turned its attention to black suffrage, the women's rights movement divided sharply on whether to support the Fifteenth Amendment, which said nothing about sex, politicians having concluded that to marry two controversial provisions would likely doom any reform. Lucy Stone was happy to accept the amendment, "thankful in [her] soul" to see anyone win the right to vote. The black abolitionist Frederick Douglass, an early supporter of women's rights, was not bothered by the exclusion of sex: "Black men first and white women afterwards," he said in 1869. Years earlier, he had questioned the parallels between black and women suffrage:

> I do not see how anyone can pretend that there is the same urgency in giving the ballot to women as to the Negro. With us, the matter is a question of life and death. . . . When women, because they are women . . ., are objects of insult and outrage at every turn; when they are in danger of having their homes burnt down over their heads; when their children are not allowed to enter schools; then they will have an urgency to obtain the ballot equal to our own. (Gurko 1974, 231)

But others were bitter that Republicans had not done more to embrace female suffrage. Stanton believed that the two amendments established "an aristocracy of sex." Susan B. Anthony thought the Fifteenth Amendment "an open, deliberate insult to American womanhood" to enfranchise ignorant blacks while leaving disenfranchised native-born, educated white women. The divide led to a split in the movement. The American Woman Suffrage Association (AWSA), headed by Stone, focused its reform efforts at the state level. The National Woman Suffrage Association (NWSA), led by Stanton and Anthony, concentrated its resources on national reform.

Given the Fifteenth Amendment's silence on sex, suffragists looked to the Fourteenth Amendment, two clauses of which presented the possibility of voting rights for women. The Privileges or Immunities Clause read, "No State shall make or enforce any law which shall abridge the privileges or immunities of citizens of the United States." When Anthony was prosecuted for casting a ballot in a federal election in 1872, she argued that voting was a privilege of citizenship and, therefore, a state law denying her the franchise violated the amendment. A federal court rejected her argument. The amendment also prohibited a state from denying to "any person within its jurisdiction the equal protection of the law." Whatever hope this Equal Protection Clause held for women's suffrage was dashed in 1875 when the Supreme Court ruled in *Minor* v. *Happersett* that "the Constitution of the United States does not confer the right of suffrage upon anyone." With the exception of the Fifteenth Amendment's prohibition of race as a criterion for voting, suffrage remained a state prerogative well into the twentieth century.

Constitutional defeats aside, the movement had some successes beginning around 1870. By the new century, four states and one territory—all west of the Mississippi River—had fully enfranchised women. (Compared to the North, the West was more receptive, and the South more resistant, to women's suffrage. No former state of the Confederacy, save for Louisiana, which permitted women to vote on tax issues only, granted any form of limited suffrage upon woman before 1900.) The Wyoming Territory was first, in 1869, in its commitment to women's suffrage, reaffirmed with statehood in 1889. Partial suffrage was adopted in other states, the most common of which was "school suffrage" in municipal elections: Because of their expertise in rearing children, women were allowed to vote in school elections. Kentucky did this in 1838, Michigan (for taxpaying women) in 1855, and Kansas in 1861. By 1900, twenty-eight states or territories conferred "school suffrage" of some sort.

The last decades of the nineteenth century gave rise to some nontraditional arguments for women's suffrage. First, women were temperamentally different and their unique virtues would improve the quality of politics. In other words, women should be enfranchised not because they were *equal* to men but because they were *better* than men. Second, voting rights would give economic protection to the growing number of working women. And a third argument was grounded in racism: Women would outvote blacks and foreigners, thus preserving "American" dominance.

The dearth of sufficient political success led the two suffrage organizations to merge in 1890 to form the National American Woman Suffrage Association (NAWSA), led by Carrie Chapman Catt. Its objective was full female suffrage by constitutional amendment. NAWSA adopted structural changes that mirrored political party organizations, with activists at the precinct, ward, city, county, state, and national levels. The movement's traditionally middle-class base became more diverse through recruitment of college-educated, privileged, and urban women. NAWSA borrowed operational tactics from the antislavery, temperance, British suffrage, and American labor movements. The association erected banners and billboards; sponsored parades, pageants, and speaking tours; hosted mass meetings; published periodicals; held nonviolent demonstrations; engaged in acts of civil disobedience; distributed political paraphernalia; mobilized supportive male voters; lobbied politicians; targeted reluctant legislators; and recruited sympathetic candidates for political office. Acquiring the right to vote was particularly resonant with wage-earning women, who comprised roughly 20 percent of the workforce and demanded the ballot to press for legislation that would improve their wages, hours, and working conditions. By 1910, the interest of organized labor and women's suffrage had converged.

Between 1910 and 1914, seven states and one territory—again, all in the West—granted women the right to vote. (Though Illinois is not on that list, of particular interest is what happened there in 1913. According to Article I of the Constitution, members of Congress are elected by those who are qualified to vote for members of the most numerous branch of the state legislature. Because the qualifications for electors of state legislators were fixed by the Illinois Constitution, the Illinois Legislature could not alter them. But Article II of the Constitution permits state legislatures to fix the qualifications of voters for presidential electors. In 1913, the Illinois Legislature granted suffrage to women, but only for presidential electors, thus creating an anomalous situation in which women could not vote for members of Congress or state legislatures, but could cast ballots for presidential electors.) The East continued to resist, with Massachusetts, New York, New Jersey, and Pennsylvania debating but rejecting referenda on women's suffrage in 1915.

Women's suffrage did not divide the political parties as black suffrage had. For much of the preceding half century, neither party sensed much to gain or lose from it, but neither party was willing to risk alienating male voters for whom women's suffrage was unpopular. By 1916, the Democratic and Republican parties supported women's suffrage, but only on a state-by-state basis.

The Democratic Party recommended extension of the franchise to women "by the States, upon the same terms as men." The Republicans also favored extension, but recognized "the right of each state to settle this question for itself." Thus, neither party supported a constitutional amendment.

American intervention in World War I in 1917 changed that. "In a military crusade being publicly justified 'to make the world safe for democracy,' the claims of those Americans excluded from full democratic rights took on special urgency"

(Amar 2005, 424). Fighting for ideals required that one live up to them also. All across the world, women were gaining suffrage. Additionally, women were contributing to the war effort by filling government positions made vacant as men went to Europe to fight. The momentum was turning. New York, an Eastern heavyweight, became the first state east of the Mississippi River to grant full political equality to women, in 1917, only two years after rejecting a similar referendum. Three other states soon followed. By 1918, fifteen states and one territory had fully enfranchised women. President Woodrow Wilson, who had only two years earlier shared the "suffrage-as-a-state-matter" view, threw his support behind a woman suffrage amendment as "an act of right and justice" and "a vitally necessary war measure."

By 1920, the "women's hour" had arrived. Following congressional assent, the proposed amendment—"The right of citizens of the United States to vote shall not be denied or abridged by the United States or by any State on account of sex"—was sent to the states for ratification. The only opposition came from the South. On August 26, 1920, the Nineteenth Amendment was certified. Three months later, more than eight million women cast ballots for the first time. Charlotte Woodward Pierce had signed the Declaration of Sentiments at Seneca Falls in 1848; she was the only signatory to live long enough to cast a ballot after the Nineteenth Amendment (Gurko 1974, 102).

Electoral Reforms

Beginning in the late 1880s, jurisdictions adopted the Australian ballot. Until that time, voters used ballots prepared by political parties that listed only one party's candidates. All voters had to do was select a party ballot and drop it in the box. Literacy was hence not required. Additionally, any poll watcher, party enforcer, or employer could see which party's ballot was selected. A man's vote was not secret. To promote a literate electorate and reduce voter intimidation, states began printing ballots that contained the names of all candidates for

office. Voters were instructed to mark the names of their preferred candidates before depositing the nonidentifying ballot
in the box. The Australian ballot, which was commonplace
by the turn of the century, proved a hindrance to voting by
illiterates.

Another reform was the initiative and referendum. An initiative allows citizens to bypass the legislative process by placing proposed laws or constitutional amendments on the ballot
for voters to support or oppose. A referendum permits citizens
to hold a popular vote on laws or constitutional amendments
passed by legislatures. Both devices sought to shift political
power from the state legislatures to the people. If voters could
make and veto laws, they could curb special interest legislation and reassert control over the institutions of government by
encouraging political accountability. Between 1898 and 1918,
twenty-two states allowed for statewide initiative or referendum or both (Piott 2003, 257).

During the nineteenth century, political parties typically
selected their candidates for office in a closed-door meeting
of party chieftains known as a caucus. Progressives disliked
the antidemocratic nature of, and political corruption in, this
candidate-selection-by-a-few-influential-party-leaders method.
A direct primary, by contrast, empowered ordinary voters to
elect the party's candidates. Wisconsin was the first state to
implement the direct primary in 1906. By the end of World
War I, almost every state insisted upon the direct primary in
some or all elections. A similar reform was the presidential
primary. Historically, party bosses hand-picked delegates to
the national party conventions. Shortly after the turn of the
century, Florida, Wisconsin, Pennsylvania, and South Dakota
provided for the direct election of delegates to the national
conventions. By 1916, half of the states had some form of presidential primary.

A final reform was the direct election of U.S. senators,
accomplished by the Seventeenth Amendment in 1913. Under
the unamended Constitution, senators represented their state

governments and were chosen by state legislatures. This democ-ratization of the Senate was fueled in part by the people's desire to possess sufficient power to counteract the alleged concen-trated and corrupting power of corporations and trusts, both of whom wielded outsized influence in state legislatures and supposedly worked against the people's interest. The Seven-teenth Amendment altered the principle-agent relationship. No longer were senators expected to act on behalf of their state legislatures; their new principle was the people.

The Franchise Limited

Between the Civil War and World War I, the universe of voters contracted. The era did not witness "an ongoing enlargement of democracy, marred only by the well-known and exceptional disfranchisement of [S]outhern blacks" (Keyssar 2000, 79–80). To the contrary: The "exceptional" event was the temporary enfranchisement of blacks. Racial, class, ethnic, and cultural prejudices clashed with "professed political values," resulting in a "piecemeal rolling back" of suffrage. The lone exception was the grant of full political equality to women at the end of this period. And that was no small accomplishment: It nearly doubled the size of the electorate.

Suffrage Delayed, Suffrage Earned: 1920–2000

The twentieth century witnessed a second democratization of the electorate. By its conclusion, nearly all adult citizens had legally earned the franchise. Between the world wars, Congress had little interest in suffrage, and the federal courts seemed incapable of doing much. Whatever progress was made was minimal, at least when compared to what happened during and after World War II. Once again, war served as motiva-tion to expand the electorate. By the 1960s, Congress and the federal judiciary had severely limited the ability of the states to prevent citizens from voting. "Will and means had caught up with authority" (Stephenson 1988, 65).

The Interwar Period: Disenfranchisement Unscathed

Suffrage laws remained relatively unchanged between 1920 and the mid-1940s. Though asked to intervene to prevent state and private efforts to keep blacks and others from the polls, federal courts mostly demurred. Only the most blatantly racially discriminatory laws were nullified.

The "white primary" illustrates well the reluctance of, and limitations on, federal courts to challenge the most routine aspects of white supremacy. The final choice in any political race is made in a general election, which is usually a contest between candidates from opposing parties. But from the Compromise of 1877 to the mid-1900s, the South voted overwhelmingly Democratic. This one-party dominance meant that the winner of the Democratic primary was the de facto winner of the general election. Limiting participation in Democratic primaries to whites, therefore, would be an effective way to keep blacks from meaningful participation in electoral politics. By 1908, eight Southern state legislatures had conferred upon political parties the legal privilege of determining their membership. And in each, the Democratic Party had denied membership to blacks.

After the Supreme Court, in *Newberry* v. *United States* (1921), held that primaries were exempt from the Fifteenth Amendment's prohibition on racial discrimination, the Texas legislature, disregarding any pretense of legal subtlety, precluded blacks from voting in primaries. In *Nixon* v. *Herndon* (1927), the Supreme Court struck down the law as violative of the Fourteenth Amendment's Equal Protection Clause. The Court did not consider a Fifteenth Amendment claim, perhaps because doing so would have required the justices to equate primaries with elections, a contention they had rejected in *Newberry*.

The Texas legislature responded by authorizing parties to determine who was qualified to vote in their primaries. The Texas Democratic Party then declared that only white

Democrats were so qualified. In *Nixon* v. *Condon* (1932), the Court, once again relying upon the Equal Protection Clause, struck down the rule because the party's decision to enact it could be traced to the power conferred upon it by the state legislature. Subsequently, and in the absence of any state legislation, the Texas Democratic Party limited participation in its primaries to "white citizens." In *Grovey* v. *Townsend* (1935), a unanimous Court upheld the resolution, though it was obviously and admittedly discriminatory, on the grounds that Fourteenth and Fifteenth Amendments restricted state action only. While the *state* may not deny equal protection of the laws or deprive individuals of the right to vote on the basis of race, *private* actors—of which the Democratic Party was one—were free to engage in discriminatory practices. *Nixon I* and *Nixon II* hinted that the Court would scrutinize Southern efforts to discriminate at the polls; *Grovey* made clear that judicial authority was constitutionally circumscribed. Texas (and other Southern states) had stumbled into an acceptable way to retain the white primary.

Judicial restraint was also on display two years later in *Breedlove* v. *Suttles* (1937), where the Court rejected a constitutional challenge to Georgia's poll tax. Though this case was brought by a white male and said nothing about racial motivation or racial effect of poll taxes, its consequences were clear: States were free to employ a well-known symbol of black disenfranchisement. In 1940, the poll tax persisted in eight Southern states.

The effects of Southern racial hostility and constitutional limitations mattered. In 1940, roughly five million voting-age blacks lived in the South, but only 150,000, or 3 percent, were registered to vote. Even fewer actually cast ballots (Key 1949, 504–535). Black voting remained low in the South until intense voting rights drives and congressional and judicial intervention in the 1960s.

In the North, enhanced black political power led to the abandonment of poll taxes by 1940, although some property and taxpaying requirements persisted. Black migration to Northern cities resulted in closer living arrangements, better communication and transportation, and shared social networks, such as black colleges and churches. These changes helped urban blacks overcome some of the standard organizational obstacles to social protest, but not all of them (Klarman 2004, 103). Literacy tests, for example, persisted in eighteen states (eleven in the North). Registration and voter turnout among blacks in the North, while much higher than for blacks in the South, lagged behind whites in the North.

One notable occurrence during this interwar period dealt with paupers (Keyssar 2000, 237–244). The Great Depression turned millions of workers into relief recipients, who in many states could be denied the vote because of pauperage laws. Most citizens, however, were keenly aware that the unemployed were not lazy, but sought relief due to terrible economic conditions. As such, pauperage laws, though not abolished, were sometimes ignored.

Every state (North and South) retained residency and registration requirements.

In 1940, *The New Republic* declared state suffrage laws a "poor substitute for the 'universal suffrage' guaranteed by the Constitution" and reported that citizens could be disqualified from voting for more than fifty reasons. When threats and violence against unpopular minorities were also considered, "the wonder is that anyone is left to go to the polls" ("Restricted Voting" 1940, 260).

A "Second Reconstruction"

It was only after 1940 that blacks began to reclaim that which was promised in 1870. Grassroots political activism, congressional action, presidential leadership, and judicial engagement ended a century of discriminatory practices. Many of these changes were prompted by American intervention in World War II. War and suffrage, once again. Aside from the obvious hypocrisy of denying suffrage to anyone who took up arms for the country, the war was fought to rid the world of a political ideology based on racism and antisemitism. And yet blacks, including black soldiers, still suffered from racist and discriminatory practices. To fight against discrimination abroad while enduring it at home made no sense; nothing but the full rights of citizenship did. The war "spawned a popular embrace of democracy more vigorous than any that had occurred since the most optimistic moments of Reconstruction" (Keyssar 2000, 245). One of the first steps was the Soldier Voting Act of 1942, which entitled persons in military service to vote by absentee ballot and exempted them in federal elections from any poll tax.

Of equal importance was the change in Supreme Court jurisprudence. By midcentury, the justices had begun to wrestle with schemes employed to deny blacks and others the right to vote. Between 1944 and 1972, the Court invalidated the white primary; prohibited racial gerrymandering to exclude blacks; struck down poll taxes in state elections; declared voting to be a fundamental right; effectively barred property and taxpaying requirements and pauperage exclusions; upheld congressional authority to outlaw voting qualifications, including literacy tests, that had the effect of discriminating on the basis of race; and limited the ability of states to impose lengthy residency qualifications in state elections.

In *Smith* v. *Allwright* (1944), the Supreme Court—relying upon *United States* v. *Classic* (1941), which held that the right to vote guaranteed by the Fifteenth Amendment also applied to primaries—struck down the white primary, the most effective method of preventing blacks from voting. A state that makes primaries an integral part of the electoral process, the justices said, cannot treat the parties that run those primaries as private actors free from constitutional constraints. Accordingly, the white primary, even if adopted absent formal participation by the state, constituted a violation of the Fifteenth Amendment.

Following the war, the National Association for the Advancement of Colored Persons (NAACP) and other civil rights organizations continued to press for full citizenship rights. An increase in black voting in the North had given those groups some leverage. Political pressure and racial violence in the South prompted President Harry Truman to establish the Committee on Civil Rights (CCR) in 1946, which called upon the nation to safeguard the civil rights of all citizens. Per voting, the report suggested abolishing poll taxes, enfranchising "Indian citizens" in Western states, and creating a Civil Rights Division in the DOJ to enforce the rights of citizens to participate in electoral politics. Relatively quickly, the five Western states that had denied the franchise to "Indians, not taxed" repealed their statutes.

In *Schnell* v. *Davis* (1949), the Court struck down an Alabama law that expanded its literacy test to include an "understanding" of what was read; the test was "merely a device to make racial discrimination easy," said the justices. (In 1959, *Lassiter* v. *Northampton County Board of Elections* clarified that in the absence of any discriminatory application, a literacy test was constitutional.)

On multiple occasions throughout the 1950s, the House of Representatives approved civil rights bills; almost all fell victim to the Southern filibuster in the Senate. The one notable exception came in 1957, when Congress created the Civil Rights Division in the DOJ and authorized the attorney general to bring civil suits and obtain injunctions in federal courts where the right to vote was threatened or denied. Subsequent federal legislation in 1960 and 1964 gave federal courts power to appoint voter referees to register voters and barred unequal application of voter registration requirements. These legislative actions were inspired by a massive grassroots movement that included petitions, demonstrations, sit-ins, freedom riders, and voter registration drives. That movement was met with fierce resistance and brutal racial violence in the South.

Some Southern states devised novel plans to minimize black voting. White residents of Tuskegee, Alabama, fearful of black migration and the effects of black suffrage, persuaded the

Alabama Legislature to alter the city limits. The redrawn city boundary was twenty-eight sided, excluded almost all blacks, and left whites unaffected. The legislature's intent was unhidden: To deny voting rights by any means that would not run afoul of existing law. When challenged, the Supreme Court held that state power to establish political subdivisions could not be used as an instrument to circumvent a federally protected right. The upshot of *Gomillion* v. *Lightfoot* (1960) was that racial gerrymandering (as employed here) violated the Fifteenth Amendment.

Federal efforts to abolish poll taxes failed numerous times in the 1940s and 1950s, mostly due to Southern opposition. By 1960, only five states, all Southern, retained poll taxes. Nevertheless, because the Supreme Court had in 1937 upheld the constitutionality of poll taxes, Congress proposed in 1962 the Twenty-Fourth Amendment, which abolished the use of poll or other taxes in *federal* elections. The amendment, despite Southern opposition, was ratified on January 23, 1964. Even before the amendment was ratified, Virginia, attempting to escape its effects, enacted legislation that required a prospective voter in any federal election to file a certificate of residence six months in advance or pay a poll tax. In *Harman* v. *Forssenius* (1965), the justices unanimously struck down the law, noting that the poll tax "was born of a desire to disenfranchise the Negro."

The Twenty-Fourth Amendment was silent on state elections. When Virginia's $1.50 annual poll tax for state elections was challenged in *Harper* v. *Virginia State Board of Elections* (1966), the Supreme Court held that poll taxes for any election violated the Fourteenth Amendment's Equal Protection Clause. The majority declared that suffrage was a fundamental right that could not be abridged on account of wealth, property, or economic status. (*Harper* had one other effect: the end of pauperage exclusions. If wealth and economic status were unrelated to a citizen's ability to participate in the electoral process, pauperage exclusions were likewise unconstitutional.)

Not long after the nation witnessed the bloody scenes from Selma, Alabama—where peaceful black and white activists began their march to Montgomery to draw attention to black voter registration and were viciously assaulted by state law enforcement officers in March 1965—President Lyndon Johnson called upon the nation to eliminate root and branch all vestiges of discrimination and oppression based on race. Congress responded by passing the Voting Rights Act (VRA) of 1965, inarguably the single most important voting law in American history. The Act authorized federal examiners to register voters in any jurisdiction where the attorney general deemed that it was necessary to enforce the Fifteenth Amendment. It outlawed any "voting qualification or prerequisite to voting" that denied the right to vote based on race, including literacy tests, tests for educational achievement and understanding, and proofs of good moral character. But it was not enough to prohibit only those methods currently employed; Southern states would find other ways. So, the Act further required that states and localities with histories of racial discrimination obtain approval (or "preclearance") from a federal court or the attorney general prior to any changes to voting laws taking effect. (This "preclearance" requirement will be discussed in chapter 2.) The Supreme Court, on the one-year anniversary of the events in Selma, upheld the VRA in *South Carolina* v. *Katzenbach* (1966) as an appropriate exercise of Congress's enforcement authority in the Fifteenth Amendment. The effect of the VRA was near immediate: In 1964, black voter registration in Mississippi was under 10 percent; by 1968, it was 60 percent. In Alabama, black voter registration had grown from 24 to 57 percent in the same four years (Keyssar 2000, 264).

Congress renewed the VRA in 1970, 1975, 1982, and 2006, with some amendments. The 1970 amendments limited state residency requirements (which were constitutionally permissible to minimize voter fraud and promote a voting populace familiar with the problems and resources of the community) to no more than thirty days in presidential elections and created uniform standards to registration and absentee voting in federal elections. But the 1970 amendments said nothing about state elections. Nevertheless, when a Tennessee law that required a one-year residency for state elections was challenged in *Dunn v. Blumstein* (1972), the justices suggested that thirty days was "ample time" for states to protect against electoral fraud. The 1975 amendments mandated bilingual registration materials and ballots.

Reapportionment, Redistricting, and Gerrymandering

Despite disenfranchisement of large segments of the population, Congress and the states have largely adhered to the principle of representation based on equal population. The one notable exception to this is the Senate, where each state, regardless of its population, has two senators. By contrast, Article I, Section 2, of the Constitution stipulates that seats in the House of Representatives be apportioned among the states in accordance with population, as determined every ten years by the national census. But it is federal law that determines the size of the House. For decades, Congress increased the number of seats in the House to reflect the growing population. Since 1911, the number of seats has been 435, save for a brief period following the admissions of Alaska and Hawaii. After each decennial census, Congress determines the number of seats to which each state is entitled. Mathematical exactitude is not possible because of constant population shifts and the constitutional requirement that each state, regardless of its population, receive at least one seat. After seats are apportioned, state legislatures redraw district lines, known as redistricting, with each district relatively equal in population to all others.

The Constitution is less clear on the principle of representation at the state level, merely insisting that every state have "a Republican form of Government." Every state admitted to the Union between 1790 and 1889 guaranteed representation in its state legislature based on population. In the twentieth century, however, urbanization led to state legislative districts that were proportionately out-of-whack. A large city with a million residents may have been represented in the state legislature by a single lawmaker, while a rural area with far less population also had one lawmaker. This is known as malapportionment: the creation of electoral districts with disparate ratios of voters to representatives. The simple solution to malapportionment is for state legislatures to redraw districts every decade or so, to reflect population shifts. For a variety of political reasons, many declined to do so.

When the Supreme Court first confronted state legislative malapportionment in *Colegrove* v. *Green* (1946), the justices held that it was a "political question" and thus nonjusticiable— beyond the authority of the federal judiciary. "Courts ought not to enter this political thicket," said the majority opinion. Only Congress could determine if states had "a Republican form of Government." Sixteen years later, however, *Baker* v. *Carr* (1962) held that malapportionment claims brought under the Fourteenth Amendment's Equal Protection Clause were justiciable. *Baker* signaled a veritable revolution in American politics by inviting litigation challenging malapportioned legislatures. The revolution came swiftly. In *Gray* v. *Sanders* (1963), the justices declared that political equality meant "only one thing—one person, one vote." The next year, the Court handed down seventeen apportionment rulings. The two most important were *Wesberry* v. *Sanders* (1964) and *Reynolds* v. *Sims* (1964), which extended the principle of "one person, one vote" to congressional districts and state legislative districts, respectively. Years later, Earl Warren, who had been chief justice during this period, called *Baker* the "most important case" of his tenure because it led to the transformation of the electoral landscape by shifting political power from rural areas to the urban and suburban ones where most Americans lived. Today, congressional and state legislative districts are relatively equal in population.

Redrawing congressional and state legislative districts has long been a highly political process. In 1811, Elbridge Gerry, the governor of Massachusetts, thought it wise to draw district lines to benefit his political allies. Commenting on his plan, a critic noted that one of the districts looked like a salamander and labeled it at "Gerry-mander." Partisan gerrymandering is drawing districts to advantage or disadvantage a particular party. Racial gerrymandering, a major consideration since the 1982 amendments to the VRA, is drawing district lines to advantage or disadvantage a particular race or ethnicity. (Both will be discussed in chapter 2.)

Age Appropriate

For centuries, twenty-one was the age at which one joined the body politic. In the 1950s and 1960s, youth organizations, veterans groups, educational associations, the NAACP, and the United Auto Workers pressured states to lower the minimum age. Successes were few. Every state except Georgia, Kentucky, Alaska, and Hawaii limited the franchise to those twenty-one years of age and older; of those four, only Georgia permitted eighteen-year-olds to vote. The Vietnam War provided the backdrop for lowering the voting age to eighteen: "Old enough to fight, old enough to vote." Congress responded. The 1970 amendments to the VRA lowered the voting age in federal and state elections to eighteen. But the Supreme Court, in *Oregon v. Mitchell* (1970), ruled that while Congress had the authority to set the voting age in federal elections, it could not by simple statute do so in state elections.

The prospect of holding an election in 1972 in which eighteen-year-olds would be allowed to vote in state but not federal elections prompted the Twenty-Sixth Amendment: "The right of citizens of the United States, who are eighteen years of age or older, to vote shall not be denied or abridged by the United States or any State on account of age." The ratification process took less than four months.

The Special Case of the District of Columbia

The District of Columbia has long occupied a special place in American constitutional framework. Carved from land ceded by Maryland and Virginia, the District is the "Seat of the Government of the United States." (In 1846, Congress returned the land donated by Virginia. The District now sits entirely in land once part of Maryland.) For its first century-and-a-half, D.C. inhabitants had no means to participate in federal electoral politics. That changed in 1961. The Twenty-Third Amendment integrated the District into the Electoral College. The D.C. Suffrage Amendment granted to the District the number of electoral votes in the Electoral College equal to the number of votes to which it would be entitled if it were a state, but not to exceed the electoral votes allocated to the smallest state. But because the District is not a state, it has no *voting* representation in Congress, even though its inhabitants are subject to all federal taxes. D.C. residents thus have, as their vehicle license plates declare, "taxation without representation."

Electoral Reforms

Although the last half of the twentieth century witnessed extraordinary gains in securing the right to vote and ensuring that those votes would be weighted equally, it also marked a decline in voter turnout. According to the U.S. Census Bureau, between 1960 and 2000, voter turnout declined from 63 to 50 percent in presidential elections. This decline is even more remarkable when considering the various reforms enacted by states to make registering and voting easier—relaxing residency requirements for students and military personnel, adopting registration deadlines close in time to elections, allowing mail-in registration, authorizing "agency registration" (registration at public facilities), approving early voting, and permitting absentee voting. Voter registration increased almost everywhere, but that increase did not appear to affect the number of citizens who voted (Piven and Cloward 2000, 261–262).

Congress considered registration reform repeatedly in the 1970s and 1980s, but with little success due to steadfast Republican opposition. Finally, in 1993, Congress passed the National Voter Registration Act. The Act, colloquially known as "Motor Voter," required states to register voters in federal elections at public agencies (driver's license centers, libraries, and welfare agencies), by mail, and by attaching voter registration forms to driver's license applications.

In 1998, Oregon became the first state to require that all elections be conducted by mail. (By 2020, three other states mandated "postal voting.")

The Return to Democracy

The twentieth century beheld a remarkable expansion of suffrage. At its dawn, many white males could vote. Women could not. Black males were effectively denied the ballot, at least in the South, by all manner of skillfully contrived legal discrimination, violence, and fraud. Those without economic means were kept away by poll taxes. Cities were grossly underrepresented in legislative chambers. And those under twenty-one were excluded from the electorate. By its conclusion, constitutional amendments had enfranchised women, barred poll taxes, and lowered the voting age in federal elections to eighteen. Congress had legislated against the obvious and subtle state regulations that had the effect of denying suffrage to citizens on the basis of race and economic status and rendered less burdensome registration requirements. And the federal judiciary had invalidated a myriad of franchise-narrowing laws and practices, declared voting to be a fundamental right, and rewrote constitutional standards of representation. It was a century of difference.

Conclusion

That voting rights in the United States are important is undeniable: Constitutional amendments deal with voting rights more than any other issue. Seven of the seventeen post-Bill of Rights amendments—the Fourteenth, Fifteenth, Seventeenth, Nineteenth, Twenty-Third, Twenty-Fourth, and Twenty-Sixth—either make the franchise more inclusive or the electoral process more democratic.

The forces that prompted this democratization were numerous. They included the power of democratic ideals, basic notions of justice and equality, socioeconomic changes, westward expansion, the rise of political parties, political and individual self-interest, protest movements, and war. War really mattered. Nearly every major suffrage extension in American history occurred during or shortly after wars. The Revolutionary War and the Wars of 1812 and 1848 accelerated the demise of property and taxpaying requirements. The Civil War brought about black male suffrage. The contributions of women during World War I advanced women's suffrage. Black soldiers returning from World War II played a prominent role in the political emancipation of blacks between the 1940s and 1960s. And the Vietnam War led to the lowering of the voting age to eighteen.

Today, nearly all adult citizens are legally entitled to vote. A few—felons and noncitizens, most notably—remain disenfranchised. But the rest enjoy relatively unmatched opportunities to participate in electoral politics. Since suffrage is the chief means by which citizens safeguard other rights, voting is the most basic civil right. As this history shows, however, the right to vote is "as fragile as it is fundamental" (Keyssar 2006, 219).

References

Amar, Akhil Reed. 2005. *America's Constitution: A Biography*. New York: Random House.

Annbinder, Tyler G. 1992. *Nativism and Slavery: The Northern Know Nothings and the Politics of the 1850s*. New York: Oxford University Press.

Beard, Charles. 1913. *An Economic Interpretation of the Constitution*. New York: The Macmillan Company.

Beeman, Richard. 2009. *Plain, Honest Men: The Making of the American Constitution*. New York: Random House.

Blackstone, Sir William. [1765–1769] 1872. *Commentaries on the Laws of England*. 4 vols. Chicago, IL: Callaghan and Company.

Bowen, Catherine Drinker. 1966. *Miracle at Philadelphia: The Story of the Constitutional Convention, May to September 1787*. Boston, MA: Little, Brown and Company.

Crotty, William J. 1977. *Political Reform and the American Experiment*. New York: Thomas Y. Crowell.

Donald, David Herbert. 1995. *Lincoln*. New York: Simon and Schuster.

Elliot, Jonathan. 1859. *Debates on the Adoption of the Federal Constitution, in the Convention held at Philadelphia, in 1787, with a diary of the debate of the Congress of the Confederacy; as reported by James Madison, a member, and deputy from Virginia*. 5 vols. Philadelphia, PA: J. B. Lippincott and Company.

Farrand, Max, ed. 1966. *The Records of the Federal Convention of 1787*. 4 vols. New Haven, CT: Yale University Press.

Foner, Eric. 2014. *Reconstruction: America's Unfinished Revolution, 1863–1877*. New York: Harper Collins.

Gurko, Miriam. 1974. *The Ladies of Seneca Falls: The Birth of the Women's Rights Movement*. New York: Schocken Books, Inc.

Hamilton, Alexander, James Madison, and John Jay. [1787–1788] 1961. *The Federalist Papers*. Edited by Clinton Rossiter. New York: Mentor.

Hayden, Grant M. 2002. "Voting and Political Participation." In Kermit L. Hall, ed., *The Oxford Companion to American Law*. New York: Oxford University Press.

Hill, Adams Sherman. 1868. "The Chicago Convention." *The North American Review*, 107 (220): 167–186.

Key, V. O., Jr. 1949. *Southern Politics in State and Nation.* New York: Alfred A. Knopf.

Keyssar, Alexander. 2000. *The Right to Vote: The Contested History of Democracy in the United States.* New York: Basic Books.

Keyssar, Alexander. 2006. Written Testimony of Alexander Keyssar Submitted to the Subcommittee on the Constitution, Civil Rights, and Property Rights of the Senate Committee on the Judiciary. *Reauthorizing the Voting Rights Act's Temporary Provisions: Policy Perspectives and Views from the Field.* 109th Cong., 2nd sess., 21 June. https://www.govinfo.gov/content/pkg/CHRG -109shrg31269/html/CHRG-109shrg31269.htm

Klarman, Michael J. 2004. *From Jim Crow to Civil Rights: The Supreme Court and the Struggle for Racial Equality.* New York: Oxford University Press.

Kousser, J. Morgan. 1984. "Suffrage." In Jack P. Greene, ed., *Encyclopedia of American Political History.* New York: Charles Scribner's Sons, 1236–1258.

Lane, Charles. 2008. *The Day Freedom Died: The Colfax Massacre, the Supreme Court, and the Betrayal of Reconstruction.* New York: Henry Holt.

Levine, Bruce. 1992. *Half Slave and Half Free: The Roots of the Civil War.* New York: Hill and Wang.

Litwack, Leon. 1998. *Trouble in Mind: Black Southerners in the Age of Jim Crow.* New York: Knopf.

Mason, Alpheus Thomas. 1965. *Free Government in the Making: Readings in American Political Thought.* 3rd ed. New York: Oxford University Press.

Mason, Alpheus Thomas, and Richard H. Leach. 1959. *In Quest of Freedom: American Political Thought and Practice.* Englewood Cliffs, NJ: Prentice Hall.

Mayer, Henry. 1998. *All on Fire: William Lloyd Garrison and the Abolition of Slavery*. New York: St. Martin's Press.

Oakes, James. 2007. *The Radical and the Republican: Frederick Douglass, Abraham Lincoln, and the Triumph of Antislavery Politics*. New York: W. W. Norton.

Padover, Saul K. 1962. *To Secure These Blessings: The Great Debates of the Constitutional Convention of 1787*. New York: Washington Square Press.

Parkman, Francis. 1878. "The Failure of Universal Suffrage." *The North American Review*, 127 (263): 1–20.

Peterson, Merrill D., ed. 1966. *Democracy, Liberty, and Property: The State Constitutional Conventions of the 1820s*. Indianapolis, IN: Bobbs-Merrill.

Piott, Steven L. 2003. *Giving Voters a Voice: The Origins of the Initiative and Referendum in America*. Columbia, MO: University of Missouri Press.

Piven, Francis Fox, and Richard A. Cloward. 2000. *Why Americans Still Don't Vote, and Why Politicians Want It That Way*. Boston, MA; Beacon Press.

Porter, Kirk Harold. 1918. *A History of Suffrage in the United States*. Chicago, IL: The University of Chicago Press.

"Restricted Voting." 1940. *The New Republic*, 103 (9): 260.

Seymour, Charles. 2017. *Electoral Reform in England and Wales: The Development and Operation of the Parliamentary Franchise, 1832–1885*. London, England: Forgotten Books.

Seymour, Charles, and Donald Paige Frary. 1918. *How the World Votes: The Story of Democratic Development in Elections*. 2 vols. Springfield, MA: C. A. Nichols Company.

Stephenson, D. Grier, Jr. 1988. "The Supreme Court, The Franchise, and the Fifteenth Amendment: The First Sixty Years." *UMKC Law Review*, 57: 47–65.

Stephenson, Donald Grier, Jr. 2004. *The Right to Vote: Rights and Liberties under the Law*. Santa Barbara, CA: ABC-CLIO.

Sydnor, Charles S. 1962. *American Revolutionaries in the Making: Political Practices in Washington's Virginia*. New York: Collier.

Turner, Frederick Jackson. 1920. *The Frontier in American History*. New York: Henry Holt.

U.S. Congress. 1834. *Annals of Congress*. 42 vols. Washington, DC: Gales and Seaton.

Waldman, Michael. 2016. *The Fight to Vote*. New York: Simon and Schuster.

Wilentz, Sean. 1992. "Property and Power: Suffrage Reform in the United States, 1787-1860." In Donald W. Rogers, ed., *Voting and the Spirit of American Democracy: Essays on the History of Voting and Voting Rights in America*. Urbana, IL: University of Illinois Press.

Williamson, Chilton. 1960. *American Suffrage from Property to Democracy, 1760–1860*. Princeton, NJ: Princeton University Press.

Woodward, C. Vann. 1957. *The Strange Career of Jim Crow*. New York: Oxford University Press.

2 Problems, Controversies, and Solutions

Introduction

In examining who has the right to vote in the twenty-first century, it is tempting to conclude that the right has undergone a simple linear expansion since the early colonial period in which only white male property owners were entrusted with the responsibility of electing officials. This view is understandable if comparing eighteenth-century voting laws and practices with contemporary ones. Since the colonial period, voting rights have been preserved in constitutional amendments, and the national and state governments have passed laws to enlarge voting rights, expanding the franchise to previously disenfranchised groups and, in many circumstances, extending the conveniences of voting by providing for mail-in, online, and early voting. Generally, under current state law, any citizen eighteen years or older who is not a convicted felon has the right to vote. This chapter will shed additional light and provide greater context for many of the contemporary controversies related to voting rights—felon disenfranchisement laws, voter ID requirements, voter registration reform, voter roll purging, voting reforms, partisan and racial gerrymandering, and the Electoral College.

Over half of the states require voters to present some form of identification prior to voting. Voter ID laws have been challenged in courts across the country, with mixed results. In 2008, the U.S. Supreme Court upheld Indiana's strict voter ID law. (Auremar/Dreamstime.com)

Felon Disenfranchisement

One longstanding voting restriction became particularly salient in 2000 when George W. Bush beat Vice President Al Gore by 537 votes in Florida, after a month-long litigation battle. Many observers noted that Gore would have easily beaten Bush if not for Florida's restrictive felon disenfranchisement laws. Currently, forty-eight states prohibit convicted felons, to one degree or another, from voting. Especially since 2000, felon disenfranchisement laws have received extensive legal and political scrutiny given our nation's extremely high incarceration rate. By one estimate, approximately 2.5 percent of the voting-age population is disenfranchised as a result of state criminal disqualification statutes (Uggen, Larson, and Shannon 2016).

For centuries, the body politic has debated the merits of limiting the franchise to those who obey the law. Social contract theorists like Thomas Hobbes, John Locke, and Jean-Jacques Rousseau argue that a political compact is formed when citizens consent to be governed by, and submit to, the laws of society in exchange for the protections that government affords. These philosophers also contemplate how to deal with those who reject the compact by violating the laws of society. Felon disenfranchisement thus finds some support in social contract theory. John Locke, in *Two Treatises of Government* (1690), for example, suggests that those who commit crimes against others separate themselves from society and, as such, may forfeit their right to vote. (Of particular note, however, Locke does not recommend that said lawbreakers be disenfranchised; rather, he leaves that decision to the legislature.)

Felon disenfranchisement also has deep roots in the American experience. From the founding through 1821, eleven states disenfranchised persons convicted of certain infamous crimes (Clegg, Conway, and Lee 2006, 6). By 1868, twenty-nine states did so.

The idea underlying felon disenfranchisement laws—that breaking the penal code carries numerous costs, some even after incarceration—is also the basis for restrictions that society finds less problematic. For example, federal law prohibits anyone convicted of a felony from possessing a firearm or serving on a federal jury. And twenty-eight states preclude a convicted felon from serving on a state jury (Binnall 2017, 4). Supporters of felon disenfranchisement note that most Americans deem it reasonable that convicted felons are prohibited from possessing guns or serving on juries.

Of course, denying the right to vote might be functionally different than prohibiting firearm possession or jury duty, since the former infringes upon a right most Americans deem fundamental. For this reason, felon disenfranchisement laws have faced greater scrutiny in recent years on both legal and policy grounds, and many states have revised their laws in response to public pressure.

Currently, only two states—Maine and Vermont—allow convicted felons to vote while in prison. In fourteen states and the District of Columbia, felons lose the right to vote while incarcerated but regain the right to re-register to vote upon completion of their sentences. An additional twenty-two states extend the vote denial until the completion of the felon's parole or probationary period. In the most restrictive situation, twelve states impose a postsentence waiting period and require additional action on the part of the felon before reinstatement of voting rights. For many of these states, the additional action is petitioning a court or the governor for voting reinstatement.

At first glance, it appears that felon disenfranchisement laws remain severe and restrictive. A cursory look at the numbers, however, does not tell the full story. In recent decades, felon disenfranchisement laws have been weakened and many states have allowed felons to vote upon leaving prison and completing their sentences. These changes have been met with controversy and, in some cases, resulted in pushback from more conservative forces.

Recent changes in Florida's election laws serve as a useful case study for understanding the competing arguments on felon disenfranchisement. In November 2018, 65 percent of Florida voters approved Amendment 4 to the state constitution, which reinstated voting rights to felons once they completed all terms of their sentences, including parole and probation. (The amendment does not apply to those convicted of murder or sexual offenses.) This amendment was lauded by opponents of felon disenfranchisement because it allowed felons to register to vote upon the completion of their sentences rather than having to seek permission from a state board on a case-by-case basis.

Upon passage of the amendment, Florida legislators debated whether the amendment was "self-executing" or required additional legislation to enforce its terms. The Republican-controlled legislature and Republican governor determined that a law was necessary to clarify the language of the amendment. The controversy involved what "completion of sentence" meant and, specifically, whether felons needed to pay all outstanding fees and fines before being allowed to register to vote. In early 2019, Florida statutorily required all felons to pay fees and fines before having their voting rights restored. This action significantly curtailed the reach of Amendment 4 because many felons had fines and restitution arrangements as part of their official sentences.

The increased financial obligations led many to argue that Florida had imposed an unconstitutional "poll tax" on potential voters and that black felons were less able to pay the fees. Opponents of the law alleged that there was no functional difference between the poll taxes prohibited by the Twenty-Fourth Amendment and Florida's requirement that felons meet certain financial obligations before voting. Both the intent (erecting barriers to black voting) and effect (depressing black voting power) of the law were indistinguishable from the constitutionally discredited poll tax.

Those arguments aside, the legality of felon disenfranchisement laws has been largely established. States have long prohibited felons from voting while in prison and even after they have completed their prison terms. In recent years, many states have liberalized felon disenfranchisement laws by allowing felons to regain voting rights upon completion of their sentences but the legal complaints continue, mostly surrounding the laws' racially disproportionate effects.

Decades prior to felon disenfranchisement laws receiving significant public attention, the Supreme Court, in *Richardson* v. *Ramirez* (1974), upheld provisions of the California Constitution and the implementing statutes that disenfranchised ex-felons over a Fourteenth Amendment Equal Protection Clause challenge. The majority relied heavily upon Section 2 of the amendment, which, among other things, punished a state for denying the right to vote to any of its male inhabitants, being twenty-one years of age and citizens of the United States, "except for participation in rebellion, or other crime," by reducing its representation in the House of Representatives. The Court also noted that, in 1868, when the amendment was ratified, twenty-nine states had provisions in their constitutions which prohibited, or authorized the legislature to prohibit, exercise of the franchise by persons convicted of felonies or infamous crimes. *Ramirez* thus held that states may disenfranchise convicted felons, even those who have completed their sentences.

Dissenting justices argued that the majority had misread the intent of Section 2, which was *not* to authorize states to disenfranchise felons but to give states a choice: Enfranchise blacks or face reduced representation in the lower chamber. Furthermore, even if Section 2 once allowed states to disenfranchise felons, that meaning was not frozen in time. In the years preceding *Ramirez*, for example, the Court had interpreted the Fourteenth Amendment to prohibit certain state practices that had previously been ruled constitutional, such as a one-year residency requirement before voting (*Dunn* v. *Blumstein*, 1972). Equally important, California had failed to provide a compelling justification for stripping ex-felons of the "fundamental" right to vote. The dissent rejected the majority's conclusion that former felons could be denied the franchise because their voting pattern might be "subversive to the interests of an orderly society." While the Supreme Court had previously justified the exclusion of voters for fear that they would change laws considered important by a temporal majority—in *Murphy* v. *Ramsey* (1885), the Court upheld the disenfranchisement of anyone who had ever entered into a bigamous or polygamous marriage; in *Davis* v. *Beason* (1890), the justices sanctioned, as a condition to the exercise of the franchise, the requirement of an oath that the elector did not teach, advise, counsel, or encourage any person to commit the crime of bigamy or polygamy—the dissent had "little doubt" that the Court would countenance such a purpose today: "To fence out from the franchise a sector of the population because of the way [it] may vote is constitutionally impermissible."

As a result of *Ramirez*, a state's decision to disenfranchise permanently convicted felons does not, *in and of itself*, run afoul of the Equal Protection Clause. The Court also made clear, however, in an unanimous opinion in *Hunter* v. *Underwood* (1985), that such laws passed with the *intent* of racial discrimination violate the Equal Protection Clause.

Litigation continued after *Ramirez*, even though the legal strategies shifted to include statutory grounds. In this century, lower courts have wrestled with whether felon disenfranchisement laws violate Section 2 of the Voting Rights Act (VRA) of 1965. Section 2, as amended in 1982, reads as follows: "No voting qualification or prerequisite to voting, or standard, practice or procedure shall be imposed or applied by any State or political subdivision in a manner which results in a denial or abridgement of the right of any citizen of the United States to vote on account of race or color." In short, Section 2 bars any state voting practice that has the *effect*, not merely the *intent*, of racial discrimination. Given that felon disenfranchisement laws have a disproportionate negative effect on racial minorities due to a much higher incarceration rate, many lawyers and interest groups have argued that such laws run afoul of the VRA. Most of those claims, however, have been rejected.

Johnson v. *Governor of Florida* (2003) is illustrative. Here, the U.S. Court of Appeals for the Eleventh Circuit entertained constitutional and statutory challenges to Florida's constitutional amendment disenfranchising ex-felons. The constitutional challenge was simple and direct: Though the Florida amendment disenfranchising ex-felons was facially neutral, it was motivated by racial animus and, therefore, violated the Equal Protection Clause. The court, relying on the precedent and logic of *Ramirez*, quickly dispensed with this challenge: Section 2 of the Fourteenth Amendment explicitly allows a state to disenfranchise felons, even those who have completed their prison sentences. With respect to whether the facially neutral felon disenfranchisement provision was enacted with racially discriminatory intent, the court conceded that Florida's original constitutional amendment, adopted in 1885, may have been so motivated, but no evidence existed to show that the state's current amendment, adopted in 1968, was adopted with racially discriminatory intent. The judges thus rejected the equal protection argument.

The statutory challenge to the Florida amendment alleged a violation of Section 2 of the VRA. The court dismissed this argument as well, noting a constitutional conflict: While Section 2 typically applies to facially neutral laws that have a racially disparate impact, the Fourteenth Amendment explicitly protects a state's right to disqualify felons. If the court were to strike down the Florida amendment as violative of the VRA, it would in essence allow a congressional statute (the VRA) to override the text of the Constitution (the Fourteenth Amendment). To the disappointment of voting rights activists, the court thus held that a facially neutral felon disenfranchisement provision cannot be challenged on the basis of its racially disparate impact under the VRA.

Other state and federal courts have addressed felon disenfranchisement laws as well, most drawing the same conclusion and for similar reasons. Generally, courts have granted state legislatures wide latitude in passing felon disenfranchisement laws as long as the *intent* is not discriminatory. Though courts have upheld them, many state legislatures—and in some circumstances, governors—have amended their felon disenfranchisement laws to make it easier for felons to regain their voting rights upon leaving prison. In the future, we are likely to see additional felon disenfranchisement reforms, especially in those states with Democratic-controlled legislatures.

In recent years, scholars and activists have brought attention to felon disenfranchisement laws by emphasizing their effect on the American electorate and have tied them to the nation's world-leading incarceration rate. While the United States has approximately 4.4 percent of the world's population, it has around 22 percent of the world's prisoner population. America leads the world with an incarceration rate of 655 people per 100,000. The next highest country, Turkey, has an incarceration rate of 287 people per 100,000 (World Prison Brief Data 2018). While there are a multitude of reasons for America's high incarceration rate, strict drug laws, overcriminalization, and mandatory sentences are three powerful factors. This "tough on crime approach," therefore, also had a profound effect on disenfranchising a much higher percentage of the population than before.

The Sentencing Project is an advocacy organization dedicated to reducing incarceration rates. Among other interests, it assesses the effect of sentencing practices on individuals, families, and broader communities. Because of the profound effect that high incarceration rates have on voting and democratic politics, The Sentencing Project has long been interested in felon disenfranchisement laws and shedding light on the staggering numbers of individuals who are excluded from the democratic process. In 2016, The Sentencing Project detailed the extent that our incarceration practices have on disenfranchisement.

According to that report, in 2016, approximately 6.1 million people in the United States were disenfranchised due to a felony conviction, an 85 percent increase from the 3.34 million felons who were disenfranchised in 1996. Roughly 2.5 percent of the total voting-age Americans is ineligible to vote on account of a felony conviction. Interestingly, about half of the 6.1 million disenfranchised reside in one of the twelve states that disenfranchise felons even *after* they complete their prison sentences.

While disenfranchising individuals who have committed a felony might seem reasonable to many, the laws' effect on American elections is substantial, especially when considered in conjunction with the Electoral College. In 2016, for example, Hillary Clinton earned three million more votes than Donald J. Trump, but still lost the presidency because Trump won the popular vote in Wisconsin, Michigan, and Pennsylvania by a combined seventy-seven thousand votes. Had Clinton won those three states and their combined forty-six electoral votes, she would have won the presidency. Evaluating the number of disenfranchised voters in key Electoral College states is, therefore, one way of analyzing the effect that felon disenfranchisement laws have on American elections. A number of important states—like Florida, Virginia, and Wisconsin—disenfranchise even after completion of the sentences, thereby disenfranchising hundreds of thousands in states crucial to presidential electoral politics. Of the 6.1 million felons who are disenfranchised nationally, approximately 27 percent reside in Florida, and its 1.5 million felons disenfranchised *postsentence* comprise 48 percent of the national total (Uggen, Larson, and Shannon 2016). The high number of disenfranchised felons in Florida, combined with its important place in presidential politics as a swing state, makes felon disenfranchisement a particularly salient issue in that state.

Felon disenfranchisement laws have also received increased attention due to the racial inequalities in the criminal justice system. This burden has been borne disproportionately by blacks. Approximately one in seven blacks has been disenfranchised, more than four times the number of nonblacks. Furthermore, about 7.4 percent of the adult black population is disenfranchised, compared to 1.8 percent of the nonblack population (Uggen, Larson, and Shannon 2016).

Although felon disenfranchisement laws passed with the *intent* to discriminate on the basis of race are unconstitutional, intent is often tough to demonstrate, as individual legislators do not voluntarily divulge their intent (and contest vehemently allegations of racial motivation).

Additionally, subsequent legislation has made it *easier* for states to disenfranchise felons. Under the terms of the National Voter Registration Act (NVRA) of 1993—more commonly known as the "Motor Voter" law—federal prosecutors are required to notify state election officials of a person's federal felony conviction, and under the Help America Vote Act (HAVA) of 2002, state election officials are instructed to purge disenfranchised felons "on a regular basis." In addition to the federal legislative support for felon disenfranchisement laws, supporters of such laws maintain that the denial of voting rights for felons is not the result of race but rather the result of a criminal conviction.

The legality of felon disenfranchisement laws has been largely established. Courts have consistently upheld felon disenfranchisement laws against Fourteenth Amendment Equal Protection challenges and VRA Section 2 lawsuits. Opponents of felon disenfranchisement laws, however, may experience greater success at the ballot box than in the courtroom. In a survey conducted in 2002, Manza, Clem, and Uggen (2004) found that 80 percent of Americans supported reinstating voting rights for ex-felons; but when asked about subcategories of felons, public support dropped. For example, 66 percent supported voting rights reinstatement for ex-felons convicted of a violent offense, 63 percent for white-collar ex-felons, and only 52 percent for sex offenders. Only 31 percent, however, supported extending voting rights to the incarcerated.

Support for restoring voting rights for ex-felons has remained strong since that survey. In a Huffington Post/YouGov poll conducted in 2018, 63 percent of Americans favored the reinstallation of voting rights for felons upon leaving prison (Levine and Edwards-Levy 2018). Supporters disagree on *how* to accomplish that, however. Of those who favor allowing ex-felons to vote, a narrow majority—53 percent—indicate that it should occur automatically, while 40 percent believe that ex-felons should follow some procedure or process to be reinstated as a voter. Support for extending voting rights to felons in prison was also lower than the 2002 survey, with only 24 percent in support in the 2018 poll. The Huffington Post/YouGov poll also indicated that support or opposition to felon disenfranchisement laws varied significantly depending on party affiliation and vote choice in the 2016 election. Nevertheless, public support for extending voting rights to ex-felons remained very high. Eighty percent of those who voted for Hillary Clinton, and 58 percent of those who voted for Donald Trump, support felon re-enfranchisement.

While an overwhelming majority of states still disenfranchise felons, to varying degrees, public opinion in favor of extending voting rights to ex-felons has remained largely consistent. Changes to felon disenfranchisement laws are likely to continue for years to come.

Voter ID

The fundamental question in the felon disenfranchisement debate is who gets access to the ballot: Is voting a right or a privilege, and what kinds of restrictions or burdens are governments allowed to place on its exercise? This divide has also been apparent in the debate over whether states may require prospective voters to present identification (ID) before casting ballots. Many states have long required some form of identification prior to voting. In recent years, however, a number of states, mostly led by Republicans, have pressed for *photo* ID.

Voter ID has become a popular reform to address the perceived problem of voter fraud. Concerns have grown that, without identification, individuals could be voting when they did not have the legal right to do so, or that individuals were voting more than once in states that did not require individuals to present some form of identification. By 2000, fourteen states either requested or required some form of identification for voting ("Voter ID History" 2017).

Voter ID became a central reform effort a few years after the 2000 disputed election between Al Gore and George W. Bush. The Florida recount procedures resulted in many Americans losing trust in the rules of the electoral process. The Florida recounts exposed some unfortunate truths about how states conduct elections, specifically how counties employed different rules for interpreting the intent of the voter if a ballot were challenged. As a result of the voting irregularities raised in that election, a National Commission on Federal Election Reform was founded by the University of Virginia's Miller Center of Public Affairs and the Century Foundation; it was cochaired by former presidents Gerald Ford and Jimmy Carter. The goal of the Commission was to present to Congress bipartisan solutions on electoral reform. A separate entity, the U.S. Commission on Civil Rights, simultaneously examined the problems in that election with the intent of providing recommendations to Congress on how to improve voting rules and advance electoral reform.

The work of the two commissions found disturbing levels of voting anomalies in Florida. The National Commission concentrated its efforts on election laws that placed barriers to the right to vote. For example, it analyzed the effect that registration laws had on voting rates. The U.S. Commission focused on the effect that Florida's voting laws had on minority voters. Many of the proposals found in these two documents aided Congress when it considered what became the HAVA of 2002.

Faced with growing discontent over Florida's handling of the 2000 election and a body of recommendations from two reform commissions, Congress sought to address the glaring weaknesses in the states' election laws and provide financial assistance for state reforms moving forward. The HAVA mandated that every state create a unified voter registration list; replace outdated voting technology, like the punch card system used by many Florida counties; and allow individuals to vote on a provisional basis if there were a disagreement about whether the person was lawfully permitted to vote in that jurisdiction. Congress also created the Election Assistance Commission (EAC) as a resource for states in administering elections; and provided funds for states to update their voting machinery (without mandating a single system), provide for voter education, and train election workers.

While the HAVA helped states with their election administration, problems in the 2004 election, particularly in Ohio, generated additional complaints about electronic voting machines, the lack of appropriate paper trails, the accuracy of voter registration rolls, the purging of voters from state voter rolls, and allegations concerning voter suppression. Many voting precincts also experienced long lines, which raised questions about how states had allocated their voting machines and whether partisan bias had affected decisions regarding how many voting machines each voting precinct received.

These problems led to additional calls for election reform. After the 2004 election, an independent, bipartisan group was tasked with studying elections and making recommendations to improve election administering. The Commission on Federal Election Reform, cochaired by former president, Jimmy Carter, and former secretary of state, James Baker, offered eighty-seven recommendations for states with the goal of increasing public confidence in our nation's elections. While most of the Carter-Baker Commission's recommendations were uncontroversial, one was highly controversial. Recommendation 2.5 suggested that states require would-be voters to obtain and show a REAL ID prior to voting. It reads as follows:

> To ensure that persons presenting themselves at the polling place are the ones on the registration list, the Commission recommends that states require voters to use the REAL ID card. . . . The card includes a person's full legal name, date of birth, a signature (captured as a digital image), a photograph, and the person's Social Security number.

> This card should be modestly adapted for voting purposes
> to indicate on the front or back whether the individual is
> a U.S. citizen. States should provide an EAC-template ID
> with a photo to non-drivers free of charge.

The recommendation was immediately criticized by the Brennan Center for Justice, the League of Women Voters, the American Civil Liberties Union (ACLU), and other organizations as an unnecessary and costly requirement that would lead to the disenfranchisement of many poor and uneducated citizens who lacked the means and ability to produce documentation necessary to prove their identity. The Brennan Center challenged the voter ID recommendation, arguing that as many as 10 percent of eligible voters did not have the documentation required to obtain a REAL ID, and that the added burdens on voters would be felt disproportionately by citizens who traditionally had experienced difficulty at the polls, including the elderly, students, low-income individuals, and those with disabilities ("Policy Brief on Voter Identification" 2006).

To reduce the financial burden on voters, the Carter-Baker Commission urged states to provide REAL ID cards at no cost to those who did not possess a driver's license and to make the procedures for acquiring a REAL ID as seamless as possible. By contrast, proponents of voter ID argued that it would reduce voter fraud by eliminating the possibility that a person could vote more than once or vote assuming another person's identity. The Commission admitted that there was "no evidence of extensive fraud in U.S. elections or of multiple voting" ("Building Confidence in U.S. Elections" 2005, 18) but noted that voter ID was nevertheless useful for two reasons. First, requiring voters to present some form of ID would eliminate the incentive to engage in fraud regardless of how prevalent it might actually be. A voter ID requirement might prevent a very close election from being decided by voter fraud. Second, a voter ID requirement might help improve citizens' trust in the electoral process. With improved voter confidence, voting and participation in the electoral process would increase.

The REAL ID Act, enacted by Congress in 2005, modified federal law by establishing guidelines for the issuance of state driver's licenses and identity documents. To receive a REAL ID, citizens were required to prove their identity by presenting a birth certificate, passport, or similar documents.

With the Carter-Baker Commission's recommendations providing political cover—and since the passage of the REAL ID Act—many states enacted voter ID laws with the stated goal of reducing voter fraud. In 2004, thirty states did not require any form of identification to vote. Though the number of states requiring some form of voter ID increased significantly after the Commission's recommendations, those laws were subjected to judicial scrutiny.

Indiana was among the first states to enact a voter ID bill in 2005. The Indiana statute was considered to be a strict form of voter ID because it required voters who failed to present a government-issued photo ID at the voting booth to bring that ID to the circuit county clerk's office within ten days of the election for their provisional ballot to be counted.

The Indiana Democratic Party and others filed suit, arguing that the photo ID requirement violated the Equal Protection Clause of the Fourteenth Amendment by imposing a substantial and unjustified burden upon on those who cannot readily obtain such identification. The federal district court upheld the law, noting that the plaintiffs had failed to produce a single individual ineligible to vote as a result of the law. After a divided U.S. Court of Appeals for the Seventh Circuit affirmed, the Supreme Court considered the matter in *Crawford* v. *Marion County Election Board* (2008).

Writing for the majority, Justice John Paul Stevens first articulated the standard the Court would use to evaluate the competing arguments. Rather than trying to adopt some bright-line rule that delineated permissible and impermissible state electoral rules, the Court declared that it would evaluate the constitutional challenge to an election regulation by weighing "the asserted injury to the right to vote against the 'precise interests put forward by the State as a justification for the burden imposed by its rule.'"

Indiana offered three justifications for the law. First, it had a valid interest in "participating in a nationwide effort to improve and modernize election procedures that have been criticized as antiquated and inefficient." Second, the law would prevent in-person voter fraud; specifically, individuals attempting to vote on behalf of dead people or attempting to vote in Indiana when they do not lawfully reside in the state. And third, the law would help instill voter confidence in the electoral process. Indiana even pointed to the Carter-Baker Commission for support, noting that "the electoral system cannot inspire public confidence if no safeguards exist to deter or detect fraud or to confirm the identity of voters" ("Building Confidence in U.S. Elections" 2005, §2.5). With increased trust in the election system, Indiana suggested that citizens will be more likely to participate in the state's elections.

The challengers focused almost exclusively on the significant burden the law placed on the purported thousands of individuals in Indiana who did not have a valid state driver's license. The number of individuals affected was suggested to be as high as forty-three thousand. Petitioners further maintained that disproportionately included in the large number were the disabled, homeless, low-income, and racial minorities.

The majority maintained that two recent statutes—the NVRA and the HAVA—placed significant challenges on Indiana and other states to update and modernize their voter rolls. Under the former, states were required to use driver's license applications as voter registration applications, thereby increasing the number of registered voters. Under the latter, states were required to maintain computerized statewide voter rolls and were mandated to verify a voter registration application by social security or driver's license number. While Indiana was not *required* to adopt a photo ID, it was a reasonable measure to help determine legal voters. After all, if photo ID were required to board a plane, enter federal buildings, or engage in bank transactions, it was rational that Indiana could require citizens to present an ID card before voting.

Missing from Indiana's voter fraud argument was evidence of an actual voter fraud problem. The majority even admitted that "[t]he record contains no evidence of any such fraud actually occurring in Indiana at any time in its history." Furthermore, under Indiana's criminal code, voter fraud was felony conduct punishable by prison time. In other words, the costs associated with committing in-person voter fraud were significantly higher than the marginal benefit of adding a vote to one's preferred candidate in a race that might be separated by thousands or tens of thousands of votes. Nevertheless, the Court noted that historians and journalists had documented instances of voter fraud in elections and that even Indiana experienced voter fraud—albeit absentee ballot fraud—in the 2003 Democratic mayoral primary for East Chicago. The need for "orderly" and "accurate" elections, the majority reasoned, overrode the need for precise and documented evidence of in-person voter fraud.

After evaluating Indiana's stated interests for the voter ID law, the majority transitioned to a discussion of the burdens imposed by the law. The burdens felt by those who do not have a valid driver's license or other acceptable form of identification, however, were mitigated by Indiana providing a free photo ID card for those who provided the needed documentation. The real burden was borne by those who faced steep difficulties in obtaining the free photo ID card, like the elderly, the homeless, or those who could not easily obtain the birth certificate or documentation needed to receive the card. While the justices were sympathetic to the burdens imposed on Indiana voters, the underlying problem was the facial challenge by Indiana Democrats. With a facial challenge, the Democrats were asking the Court to declare the Indiana voter ID requirement unconstitutional in all circumstances. A majority of the

Court was unwilling go that far because the trial court record was unclear on the magnitude of the law's effect. Therefore, the Court ruled that "on the basis of the record that has been made in this litigation, we cannot conclude that the statute imposes 'excessively burdensome requirements' on any class of voters." By using this language, the majority left open the possibility that with a more fully developed evidentiary record that clearly establishes how many people are harmed, the Court might be willing to entertain a challenge to a different voter ID law.

In dissent, Justice David Souter, joined by Justice Ruth Bader Ginsburg, agreed with the legal standard articulated by the majority but disagreed on the nature and scope of the injury. First, there were travel costs and fees associated with acquiring the ID card. While wealthier people might find the travel and fees as more of an "inconvenience," those burdens would be cost prohibitive for the poor and disabled. For example, while Marion County had over nine hundred active voter precincts, it had only twelve Bureau of Motor Vehicles (BMV) license branches, meaning that many without a driver's license had to use public transportation, or had to ask a friend or family member, to get to the BMV. That burden was exacerbated because, as of 2007, twenty-one of Indiana's ninety-two counties had no public transportation system at all and, as of 2000, nearly 10 percent of voters lived in one of those twenty-one counties. For those counties that had public transportation, many of the services reached only certain cities, leaving thousands of citizens in towns and cities without any reasonable means of public transportation.

Second, assuming that individuals without an ID card could get to a BMV, Souter argued that many faced a "second financial hurdle" because, to obtain proper identification, individuals needed to present a birth certificate, a certificate of naturalization, U.S. veterans photo identification, or a U.S. passport. Since Indiana counties levied fees for obtaining birth certificate copies and the U.S. Department of State charged upward of one hundred dollars to obtain a passport, the costs associated with obtaining a ID card might be cost prohibitive for the poor, elderly, and disabled.

While the law allowed those without an ID card to cast a provisional ballot, to have the provisional ballot accepted, the voter had to appear before the circuit court clerk or county election board within ten days of the election and sign an affidavit stating the reason for not having a photo ID card was due to indigency or a religious objection. This required poor voters without a proper ID card to travel to the county office within ten days of *each election* if they wanted their votes counted. Souter noted that this onerous requirement was demonstrated in the 2007 municipal elections in Marion County when thirty-four provisional ballots were cast but *only* two of those provisional voters made it to the county seat within ten days after the election.

Not only were the costs associated with the voter ID requirement too excessive, the dissent argued, but Indiana's stated interests were flimsy, unpersuasive, and most likely masked the state's true motivation. At its core, the voter ID law was intended to reduce or eliminate in-person voter fraud even though the Indiana legislature and the district court were never provided one example of in-person voter impersonation in the state. In fact, the trial court record included affidavits from poll workers who testified that they had never witnessed any *attempts* to engage in in-person voter fraud. The voter ID requirement was thus an expensive solution in search of a problem. Given the complete absence of any in-person voter impersonation problem in the state or in the nation, many voter ID opponents wondered whether the requirement was simply a pretext for a law designed to make it more difficult for Democratic-leaning voters to exercise the franchise.

Following *Crawford*, states were largely free to proceed with voter ID requirements as long as the laws were not intentionally discriminatory or in violation of a state constitutional provision. In 2019, thirty-five states had some form of voter ID requirement. Seventeen of the thirty-five states required a

photo ID to vote while eighteen accepted other forms of identification, like a utility bill, to document the voter's identity.
Since the Court upheld Indiana's voter ID law, lower courts
have wrestled with voter ID laws across the country. Some have
been upheld; others struck down. The debate over whether
voter ID laws are needed for ballot integrity or whether they
are a way to discourage Democratic voters has developed in
different ways in the states.

One major factor contributing to the recent growth in
voter ID laws has been the Supreme Court's decision in *Shelby
County* v. *Holder* (2013), which dealt a serious blow to a key
provision of the VRA. Under Section 5 of that Act, many states
and localities were required to receive preclearance from the
U.S. District Court for the District of Columbia or the U.S.
attorney general prior to changing their election laws. The
jurisdictions under the Section 5 preclearance requirement had
a documented history of racial discrimination in their voting
practices. In *Shelby County*, the Supreme Court did not declare
the preclearance requirement unconstitutional, but rather the
Section 4 formula for determining which jurisdictions were
required to receive preclearance, in essence suspending the preclearance requirement until Congress passed an updated coverage formula. Given that many southern states were covered
under the Section 5 preclearance requirement, passing voter ID
laws were problematic, since high percentages of those without
the proper identification were racial minorities and would be
disproportionately affected by such laws. Since the Supreme
Court gutted the VRA in 2013, covered jurisdictions—like
Texas, Virginia, and North Carolina—have been free to pass
voter ID laws without receiving prior federal approval.

Opponents of voter ID laws have long complained that such
laws can make voting more costly, which is likely to depress
voter turnout. Such claims raise important empirical questions
regarding the extent of voter disenfranchisement and the effect
that such laws have on turnout. The calls for voter ID requirements have been based on claims that elections have been

tainted by various degrees of voter fraud as well. Usually, voter fraud has been defined as in-person voter fraud. In-person voter fraud requires that individuals try to vote more than once by claiming to be another person, whether that person be alive or dead. Fortunately, research has been conducted on the empirical reality of voter fraud.

Since 2000, voter fraud has become an important rallying cry for those seeking to pass additional restrictions on voting rights. The concern is that corruption at the ballot box is rampant and that many individuals are voting more than once. A further concern is that this illegal behavior benefits Democratic candidates. One elected official who has long voiced, often without evidence, both of these claims is Kris Kobach, Kansas's Secretary of State from 2011 to 2019. Kobach has also supported and helped draft voter ID laws and anti-immigration laws across the country. For example, a 2013 Kansas law required people to prove their citizenship with a birth certificate or passport when registering to vote. The ACLU of Kansas challenged the law's constitutionality (Fish v. Kobach, 2018).

At a trial that proved to be an embarrassment to Kobach, he failed to provide any evidence that noncitizens were registered to vote in any great number (or with intent to vote) or that noncitizens were the key factor in deciding any election. Kobach's experts relied upon faulty data, most notably a spreadsheet from one county in Kansas that purportedly showed that dozens of noncitizens attempted to register to vote in an eighteen-year period. The actual number of noncitizens showing up on voter registration rolls was thirteen and these were the result of administrative error, not criminal intent to vote. (None had even showed up at the polls or attempted to cast a ballot.) Though provided the opportunity to demonstrate with empirical evidence the existence of voter fraud in Kansas, Kobach and his supporters failed to do so. The case was dismissed.

Other supporters of voter ID and more restrictive voter registration procedures have also largely been unable to support their claims with verifiable data. Following the 2016 election, President Donald Trump promised to provide support and evidence for his claim that millions of noncitizens had voted in the election, tipping the popular vote to Hillary Clinton. Soon after taking office, Trump created the Presidential Advisory Commission on Election Integrity to examine voting irregularities and propose possible reforms. In early 2018, the Commission was disbanded after many states refused to share voting data out of concern for privacy and possible violations of state law.

The empirical evidence regarding in-person voter fraud suggests that the problem is minimal to nonexistent. Justin Levitt (2007) and Lorraine Minnite (2010), using election incident reports, journalistic accounts, and allegations of voter fraud, have concluded that in-person voter fraud is essentially nonexistent. More recent academic studies have supported these findings. Philip Bump (2016) also scoured the secondary voter data in 2016, looking for reports of voter impersonation in the 2016 election and found only four such instances. Those who believe that voter fraud is prevalent argue that the reason it is so ubiquitous is because people do it so well, thereby discounting the studies that have found no voter fraud based on the absence of such evidence. Other researchers have used more refined scholarly tools, like examining statistical anomalies that would point to individuals voting for dead people or statistical analysis on the probability of double voting. The studies are consistently clear that in-person voter fraud is miniscule and has never swayed an election (Cottrell, Herron, and Westwood 2018; Goel et al. 2020).

Interestingly, voter fraud studies that demonstrate an electoral effect are those that examine the influence that voter ID laws have on elections, specifically, how many potential legitimate voters are disqualified by voter ID laws. Some early studies have found that, overall, voter ID laws did not affect voter turnout (Alvarez, Bailey, and Katz 2008; Mycoff, Wagner, and

Wilson 2009). Others indicate that photo and nonphoto ID laws decreased turnout between 1.6 and 2.2 percent, and that voter ID laws disenfranchised between three and 4.5 million voters in 2006 (de Alth 2009, 186). More recently, studies found voter ID laws to have a significant negative effect on potential voters. Researchers at the University of Wisconsin surveyed nonvoters in two counties to evaluate the effect the state's strict voter ID law had on the 2016 election and concluded that 10 percent of nonvoters in those counties lacked a qualifying voter ID or "report[ed] that voter ID was at least a *partial* reason for not voting." The researchers also noted that "voter ID requirements 'directly' affect voters who lack qualifying IDs but also 'indirectly' affect voters who are confused about their compliance with the law." Since the majority of those deterred or prevented from voting in 2016 had voted in 2012, the estimates were that the "voter ID requirement reduced turnout in [those] counties by up to one percentage point" (DeCrescenzo and Mayer 2019, 342).

Studies have also examined which groups have been most affected by voter ID laws. The Wisconsin study found that the burdens of voter ID fell disproportionately on low-income and minority populations. In a broader, more systematic look at the effect that voter ID laws have on turnout for different races and ethnicities across fifty-one elections (twenty-five primaries and twenty-six general elections) in ten states that have strict voter ID laws, researchers found that strict voter identification laws have a "differentially negative effect on the turnout of racial and ethnic minorities" in primaries and general elections. Furthermore, given the strong correlation between minority voters and the Democratic Party, the researchers concluded that strict voter ID laws "skew democracy toward those on the political right" (Hajnal, Lajevardi, and Nielson 2017, 1). In short, the research is beginning to demonstrate how voter ID laws are reducing voter participation of a key Democratic constituency.

Voter Registration Reform

Because states have broad latitude in determining the procedures and rules surrounding voter registration, a variety of different voter registration systems exist among the states. (See chapter 5 for a summary.) These rules are particularly important because, unlike many Western democracies that automatically register citizens to vote, registration remains ultimately a matter of individual choice. Additionally, some of the rules regarding when, where, and how people can register to vote have become nationalized since the NVRA was enacted in 1993.

How to Register

The oldest method to register to vote is to do so in person, typically at a county voting office or other designated location. While states have traditionally allowed citizens the right to register via U.S. mail, the NVRA codified that right. In recent years, some states have allowed individuals to register online as well. Currently, thirty-seven states allow for online registration while twelve states do not. North Dakota does not require voter registration as voters are simply required to present identification and proof of residency when voting.

State prerogatives notwithstanding, federal law has attempted to ease the voter registration process, with the expectation that voter turnout would increase. The NVRA requires states to make voter registration forms available when and where people register their cars, at welfare agencies and like offices, and by mail.

For some time, Republicans and Democrats have sparred on voter registration reform, primarily over concerns about how those prospective voters would vote. Similar to the arguments made in the voter ID debate, many believe that larger voter turnout will help Democratic candidates and lower turnout will help Republican candidates. In 1977, President Jimmy Carter proposed the National Uniform Registration Act, which would have nationalized voter registration requirements rather than allowing each state set its own rules. While that idea failed due to partisan conflict, Republicans and Democrats continued debating voter registration reform. Overall, Democrats were interested in expanding the potential electorate by making voter registration easier and Republicans were interested in combating voter fraud and ensuring the accuracy of registration lists.

The parties' competing concerns about voter registration and voter roll accuracy provided an opportunity for compromise. Curtis Gans, a nonpartisan voting scholar, suggested that "common ground existed to remove voters from lists in a responsible manner so long as the purging was accomplished by an official state agency and that no voter be removed for merely not voting" (Baldino and Kreider 2010, 477). These recommendations were eventually incorporated into the NVRA (though, to be clear, the thrust of the law was that each state must provide opportunities for motor vehicle customers to register to vote while doing business with that government agency).

Some states have begun experimenting with automatic voter registration (AVR). Oregon was the first state to adopt AVR in 2016. AVR allows states to be in compliance with the NVRA by registering individuals who do business in that state's motor vehicles offices. AVR clearly makes voter registration easier, though some critics argue that it infringes upon a person's right *not* to register, a right theoretically protected by the Free Speech Clause of the First Amendment.

When to Register

States also have a myriad of laws governing how early one must register in advance to vote in an election. Currently, twelve states require registration materials to be postmarked or in the hands of election officials thirty days prior to the election. Other states require registration materials to be submitted anywhere from six (New Hampshire, depending on the office) to twenty-nine days prior to an election. Regardless of the registration window, the burden is on the individual to know the state's registration requirements.

While the Twenty-Sixth Amendment (1972) prohibits a state from denying the right to vote based on age to those who are eighteen years of age and older, many states allow for sixteen and seventeen-year-olds to pre-register to vote. According to the National Conference of State Legislatures (NCSL), fourteen states and the District of Columbia allow sixteen-year-olds to pre-register, four states allow seventeen-year-olds the right to pre-register, and five states establish some other age for pre-registration. The advantage of pre-registration is that when those individuals reach eighteen years of age, they are registered. While twenty-six states currently have no opportunities for pre-registration, this area of voter registration law is fluid and will likely remain so. Recently, some localities have reduced the voting age so that sixteen and seventeen-year-olds can also vote in city council, school board, and other local elections. This trend is not likely to affect federal election rules as it is unexpected that there will be a groundswell of support to reduce the minimum voting age to sixteen. The supermajority needed to amend the Constitution and reduce the minimum voting age is not likely to occur in the near future.

Voter Roll Purging

In 1993, Congress responded to concerns, voiced primarily by Republicans, about the election corruption or fraud that resulted from states failing to regularly update voter registration lists. One portion of the NVRA required states to keep a general voter registration list maintenance program that makes a "reasonable effort" to remove the names of persons who had become ineligible by reason of death, moving outside the jurisdiction, or conviction of a disqualifying crime. At the same time, the Act insisted that the list maintenance program be "uniform, nondiscriminatory" and consistent with the VRA.

Specifically precluded was removing registrants solely because of a failure to vote or within ninety days of a federal election. Congress was clearly trying to strike a balance between too much leniency, which could lead to inaccurate voter registration lists, and too much security, which could strip the franchise from eligible voters.

With respect to removal for moving outside the jurisdiction, the NVRA permitted states to use change-of-address information supplied by the U.S. Postal Service. Once a state received that information, it could send to the registrant a notice requesting the registrant to return a preaddressed, postage-prepaid card either affirming or correcting the change of address. If the card were not returned *and* the registrant then failed to vote in the next two federal general elections, the state could remove the registrant from the voter list. Change-of-address information is useful in maintaining voter lists because Americans' mobility leads to the possibility that a voter could be registered to vote in more than one state. In 2012, for example, the Pew Center estimated that about 2.75 million Americans were registered to vote in more than one state ("Inaccurate, Costly, and Inefficient" 2012).

Subsequent legislation, enacted by Congress in 2002, directed that states maintain a system by which to cull ineligible persons from voter registration lists. Specifically, the HAVA authorized states to remove an individual from the list of eligible voters if the registrant (1) did not respond to the official notice regarding potential removal; and (2) did not vote in two consecutive federal elections, but insisted, as the NVRA had, that "no registrant may be removed solely by reason of a failure to vote." Read together, these federal laws appear to give states wide latitude in determining the particulars of voter roll purging so long as the states were not purging registrants *solely* on the basis of not voting.

Maintaining accurate voter rolls advances administrative convenience and decreases the likelihood that an election will be marred by controversy or scandal. The Interstate Voter

Registrant Crosscheck Program, a database that identifies potentially ineligible voters to target for possible removal, was created to expedite the process by which states find individuals who might be trying to vote in more than one state at a time. The Crosscheck Program looks for duplicate voters by first, middle, and last names, combined with the last four digits of Social Security numbers and birthdates. Possible matches are shared with states enrolled with the program. In 2018, twenty-six states shared their data with other states.

While the Crosscheck Program appears to be a valuable resource for ferreting out double voters, some states have dropped out of the program or have not shared data with other states for two important reasons. First, the data have often proven to be unreliable. Names that are flagged as possible "matches" simply do not match, as they have different middle names or the ordering of names is different. States are also apparently not provided with the Social Security numbers as promised, thereby making it more difficult to find legitimate matches. Second, many states are concerned that the program has a racial and ethnic bias because blacks and Hispanics have been overrepresented in the names that have been identified. One possible reason for this, as *Rolling Stone* has reported, is that U.S. Census data show that blacks and minorities are overrepresented in eighty-five of the one hundred most common last names (Palast 2016). This bias compounds with the NVRA's requirement that states first send postcards to flagged registrants because, according to the U.S. Census Bureau, white voters are 21 percent more likely than blacks or Hispanics to respond to official requests, homeowners are 32 percent more likely to respond than renters, and the young are 74 percent less likely than the old to respond (Palast 2016). Nevertheless, some states relied heavily on the Crosscheck Program to identify voters to purge from the voter rolls. In July 2019, for example, Ohio published a list of 235,000 voters set to be purged. After some errors were uncovered and some voters took action to remove their names from the list, approximately

183,000 registrants were set to be removed (Casey 2019). (For security reasons, the Crosscheck Program was suspended in December 2019, pending review by the Kansas secretary of state.)

Ohio's adoption of an aggressive method of purging—one that seemed more interested in voter removal than accurate voter registration lists—invited a legal challenge. The disputed part of Ohio's purging law worked as follows: If a voter missed a federal election, the state flagged the voter as possibly having moved. The state then sent official notice requesting the registrant to return the notice if still living at his or her place of residence. A returned notice ended the inquiry. A notice not returned, however, kept the name flagged and, if the registrant did not vote in either of the next two federal elections, the registrant's name was purged from the voter registration list. The plaintiff's argument was two-fold. First, Ohio was potentially removing voters who had actually not moved, thereby purging eligible voters. And second, both the NVRA and the HAVA prohibited the removal of registrants solely on the basis of not voting.

This case, *Husted* v. *A. Philip Randolph Institute*, reached the Supreme Court in 2018. By a five-to-four vote, the Court upheld the process for removing voter registrants because, consistent with the NVRA and HAVA, Ohio was not purging voters *solely* on the basis of not voting but rather as the first step in a multistep process. In other words, not voting in two consecutive years *triggered* the voter removal process but not responding to the formal notice *and* not voting in the next four consecutive years were necessary steps in the removal process. Of particular curiosity, the majority upheld an aggressive purging of voter registration lists on the basis of two laws, of which the first—the NVRA—had the defined purpose of "increasing the number of eligible citizens who register to vote" and enabling voting officials at every level to enhance "the participation of eligible citizens as voters in elections for federal office"; and the second was titled, not accidently, the HAVA.

The primary dissent, written by Justice Stephen Breyer, argued that Ohio's attempts to maintain accurate voter rolls were inconsistent with the NVRA's requirement that states take *reasonable* steps to ensure that ineligible voters were not registered. To the contrary, Ohio's efforts were wholly unreasonable. In 2012, Ohio, mailed approximately 1.5 million such postcards and received in return about 235,000. Instead of interpreting that low return rate commonsensically—most people, for a variety of reasons, do not return postcards from the government—Ohio took that as evidence that more than a million registrants had failed to vote and moved out of the jurisdiction. Ohio thus began to purge those million registrants, mistakenly concluding that failure to vote and failure to return a postcard were legitimate proxies for moving. In spite of the specific commands of the NVRA and the HAVA, Ohio was in effect removing voters "solely by reason of failure to vote." Given the importance of voting to democracy, the dissent concluded, Ohio should have been more certain as to whether individuals had, in fact, moved. Justice Sonia Sotomayor also penned a dissent, noting the disproportionate effect of the purging on "minority, low-income, disabled, and veteran voters," and suggesting that state voter purges, under the guise of statutory compliance, be treated as what they are— illegitimate attempts to suppress the votes of disfavored groups.

States engaged in more aggressive vote purging practices were handed a significant victory in *Husted*. The effect of laws like Ohio's are hard to underestimate, especially in close, contested elections. In Ohio, for example, more than one million individuals, or around 13 percent, of the state's voting population failed to return their postcards. And in December 2019, a Wisconsin judge upheld the state's decision to purge some two hundred thousand persons from the voter rolls. Republicans across the country have been pushing voter roll purging to advance and improve electoral integrity, while Democrats have argued that voter purging efforts are consistent with felon disenfranchisement and voter ID laws in that young voters and racial and ethnic minorities feel a direct and disproportionate effect of these laws. Democrats have largely maintained that as American demographics are shifting in ways that benefit Democratic candidates, Republicans have increased their efforts to disenfranchise large pockets of the American electorate to hold off expected Democratic electoral advantages.

Voter roll purging also became an issue in the Georgia gubernatorial race in 2018, which pitted Georgia Secretary of State Brian Kemp against Stacey Abrams, a member of the Georgia House of Representatives. Kemp defeated Abrams by a slim 55,000 votes out of 3.9 million votes cast. Two aspects of the race received national attention. First, under Georgia law, the secretary of state oversees the election operation. Therefore, Kemp was overseeing an election in which he was the candidate. Second, Kemp, as secretary of state, instituted many voting-related practices that made it more difficult for racial and ethnic minorities to vote. As in Ohio, Kemp instituted an extremely aggressive voter roll purging policy, resulting in approximately 1.4 million Georgians purged from the voter rolls. Kemp had also interpreted a state law to require the name on voter registration materials to be an exact match with the name on the applicant's government-issued ID. Any slight change or difference meant a hold on the voter registration application. Kemp's office was also criticized for choices regarding how many polling places were open and where those polling places would be located. Many Democrats argued that Kemp had strategically closed polling places or limited the number of voting machines to create longer lines and, therefore, greater frustration in high minority voting precincts.

As Americans become more partisan and polarized, it is likely that efforts to use voting and election law to one's electoral advantage will continue. Election law scholar Richard Hasen (2012) refers to these efforts to using election law to one's political advantage as the "voting wars."

Voting Reform

American elections are long and costly. Presidential candidates often enter the race for their party's nomination a year or more before the first primary vote is counted. Hundreds of millions of dollars are spent by candidates, parties, and interest groups to convince voters to support particular candidates (and oppose others). Even though citizens are inundated with campaign information for lengthy periods of time, a 60 percent voter turnout rate in a presidential election is considered to be high. In midterm elections, voter turnout is often in the 30 percent range and even lower for local elections. America's relatively low voter turnout rates have led many to call for reform to increase electoral participation. A November 2016 survey of individuals who were registered but did not vote in the 2016 general election found that 14.3 percent noted that they were "too busy" or had a "conflicting schedule" that kept them from voting ("Voting and Registration" 2017). Many of the topics mentioned here are designed to make election day more convenient so that voting turnout increases.

Tuesday Voting

Why are federal elections held on a single Tuesday? Congress passed a law in 1845 that required that federal elections be held on the Tuesday after the first Monday in November in odd-numbered years. This means that federal elections fall between November 2 and November 8. While most Americans are certainly accustomed to a November Tuesday as election day, that decision was made by Congress in a much different era of American life. In mid–nineteenth-century American agrarian life, election day during planting season (spring) or crop season (summer) was simply not feasible, therefore, leading to post-harvest season as the best option. The choice of Tuesday was also a vestige of mid–nineteenth-century agrarian life because individuals who lived in rural areas needed to travel relatively long distances into town to cast their vote. Having election day on a Monday was unlikely because people would have needed to start their trip on a Sunday, a day reserved for church and rest. Therefore, the choice was Tuesday and it has remained so since 1845.

Many voting reform advocates have argued that a Tuesday election day suppresses voter turnout because busy work and family schedules intervene. Therefore, many have argued for moving election day to the weekend, just like European countries, most of which vote on Sunday. Proponents of weekend voting posit that voter turnout will increase and that additional polling places, like schools, will be available. The argument against moving election day to the weekend is that it might be more difficult to find additional poll workers and that it would hamper the availability of service industry workers, many of whom have to work on the weekends.

While moving election day to the weekend has not gained traction, making the Tuesday election day more convenient has gained significant support, with many states already moving in that direction. The National Commission on Federal Election Reform recommended making election day a national holiday ("To Ensure Pride and Confidence in the Electoral Process" 2001, 5). Foreseeing the argument from the business community that having an additional national holiday would be too costly, the Commission recommended merging Veterans Day with election day. Many people believe that making election day a national holiday would increase voter turnout because more people would have off from work, and it would send a strong symbolic message from the government that voting is a valuable exercise. Making election day a national holiday would also expand opportunities for polling stations and increase the pool of poll workers. In some states, election day is a holiday for state workers. Additionally, over three hundred companies have signed on to the nonpartisan effort, "Make Time to Vote," by providing their employees paid time to vote.

The U.S. Census Bureau poll of nonvoters from the 2016 election demonstrated the limitations of making election day a national holiday. While 14.3 percent of nonvoters attributed their nonvoting to being too busy, 31.7 percent indicated they did not vote because they suffered from an illness or disability, were out of town, forgot to vote, had transportation issues, had registration problems, or had an inconvenient polling place ("Voting and Registration" 2017). Not many of these voters would be helped by making election day a national holiday. The voting reforms most likely to help these nonvoters are early voting and mail-in voting, reforms that many states have implemented.

Early Voting

The 2000 presidential election exposed many election administration problems. Following its resolution, the public's attention shifted to how states administer elections, whether voting machines or paper ballots are better for recording votes, and even how long voting lines should be. Encouraged by the HAVA, many states implemented some form of early voting starting in 2004. Generally, there are three types of early voting: vote by mail, in-person early voting, and no-excuse absentee voting (Gronke, Galenas-Rosenbaum, and Miller 2007). Like many of the other issues in this chapter, the politics of in-person early voting have been complicated because of their intersection with race and ethnicity.

According to the NCSL, thirty-nine states and the District of Columbia currently have established some form of in-person early voting. With in-person early voting, registrants may vote at an elections office or a satellite location prior to the election. The average length for early voting is nineteen days, with the earliest states (South Dakota and Minnesota) being forty-six days and the latest (Oklahoma) being the Thursday before the election. As in-person early voting grew in popularity and some states released statistics on which party registrants were more likely to vote early, some Republican-controlled legislatures began restricting the number of in-person early voting days.

For example, in 2010, Republicans gained control of the Wisconsin state legislature and governor's office. Shortly thereafter, the legislature reduced the in-person early voting window from thirty to twelve days. In 2014, Wisconsin further reduced the in-person early voting window from twelve to ten days and prohibited weekend in-person early voting (Berman 2016). In addition to legal disputes regarding whether reductions in early voting are discriminatory, other states have wrestled with other early voting issues, such as how to open early voting locations in a nondiscriminatory fashion that still adequately respond to early voting demand.

The debate over early voting and where to place voting machines is, of course, related to how long people have to wait to vote. One argument why early voting is important is that long voting lines deter registrants from voting. One study, based on survey responses, found that long voting lines probably deterred between five hundred thousand and seven hundred thousand prospective voters in the 2012 election (Stewart and Ansolabehere 2013). Two more recent studies—one based on poll observers (Stein et al. 2019) and the other examining long wait lines at the ballot box using cellphone data from 93,658 polling places (Garisto 2019)—found similar conclusions. The technology-enhanced study documented one very clear disparity: Voters in predominantly black neighborhoods waited 29 percent longer, on average, than those in white neighborhoods. The study also found that black voters were approximately 74 percent more likely to wait for more than thirty minutes. Findings like these suggest why many observers view early voting and long wait lines at the polls as a civil rights issue as minority voters in urban areas appear to have a very different voting experience than white suburban voters.

Mail-In Voting

By 2020, four states—Oregon, Washington, Colorado, and Hawaii—will provide for mail-in voting. In these states, ballots are mailed to eligible voters and must be returned by election day. In Colorado and Washington, voters can still vote in-person if desired. While many variables affect voter turnout, initial studies seem to suggest that voting by mail increases voter turnout. Voter turnout increased for Oregon, Washington, and Colorado after vote by mail went into effect. (Hawaii's system will go into effect in November 2020.)

Many scholars and analysts have examined whether in-person early voting produces higher voter turnout similar to mail-in voting. As states have expanded alternative voting methods—such as early voting and mail-in voting—voters have taken advantage of these new methods of voting. According to the U.S. Census Bureau and other studies, nearly 35–40 percent of all ballots in the 2016 and 2018 elections were cast prior to election day (Misra 2019). Overall voter turnout, however, has not seen a corresponding increase. Researchers from the University of Wisconsin in 2013 concluded that "despite being a popular election reform, early voting depresses net voter turnout" because it robs election day of its "stimulating effects" (Burden et al. 2014, 108). They concluded that the only election reform that increases voter turnout is same-day voter registration, which allows people to register and vote simultaneously.

When asked to provide reasons for not voting, nonvoters cite inconvenience. Reforms like same-day registration, early voting, and mail-in voting might increase voter turnout to some degree, but voter turnout would not likely significantly improve even if all states were to adopt these reforms. Voter turnout data from 2016 show that states that have some form of early voting do not experience higher voter turnout than those without early voting (McDonald 2018). This suggests that something else is driving nonvoting. Some argue that voting rates are depressed due to deeper, more structural features of the American political system, such as the two-party system, a dearth of quality candidates, and gerrymandered legislative districts.

Gerrymandering

Under Article I, Section 4, of the Constitution, states have the responsibility to regulate the "times, places, and manner" of elections for U.S. representatives and senators. Through a series of acts, Congress has established that representatives will be chosen from single-member congressional districts. After each decennial census, Congress apportions seats in the House of Representatives on the basis of each state's population. After apportionment, state legislatures redraw district lines, known as redistricting, with each district relatively equal in population to all others.

Gerrymandering is manipulating the boundaries of an electoral constituency (congressional or state legislative district) to favor one group of persons over another. Partisan gerrymandering occurs when districts are drawn to advantage one particular party and disadvantage another. Racial gerrymandering exists when lines are drawn to advantage or disadvantage a particular race or ethnicity.

Partisan Gerrymandering

The Supreme Court has also been asked to adjudicate claims brought by state residents who believe their legislatures improperly relied upon partisan motivations when drawing legislative districts. Though a longstanding practice in American politics, the Court first became involved with partisan gerrymandering claims in *Davis* v. *Bandemer* (1986). At issue in *Davis* was whether an Indiana gerrymander ostensibly benefiting the Republican party violated the Fourteenth Amendment Equal Protection rights of Indiana Democrats. While a majority of justices agreed that partisan gerrymandering disputes were justiciable—meaning that they could be decided by federal courts—neither the Supreme Court nor lower federal courts were able in the following decades to agree upon a reasonable and principled standard to apply in deciding partisan gerrymandering disputes.

Partisan gerrymandering reappeared before the Court in *Vieth* v. *Jubelerer* (2004) but, once again, the justices could not agree on a standard to evaluate when partisan gerrymanders ran afoul of the Constitution. The result: After the 2010 census, partisan gerrymandering cases flooded federal and state courts; and litigation from Wisconsin, Maryland, and North Carolina finally reached the Supreme Court in 2018 and 2019.

In *Rucho* v. *Common Cause* (2019), the Supreme Court was asked to determine whether congressional district maps drawn in North Carolina and Maryland were unconstitutional partisan gerrymanders. In North Carolina, Democrats alleged that the Republican-led state legislature had drawn district maps that would lead to a delegation to the U.S. House of Representations of ten Republicans and three Democrats, which was vastly out of line with statewide vote-share totals. In Maryland, Republicans filed suit against the Democratic-controlled state legislature for using the redistricting process to flip a Republican seat Democratic, leading to a seven-to-one Democratic advantage in the congressional delegation.

Writing for a five-member majority, Chief Justice John Roberts concluded that partisan gerrymandering claims presented political questions beyond the reach of federal courts because there was no discernible standard that judges could apply to evaluate when partisan dominance became too excessive. Because judges held different opinions regarding how much partisan gerrymandering was permissible, there was no clear, absolute standard that all judges could apply to distinguish between constitutional and unconstitutional gerrymandering. The *Rucho* majority was also concerned that partisan gerrymandering claims "rest[ed] on an instinct that groups with a certain level of political support should enjoy a commensurate level of political power and influence." The idea that congressional maps should be drawn so that each party could translate statewide levels of support into an equal amount of representation in the congressional or state house delegation appeared to be grounded in a desire for proportional representation, the

Court argued, a representational scheme not required by the Constitution.

Writing for the four dissenters, Justice Elena Kagan argued that extreme partisan gerrymandering disputes could and should be heard by federal courts because they turned "upside-down the core American idea that all governmental power derives from the people." By engaging in partisan gerrymanders, elected officials were insulating themselves against voters' preferences, which was the opposite of how the framers intended our democracy to work. Drawing congressional and state legislative districts using sophisticated software to unfairly advantage the party in power implicated voting rights because it removed sovereignty from the voters by insulating elected officials from shifts in voter sentiments. In short, elected officials were selecting voters rather than voters selecting elected officials, a topsy-turvy situation from the fundamental principle of democracy.

Since partisan gerrymandering claims are, at least for now, beyond the reach of federal courts, solutions will be found—if at all—in state courts, state legislatures, and state practices. *Rucho* did not preclude state courts from hearing partisan gerrymandering claims under state constitutional provisions. For example, in the fall of 2019, a state judge in North Carolina ruled that the state legislature's congressional map violated a state constitutional provision. As states redraw legislative maps following the 2020 census, it is foreseeable that many of those maps will be challenged as violative of state constitutions. State constitutions and state courts will thus continue to play a role in moderating excessively partisan gerrymanders.

Also of note, numerous state legislatures have attempted to minimize the partisanship inherent in redistricting by creating independent redistricting commissions, which are tasked with drawing legislative maps or advising lawmakers in the mapmaking process. Some have cautioned against this practice, however, noting that if only blue states (Democratic-leaning) or red states (Republican-leaning) create independent redistricting commissions, it could help solidify the opposing party's strength in the U.S. House of Representatives (and in individual state legislatures). Currently, eight states use some form of independent redistricting commission to create congressional maps: Five have commissions that *advise* or *assist* the state legislatures in the congressional redistricting process; and three use commissions as a backup in the event that the state legislature is unable to agree on a redistricting plan. (Montana's Constitution provides for a commission if and when it is allocated more than one representative in the House.) For *state* legislative redistricting, twenty-five states use some form of independent redistricting commissions: Fourteen have commissions that draw the lines, six have commissions that advise or assist the state legislature in drawing the lines, and five use commissions as a backup. (Iowa is unique in its redistricting process in that it gives nonpartisan legislative staff the responsibility of developing the maps for both chambers of the state legislature and congressional districts—with any political or election data, including the addresses of incumbents—subject to legislative approval.)

Many independent, nonpartisan public policy institutes—like the Brennan Center for Justice and the Campaign Legal Center—argue that independent redistricting commissions are beneficial to democratic engagement because they are more likely to create competitive legislative districts and enhance voter participation. A key democratic principle is that voters choose elected officials. When legislators engage in partisan gerrymandering, however, elected officials are, in essence, choosing their voters. Additionally, partisan gerrymandering creates safe legislative districts, in which candidates on the extremes of the political spectrum often win seats as they do not need to moderate their political positions to secure victory in the election. While independent redistricting commissions will not solve all democratic ills, their use will likely curtail the hyperpolarization that is now endemic in American politics.

Unless and until Congress requires states to reduce partisan bias in the redistricting process—something unlikely to occur—or the Supreme Court reverses its decision in *Rucho*, the solution to partisan gerrymandering rests with state legislatures, which can take affirmative steps to promote fairness and impartiality in the redistricting process.

Racial Gerrymandering

To understand how racial gerrymandering is possible, it is necessary to consider the Constitution and federal law. Read together, they announce a minimal set of rules that states must follow in drawing congressional and state legislative districts. According to the Supreme Court, Article I, Section 2, infers that equal representation for equal numbers of people is the fundamental goal for the U.S. House of Representatives; in short, congressional districts be as equal in population as is practicable. Similarly, the justices interpret the Equal Protection Clause of the Fourteenth Amendment to require that seats in state legislatures be apportioned on a population basis. For both congressional and state legislative districts, some minor deviation is permissible. Statutorily, Section 2 of the VRA, as amended in 1982, prohibits "any State or political subdivision" from imposing any "standard, practice, or procedure . . . which results in a denial or abridgement of the right of any citizen of the United States to vote on account of race or color."

In addition to the legal requirements associated with redistricting, states have followed various traditions or practices that have been deemed fair and impartial. Redistricting bodies are expected to create legislative districts that are *compact* (minimum distance between all parts of the district), *contiguous* (all parts of district must be connected), and respect traditional governmental lines (counties, cities, and towns) and "communities of interest" (racial, ethnic, and other groups that might have similar values).

Prior to the VRA's passage in 1965, some states and cities engaged racial gerrymanders that were overt and clearly discriminatory. For example, as mentioned in the previous chapter, the Alabama legislature redrew the boundaries of the city of Tuskegee, Alabama, to *exclude* virtually all black voters, placing them into a district with almost no whites. Charles Gomillion and other black voters filed suit against Tuskegee mayor, Phil Lightfoot, alleging that their voting rights, as guaranteed by the Fifteenth Amendment, had been denied as a result of the racial gerrymander. In *Gomillion* v. *Lightfoot* (1960), a unanimous Supreme Court held that the "unequal weight in voting distribution" based solely on racial lines violated the amendment.

While *Gomillion* made clear that states may not use gerrymanders to *harm* black voters, some states believed that Section 2 of the VRA permitted—or even encouraged—states to gerrymander to enhance black voting power by using the redistricting process to maximize the number of legislative districts consisting of a majority of minority voters. Many did so, by creating so-called majority-minority districts. In some cases, the U.S. Department of Justice (DOJ) even required states under Section 5 preclearance to increase the number of majority–minority districts.

As states were engaged in ways to increase the number of majority–minority districts, white voters were countering (often in lawsuits) that all forms of race-conscious gerrymandering, regardless of how benign the motives might be, violated the Equal Protection Clause of the Fourteenth Amendment. In a series of cases, beginning with *Shaw* v. *Reno* (1993), the Supreme Court ruled that when state legislatures draw legislative districts, race can be a factor, but not the *predominant* factor in the calculation. Such a nebulous standard invited tremendous confusion among the states. Nevertheless, this string of at-times seemingly discordant decisions caused states to curtail explicit uses of race in redistricting analyses.

The belief of many that Section 2 of the VRA placed a responsibility on states to draw legislative districts in ways to expand opportunities for minorities to elect representatives of their choice was dealt a serious blow in *Abbott* v. *Perez* (2018). Here, the Supreme Court rebuffed challenges to legislative districts drawn in Texas following the 2010 census. In upholding the districts and ruling that the Texas legislature had not intentionally diluted the voting power of minorities, the narrow majority ruled that when legislative districts are challenged under Section 2 of the VRA, challengers bear the burden of proof in showing that the legislature had not acted in good faith. This decision effectively made it harder for individuals and groups to challenge state legislative districts as being violative of the VRA.

The Voting Rights Act of 1965 and *Shelby County* v. *Holder* (2013)

As discussed in chapter 1, although voting rights for black Americans were ostensibly granted by the Fifteenth Amendment (1870), states found novel ways to deny the franchise to black Americans over the next many decades. Because the Fifteenth Amendment prohibited states from denying voting rights to individuals based on race or color of skin, states often imposed barriers to the right to vote—poll taxes, grandfather clauses, and literacy tests, for example—that, while technically not prohibited under the Fifteenth Amendment's terms, produced the same racially discriminatory effects. As desired, states that imposed these additional voting barriers experienced significantly lower rates of black voter participation.

These state efforts to discriminate against black voters were finally eradicated in 1965, when Congress passed the VRA. The most controversial provision of the VRA was Section 5, which required "covered jurisdictions" to petition the U.S. attorney general or the U.S. District Court for the District of Columbia prior to amending their election laws. Even though provisions of the VRA had been reauthorized overwhelmingly by Congress numerous times, some Republicans have long believed that the preclearance requirement in Section 5 was an unconstitutional intrusion on state sovereignty. While Republican members of Congress continued to support and vote for reauthorization of the VRA's amendments, conservative legal scholars worked hard to develop a legal strategy that would present Section 5 before a conservative-led Supreme Court sympathetic to their legal arguments.

Northwest Austin Municipal Utility District No. One v. *Holder* (2009) involved a constitutional challenge to the VRA. The Northwest Austin Municipal Utility District No. One (NAMUDNO), a small political subunit that provided city services to residents of Travis County, Texas, sought a statutory exemption from the preclearance requirement in Section 5 while simultaneously arguing that Section 5 was an intrusion on state sovereignty (under the Tenth Amendment) and should be declared unconstitutional.

Eight of the nine justices declined to rule on the broader constitutional question of whether Section 5 was unconstitutional. Instead, the justices opted for the narrow approach by deciding that NAMUDNO was entitled to an exemption from the preclearance requirement. Nevertheless, legal observers agreed that the majority opinion placed Congress on notice that the justices were concerned that Section 5 might not be "justified by current needs." The lesson of *NAMUDNO* appeared to be that if Congress chose not to correct the defects of the preclearance requirement, the Court would subject Section 5 to serious constitutional scrutiny in the future.

That scrutiny arrived in 2013, when the justices took up *Shelby County* v. *Holder*. Here, Shelby County, Alabama, launched a direct constitutional challenge to Section 5, arguing that times had drastically changed in the "covered jurisdictions" since 1965 when the VRA was passed. When the Court handed down its decision, however, the opinion, written by Chief Justice John Roberts, focused not on the Section 5 preclearance requirement but on the "coverage formula" outlined in Section 4. (An excerpt of this case is reproduced in chapter 5.)

Section 4 of the VRA outlined the criteria used to determine which jurisdictions would be subject to preclearance requirement in Section 5. Under the original terms of Section 4, any state or political subdivision that maintained a test or device as a prerequisite to voting as of November 1, 1964, and had less than 50 percent voter registration or turnout in the 1964 election was subject to the preclearance requirement. The coverage formula had changed over the years but was last updated in the 1975 reauthorization. In those amendments, Congress broadened the definition of "test or device" to include providing English-only ballots in places where over 5 percent of voting-age citizens spoke a language other than English and updated the "less than 50 percent registration or turnout" requirement, pegging it to the 1972 presidential election.

Because the VRA, generally, and Section 5, specifically, imposed significant federalism costs on only a handful of states, the Court carefully examined whether the preclearance requirement was still needed. In a stunning move, the majority struck down the coverage formula in Section 4, but left Section 5 in place. Section 4 was unconstitutional, said the narrow majority, because the VRA had been successful. Voter registration and voter turnout had vastly improved since 1965 and the covered jurisdictions had long ago forfeited any attempts to minimize the voting power of minority voters. In essence, because the VRA had been so successful, it was no longer needed. The decision left to Congress the power to create a new, updated Section 4 coverage formula. Congress has, so far, failed to act.

Noting the irony of the chief justice's words, Justice Ruth Bader Ginsburg's dissent noted that getting rid of the preclearance because it has worked so well "is like throwing away your umbrella in a rainstorm because you are not getting wet." The crux of her dissent was a worry that history would unfortunately repeat itself and that minority voters would suffer once again.

The effect of *Shelby County* may not be as benign as Roberts predicted it would be. States, many of which were previously subject to preclearance, have passed voter ID laws, which undoubtedly have a discriminatory effect, if not intent. Many states have engaged in aggressive voter roll purges, with the Court ultimately sanctioning those efforts in *Husted*. In her *Husted* dissent, Justice Sonia Sotomayor noted that even though the VRA was very successful, Congress understood that many states were engaging in efforts to protect registered voters from being unlawfully purged from voter rolls. To that end, Congress passed the NVRA to "increase the registration and enhance the participation of eligible voters in federal elections." But Sotomayor concluded that Ohio's voter roll purging very clearly "had disproportionately affected minority, low-income, disabled, and veteran voters," and that by upholding Ohio's actions, the Court "entirely ignore[d] the history of voter suppression against which the NVRA was enacted" and turned a blind eye to a "program that appear[ed] to further the very disenfranchisement of minority and low-income voters that Congress set out to eradicate." In short, the race-neutral world that Roberts envisioned in *Shelby County* might not exist. Many states continue to engage in voting practices that produce a discriminatory effect against minority voters.

The Electoral College

The framers struggled mightily with how to elect a president in a nation composed of states jealous of their own prerogatives and distrustful of centralized authority. Congressional selection was rejected, the framers fearing that the choice would be too divisive and engender too many hard feelings in Congress. Additionally, separation of powers cautioned against giving one branch "too much agency" in the appointment of the members of the others. Selection by state legislatures was discarded out of fears that a president politically beholden to those legislatures would undercut federal authority and undermine federalism, the carefully constructed division of power between two distinct governments. And direct election was not an option for two primary reasons. First, the geographic distribution of four million people, barely connected by transportation and communication, made national campaigns impracticable. Without sufficient information about all the candidates, people would naturally vote only for their "favorite sons," those with whom they were already familiar. The president would thus almost always be chosen by the most populous states. Second, direct election would likely result in no candidate emerging with a popular vote sufficient to govern the entire country. The compromise—which emerged from spirited disagreement rather than some grand political strategy by a group of the philosophical elite—was indirect election of the president by an Electoral College. Its animating purpose was to have knowledgeable and informed persons select the president.

Under Article II, Section 2, of the Constitution, each state was allocated a number of electors equal to the number of its senators and representatives. Each of those electors (in every state) would then vote for two persons, presumably a first and second choice. The person having the greatest number of votes would be president, if such number were an absolute majority of the electoral votes. If more than one candidate had a majority (or had an equal number of electoral votes with another), the House would choose one of them for president. If no candidate had a majority, the House would choose from among the five highest electoral vote getters. In choosing the president, however, each state delegation had one vote, and an absolute majority of the states was required to elect the president. (After the choice of president, the person having the next highest number of electoral votes was vice president. And if two runner-up candidates had equal votes, the Senate would select the vice president.)

The framers' views on the Electoral College were "conflicting and diverse" (Rogers 2010, 29). Even so, most thought that the Electoral College would serve as the nominating body for president, with election ultimately coming from the House. The framers assumed that many people would seek the presidency, thus depriving any one candidate of the majority of electoral votes and throwing the election to the House.

But the framers' understanding of how the Electoral College would function quickly unraveled for two reasons. First, the framers did not anticipate the rise of political parties and a strong national two-party system. Instead, they believed that state legislatures would assign their electoral votes to candidates with strong local and national reputations. By 1800, however, a party-based system had developed, and the parties assumed the role of nominating candidates. With only two major national parties, most elections came down to a contest between two people—the winners of their respective party selection processes. And with only two candidates, one was bound to earn a majority of the electoral votes, thus depriving the House of the opportunity to elect a president. Second, the election of 1800 exposed a flaw in the Electoral College operations. In that election, Thomas Jefferson and Aaron Burr—though they were running mates from the same political party—tied in the Electoral College. Jefferson and Burr tied because an equal number of electors voted for the two candidates as their first and second choices. It mattered not *constitutionally* that the party understood that Jefferson was the presidential candidate and Burr the vice-presidential candidate. Nor did it matter *constitutionally* that Jefferson had been named as the first choice on most electoral ballots. The only thing that mattered *constitutionally* was the two had tied, thus sending the election to the House. On the first thirty-five ballots in the House, neither candidate received a majority of the sixteen states, Jefferson winning eight and Burr six, with two abstaining. On the thirty-sixth ballot, the House elected Jefferson. The election of 1800 made clear that parties had become a permanent fixture in American politics. To reflect that reality—and to prevent a reoccurrence of the embarrassing election in which the House had to choose between two running mates—the Twelfth Amendment, ratified in 1804, required electors to cast two separate ballots, one for president and one for vice president. (Additionally, the amendment insisted that the vice president also secure an absolute majority of electoral votes. If no candidate obtained an electoral majority, the Senate—each senator having one vote—would chose the vice president from the top two electoral vote recipients; and an absolute majority of the senators was necessary to a choice.) The election of 1804 and every election since has been carried out under the terms of the Twelfth Amendment.

The Constitution left to the states the question of how to *apportion* electors. One way was on a proportional basis, meaning that if candidate A earned 40 percent of the state's popular vote, that candidate received 40 percent of the state's electors. Another way was the "winner-take-all" basis, sometimes referred to as the "unit rule." Under this method, the candidate with the most popular votes received all of the state's electors. Most states adopted this method, which helped solidify the two-party system by minimizing the potential growth and influence of minor parties. The Constitution also left to the states the manner of *selecting* electors. In the early decades, most state legislatures simply appointed the electors. By the Civil War, however, all states had moved to adopt the popular election of electors, a clear move away from the framers' vision of elite governance and toward a more populist democracy.

What follows is a primer on the modern-day Electoral College (Kimberling 1992, 7–13).

- Each state is allocated electors equal to the number of its U.S. senators (always two) and U.S. representatives (which may change after each decennial census).
- Political parties (or independent candidates) in each state submit to the state's chief election official a list of individuals pledged to their candidates for president and vice president and equal in number to the state's electoral vote. Typically, the political parties select these individuals either in their

state party conventions or through appointment by their state party leaders, while some third parties and independent candidates merely designate theirs.

- After caucuses and primaries, the major parties nominate their candidates for president and vice president in their national conventions, which are traditionally held in the summer preceding the election. (Third parties and independent candidates follow different procedures according to individual state laws.) The names of the nominated candidates are then submitted to each state's chief election official so that they might appear on the general election ballot.

- On the Tuesday following the first Monday of November in years divisible by four (as established by federal law), the people in each state cast ballots for the party slate of electors representing their choice for president and vice president (although as a matter of practice, general election ballots normally say "Electors for" each set of candidates rather than list the individual electors on each slate).

- Whichever party slate wins the most popular votes in the state becomes that state's electors—so that, in effect, whichever ticket gets the most popular votes in a state wins all the electors of that state. (The two exceptions to this "winner-take-all" method are Maine and Nebraska, where two electors are chosen by statewide popular vote and the remainder by the popular vote within each congressional district.)

- On the Monday following the second Wednesday of December (as established by federal law), each state's electors meet in their respective state capitals and cast their electoral votes—one for president and one for vice-president. (To prevent electors from voting only for "favorite sons" of their home state, at least one of their votes must be for a person from outside their state, though this is seldom a problem since the parties have consistently nominated presidential and vice-presidential candidates from different states.)

- The electoral votes are sealed and transmitted to the president of the Senate who, on January 6, opens and reads them before both houses of the Congress.

- The candidate for president with the most electoral votes, provided that it is an absolute majority of the whole number of electors, is declared president. Similarly, the vice-presidential candidate with the absolute majority of electoral votes is declared vice president.

- If no presidential candidate obtains an absolute majority of electoral votes, the House selects the president from among the top three contenders, with each state casting only one vote and an absolute majority of the states being required to elect. Similarly, if no one obtains an absolute majority for vice president, then the Senate makes the selection from among the top two contenders for that office, and an absolute majority of senators is required to elect.

- At noon on January 20, the duly elected president and vice president are sworn into office.

Critics of the Electoral College advance four general arguments. First, the reality of a president elected without a majority of the popular vote. Far from being unusual, this has happened nineteen times. In 1824, four candidates split the popular vote, with no candidate earning more than 42 percent. (Because no candidate earned a majority of the electoral votes either, the House decided this election, the last to be so decided. Of note, the House did *not* elect the candidate with the highest number of popular *and* electoral votes.) In fourteen elections—1844, 1848, 1856, 1860, 1880, 1888, 1892, 1912, 1916, 1948, 1960, 1968, 1992, and 1996—the victor in the Electoral College did not receive a majority of the popular vote (though in each he was the candidate with the highest number of popular votes). And in four elections—1876,

1888, 2000, and 2016—the winner of the electoral vote *lost* the popular vote.

Second, the risk of a "faithless elector" (one who is pledged to vote his or her party's candidate, but votes for another candidate). The fact that no faithless elector has ever determined a presidential election is immaterial to the risk that it proposes.

Third, the possibility that the Electoral College depresses voter turnout. Since each state is entitled to its predetermined electoral votes regardless of voter turnout, there is no incentive to promote voter participation.

And fourth, failure to reflect the national popular will. The Electoral College inarguably overrepresents people in rural states. For example, in 2020, Florida had a total population of more than twenty-one million, with twenty-nine electoral votes. The *nine* least populous jurisdictions—Wyoming, Vermont, Washington, D.C., Alaska, North Dakota, South Dakota, Delaware, Rhode Island, and Montana—had a total population of just over seven million yet owned twenty-eight electoral votes. Each Floridian's potential vote, then, carried about one-third the weight of a potential vote in the other states listed. (Opponents further point out that the "winner-take-all" method, employed in forty-eight states and the District of Columbia, distorts even further the national political will.)

Defenders of the Electoral College, though less vocal, respond with four primary arguments. First, it contributes to cohesiveness by requiring a distribution of popular support to be elected president. Without the Electoral College, presidents would be selected by the most populous region or by large metropolitan areas. Because under the current allocation of electoral votes no single region contains enough to elect a president, candidates are motivated to pull together coalitions of regions rather than to exacerbate regional differences.

Second, the Electoral College may increase voter participation, especially in swing states, as citizens know that small numbers of votes in one state (think Florida in 2000) or in several states (think Wisconsin, Michigan, and Pennsylvania in 2016) may make the difference between winning all or none of that state's electoral votes.

Third, the winner-take-all-of-the-electoral-votes method contributes to political stability by making it exceedingly difficulty for third parties to secure enough popular votes in enough states to win the presidency. On a practical level, this pressures third parties to compromise their views and to align with one of the two major parties. Equally important, it also incentivizes the two major parties to moderate their views to absorb third party movements and cater to their would-be voters. The Electoral College thus "encourages political parties to coalesce divergent interests into two sets of coherent alternatives, [which] . . . contributes to the political stability of the nation" (Kimberling 1992, 13).

And fourth, it helps maintain the federal system so coveted by the framers. The Electoral College was designed to represent the state's (not the people's) choice for the presidency. To abandon it, presumably in favor of direct popular election, would erode the federal structure of government to the detriment of the states.

Even though the Electoral College is more democratic than the framers intended and functions in ways that the framers could never have imagined, its unique features still draw significant criticism and calls for substantial reform or even abolition. Those proposals for abolition have failed because the alternatives to the Electoral College are also problematic and amending the Constitution is a politically difficult task.

Since the number of the states' electoral votes vote is based loosely upon population—and forty-eight states and the District of Columbia apportion their electoral votes on a "winner-take-all" basis—presidential candidates spend their time and resources in states that are competitive. For example, even though California is the nation's most populous state and possesses an amazing fifty-five electoral votes (more than 20 percent of the electoral votes needed to secure the presidency) in the 2012, 2016, and 2020 elections, the two major parties' candidates did not campaign in California because the state is so solidly Democratic. The candidates are more likely to campaign in "swing states," those states where both parties have a shot at winning electoral votes, like Florida, Wisconsin, Ohio, and Pennsylvania.

In the 2000 presidential election, twenty-four states, equaling 201 electoral votes, were never visited by either candidate. Only fifteen states, totaling 240 electoral votes, were visited by the candidates a total of ten times or more. The number of visits data are also supported by where the candidates targeted their television advertising. In 2000, not one dollar was spent toward advertising in twenty-five states (Shaw 2006, 79–87). The skew in campaign visits and advertising dollars remained true for the 2016 presidential election with nearly 70 percent of all campaign events held in just six states—Florida, North Carolina, Pennsylvania, Ohio, Virginia, and Michigan (Alexander 2019, 81). It is exceedingly clear that the Electoral College shapes presidential campaigns in ways that the framers never envisioned.

At first blush, the Electoral College may not appear to implicate voting rights. After all, a vote in Wyoming is equal to a vote in Pennsylvania. The voting rights concern related to the Electoral College, however, stems from two factors. First, because the electoral vote, and not the popular vote, determines who wins the presidency, some states are more important in the Electoral College calculation. It is possible that a vote in Wyoming or Kansas is not, in fact, equal to a vote in Pennsylvania or Ohio. If campaigns target certain voters in certain states and not all voters, then it appears that certain votes count more than other votes in a strategic sense. This imbalance then is the target of efforts to amend the Constitution to replace the Electoral College with popular vote. If that were to happen, the winner of the popular vote would become president and would avoid the situation that has occurred five times in American history (1824, 1876, 1888, 2000, and 2016) where the winner of the popular vote did not secure the presidency.

Replacing the Electoral College with a popular vote would seriously alter candidates' strategies with respect to where they campaign for votes but it might also help solve another voting rights concern related to the Electoral College. Since one key factor in political participation is the level of information one receives—and political campaigns saturate swing state, voters with information while often completely avoiding safe state voters—the pressure to participate is extremely high for swing state voters (Alexander 2019, 83). That same level of pressure to participate is missing in safe state voters.

Generally, voter turnout in presidential elections is higher in swing—or battleground—states than in safe states. Voters in swing states like Florida and Ohio are more likely to vote than voters in safe states like California (for Democrats) or Oklahoma (for Republicans). The voter turnout data from the 2016 election show that in twelve of the fifteen battleground states, voter turnout was higher than the national average (Kurtzleben 2016). Because there are many factors contributing to voter turnout, it is difficult to say that the battleground status *causes* the voter turnout, but some scholarly studies, which control for other contextual or political factors, indicate that living in a battleground state does make a person more likely to vote. For example, Lipsitz (2009) found that citizens in battleground states were 3 percent more likely to vote in 1988 and 2000, with a 6 percent expected difference between battleground and safe states in the 2004 election. In studying the 2000 election, Hill and McKee (2005) also found that citizens in battleground states were 1 to 2 percent more likely to vote than citizens in safe states. In short, while there are many variables effecting the decision whether to vote, where one lives and its relationship to the Electoral College appears to influence voter turnout.

One popular reform idea is to abolish the Electoral College and replace it with direct popular election. Abolishing the Electoral College, however, would require a constitutional amendment, which requires two-thirds approval in both houses of Congress and ratification by three-fourths (thirty-eight) of the states. States that benefit from the Electoral College—typically smaller states—are sufficient in number to block ratification. Many reformers have therefore shifted their focus to the National Popular Vote Interstate Compact (NPVIC). This plan, which originated in 2006, is an agreement between states and the District of Columbia to award their electoral votes to the national popular vote winner, regardless of which candidate wins their respective states (or the District of Columbia). The agreement would not go into effect until the number of states who agree to the compact have at least a combined 270 electoral votes. Currently, fifteen states and the District of Columbia, totaling 196 electoral votes, have agreed to enter into the compact. Some scholars argue that the NPVIC is unconstitutional because Article I, Section 10, of the Constitution requires Congress to approve interstate compacts. Others maintain that because of *Virginia* v. *Tennessee* (1893), Congress need only approve compacts that *increase* state power, and because states would not be exercising any more power than they already have (allocating electoral votes), congressional approval is not required.

In short, NPVIC is the best chance of Electoral College reform. Public opinion polls consistently show that Americans are ready to replace the Electoral College with the popular vote but the political prospects for such a monumental change in American politics are slim. The Electoral College is likely here to stay, even if the manner in which states award their electoral votes is modified by the NPVIC.

Conclusion

The right to vote in American life has a long and complicated history. Under current law, the percentage of Americans eighteen years or older who are denied the franchise is relatively low. This liberalization of voting eligibility is far removed from the colonial period, when voting rights were reserved for white male property owners. This chapter, however, has highlighted three major themes in the contemporary debate on voting rights. First, while voting rights are near universal, there still remain significant legal and policy fights regarding the degree to which states may place restrictions or barriers to voting in the interest of ensuring the integrity of the vote. With felon disenfranchisement laws, states have restricted the franchise of those who are either in prison or have left prison but are still under the supervision of the criminal justice system. While some states have made it easier for ex-felons to regain the right to vote, felon disenfranchisement laws are still popular.

With voter ID requirements and voter roll purging, states have placed additional requirements on those who are legally entitled to vote. Courts have been generally sympathetic to state efforts to ensure the integrity of the ballot, regardless of the dearth of evidence that voter fraud is an empirical reality. In fact, the Roberts Court has upheld voter ID requirements and aggressive voter roll purging activities even in the absence of evidence that voter fraud exists.

Second, this chapter has evaluated many of the reform efforts to increase voter turnout. While we are at near-universal suffrage, voter participation rates remain embarrassingly low in many elections. To increase voter participation, many have proposed process-based reforms, such as making voter registration easier, moving election day to the weekend, or making election day a national holiday. Many of these reforms, such as early voting and mail-in voting, have already been implemented. Nevertheless, voting rates have not increased substantially as a result.

Finally, this chapter has some of the structural rules and practices of the American political system—partisan and racial gerrymandering, the VRA, and the Electoral College—that, at times, have made it difficult for certain groups to maximize their political voice.

References

Alexander, Robert M. 2019. *Representation and the Electoral College*. New York: Oxford University Press.

Alvarez, R. Michael, Delia Bailey, and Jonathan N. Katz. 2008. "The Effect of Voter Identification Laws on Turnout." California Institute of Technology Social Science Working Paper 1267R. January. https://papers.ssrn.com /sol3/papers.cfm?abstract_id=1084598

Baldino, Thomas J., and Kyle L. Kreider. 2010. *Of the People, By the People, For the People: A Documentary Record of Voting Rights and Electoral Reform*. Vol. 2. Santa Barbara, CA: Greenwood Press.

Berman, Ari. 2016. "The GOP's War on Voting Is Working." *The Nation*, 29 June. https://www.thenation.com/article /archive/the-gops-war-on-voting-is-working/

Binnall, James. 2017. "Summonsing Criminal Desistance: Convicted Felons' Perspectives on Jury Service." *Law and Social Inquiry*, 43 (1): 4–27.

"Building Confidence in U.S. Elections: Report of the Commission on Federal Election Reform." 2005. https:// www.legislationline.org/download/id/1472/file/3b50795b2 d0374cbef5c29766256.pdf

Bump, Philip. 2016. "There Have Been Just Four Documented Cases of Voter Fraud in the 2016 Election." *Washington Post*, 1 December. https:// www.washingtonpost.com/news/the-fix/

wp/2016/12/01/0-000002-percent-of-all-the-ballots-cast
-in-the-2016-election-were-fraudulent/

Burden, Barry C., David T. Canon, Kenneth R. Mayer, and
Donald P. Moynihan. 2014. "Election Laws, Mobilization,
and Turnout: The Unanticipated Consequences of Election
Reform." *American Journal of Political Science*, 58 (1):
95–109.

Casey, Nicholas. 2019. "Ohio Was Set to Purge 235,000
Voters. It Was Wrong About 20%." *New York Times*,
14 October. https://www.nytimes.com/2019/10/14/us
/politics/ohio-voter-purge.html

Clegg, Roger, George T. Conway, III, and Kenneth K. Lee.
2006. "The Bullet and the Ballot—The Case for Felon
Disenfranchisement Statutes." *American University Journal
of Gender Social Policy and the Law*, 14: 1–26.

Cottrell, David, Michael C. Herron, and Sean J. Westwood.
2018. "A Rigged Election? Evaluating Donald Trump's
Claims of Massive Voter Fraud in the 2016 Presidential
Election." *Electoral Studies*, 51: 123–142.

de Alth, Shelley. 2009. "ID at the Polls: Assessing the Impact
of Recent State Voter ID Laws on Voter Turnout." *Harvard
Law & Policy Review*, 3: 185–202.

DeCrescenzo, Michael G., and Kenneth R. Mayer. 2019.
"Voter Identification and Nonvoting in Wisconsin—
Evidence from the 2016 Election." *Election Law Journal*,
18 (4): 342–359.

Garisto, Daniel. 2019. "Smartphone Data Shows Voters in
Black Neighborhoods Wait Longer." *Scientific American*,
1 October. https://www.scientificamerican.com/article
/smartphone-data-show-voters-in-black-neighborhoods
-wait-longer1/

Goel, Shared, Marc Meredith, Michael Morse, David
Rothschild, and Houshmand Shirani-Mehr. 2020.

"One Person, One Vote: Estimating the Prevalence of Double Voting in U.S. Presidential Elections." *American Political Science Review*, 114 (2): 456–469.

Gronke, Paul, Eva Galanes-Rosenbaum, and Peter A. Miller. 2007. "Early Voting and Turnout." *PS: Political Science and Politics*, 40 (4): 639–645.

Hajnal, Zoltan, Nazita Lajevardi, and Lindsay Nielson. 2017. "Voter Identification Laws and the Suppression of Minority Votes." *The Journal of Politics*, 79 (2): 363–379.

Hasen, Richard L. 2012. *The Voting Wars: From Florida 2000 to the Next Election Meltdown.* New Haven, CT: Yale University Press.

Help America Vote Act. Public Law 107-252, *U.S. Statutes at Large*, 116 (2002): 1666–1730.

Hill, David, and Seth McKee. 2005. "The Electoral College, Mobilization, and Turnout in the 2000 Presidential Election." *American Politics Research*, 33 (5): 700–725.

"Inaccurate, Costly, and Inefficient." 2012. Pew Center on the States. Washington, DC: Election Initiatives Brief. https://www.pewtrusts.org/~/media/legacy/uploadedfiles/pcs_assets/2012/pewupgradingvoterregistrationpdf.pdf

Kimberling, William. 1992. *The Electoral College.* Washington, DC: National Clearinghouse of Election Administration, Federal Election Commission.

Kurtzleben, Danielle. 2016. "Charts: Is the Electoral College Dragging Down Voter Turnout in your State?" *NPR*, 26 November. https://www.npr.org/2016/11/26/503170280/charts-is-the-electoral-college-dragging-down-voter-turnout-in-your-state

Levine, Sam, and Ariel Edwards-Levy. 2018. "Most Americans Favor Restoring Felons' Voting Rights, but Disagree on How." *Huffington Post*, 21 March. https://

www.huffpost.com/entry/felons-voting-rights-poll_n_5ab2
c153e4b008c9e5f3c88a

Levitt, Justin. 2007. "The Truth About Voter Fraud." Brennan
Center for Justice. https://www.brennancenter.org
/our-work/research-reports/truth-about-voter-fraud

Lipsitz, Keena. 2009. "The Consequences of Battleground
and Spectator State Residency for Political Participation."
Political Behavior, 31 (2): 187–209.

Locke, John. [1690] 1960. *Two Treatises of Government.*
New York: Cambridge University Press.

Manza, Jeff, Clem Brooks, and Christopher Uggen. 2004.
"Public Attitudes Toward Felon Disenfranchisement in the
United States." *Public Opinion Quarterly*, 68 (2): 275–286.

McDonald, Michael. 2018. "2016 November General
Election Turnout Rates." Last modified 5 September 2018.
http://www.electproject.org/2016g

Minnite, Lorraine C. 2010. *The Myth of Voter Fraud.* New
York: Cornell University Press.

Misra, Jordan. 2019. "Voter Turnout Rates among All Voting
Age and Major Racial and Ethnic Groups Were Higher
Than in 2014." *U.S. Census Bureau,* 23 April. https://www
.census.gov/library/stories/2019/04/behind-2018-united
-states-midterm-election-turnout.html

Mycoff, Jason D., Michael W. Wagner, and David C.
Wilson. 2009. "The Empirical Effects of Voter-ID Laws:
Present or Absent?" *PS: Political Science and Politics*, 42
(1): 121–126.

National Voter Registration Act. Public Law 103-31,
U.S. Statutes at Large, 107 (1993): 77.

Palast, Greg. 2016. "The GOP's Stealth War against Voters."
Rolling Stone, 24 August. https://www.rollingstone.com
/politics/politics-features/the-gops-stealth-war-against
-voters-247905/

"Policy Brief on Voter Identification." 2006. Brennan Center for Justice, 12 September. https://www.brennancenter.org /our-work/research-reports/policy-brief-voter-identification

Rogers, Michael. 2010. "A Mere Deception—A Mere *Ignis Fatuus* on the People of America: Lifting the Veil on the Electoral College." In *Electoral College Reform: Challenges and Possibilities*. Edited by Gary Bugh. Burlington, VT: Ashgate Publishing, 19–41.

Shaw, Daron R. 2006. *The Race to 270: The Electoral College and the Campaign Strategies of 2000 and 2004*. Chicago, IL: University of Chicago Press.

Stein, Robert M., Christopher Mann, Charles Stewart, Zachary Birenbaum, Anson Fung, Jed Greenberg, Farhan Kawsar, et al. 2019. "Waiting to Vote in the 2016 Presidential Election: Evidence from a Multi-County Study." *Political Research Quarterly*. https://doi. org/10.1177/1065912919832374.

Stewart, Charles H., III, and Stephen A. Ansolabehere. 2013. "Waiting in Line to Vote." Report, Election Assistance Commission. http://web.mit.edu/supportthevoter/www /files/2013/06/Charles-Stewart-Waiting-in-Line-to-Vote -White-Paper.pdf

"To Ensure Pride and Confidence in the Electoral Process." 2001. National Commission on Federal Election Reform. http://web1.millercenter.org/commissions/comm_2001 .pdf

Uggen, Christopher, Ryan Larson, and Sarah Shannon. 2016. "6 Million Lost Voters: State-Level Estimates of Felon Disenfranchisement, 2016." https://www .sentencingproject.org/publications/6-million-lost-voters -state-level-estimates-felony-disenfranchisement-2016/

"Voter ID History." 2017. National Conference of State Legislatures. https://www.ncsl.org/research/elections- and-campaigns/voter-id-history.aspx

"Voting and Registration in the Election of November 2016."
2017. U.S. Census Bureau. https://census.gov/data/tables
/time-series/demo/voting-and-registration/p20-580.html

World Prison Brief Data. 2018. https://www.prisonstudies.
org/country/united-states-america

This chapter, in ten original essays, presents the diverse views of scholars and other invested individuals on a range of topics related to voting rights; it is intended to supplement the discussions of these topics in the first two chapters. Some of the essays are historical. Others offer a balanced analysis of the topic: Here are the strongest arguments for, and against, a particular public policy. And still others specifically advocate for (or against) some specific policy or action.

Donald Grier Stephenson Jr., professor of government emeritus at Franklin & Marshall College, addresses the unfinished work of the Supreme Court's reapportionment revolution that began in the 1960s.

Kara E. Stooksbury, professor of political science at Carson-Newman University, discusses the modern history of felon disenfranchisement, and suggests that criminal disqualification is antithetical to democratic principles.

Voter fraud and its prevention are the subjects of the next two essays. Adam B. Lawrence, associate professor of government at Millersville University, examines the evidence behind

President Lyndon Johnson signs the Voting Rights Act (VRA) on August 6, 1965. Not long after the nation witnessed the bloody scenes from Selma, Alabama—where peaceful black and white activists began their march to Montgomery to draw attention to black voter registration and were viciously assaulted by state law enforcement officers in March 1965—the president called upon the nation to eliminate root and branch all vestiges of discrimination and oppression based on race. Congress responded. The VRA is inarguably the single most important voting law in American history. (LBJ Library photo by Robert Knudsen) the all-too-common allegations of voter fraud, concluding that it happens far less than is perceived. Even so, Howard Ellis, professor of business administration emeritus at Millersville University, recommends that all voters be required to produce photo identification as a means to eliminate the *potential* for in-person voter fraud.

Lori Maxwell, professor of sociology and political science at Tennessee Tech University, writes about the history, language, application, judicial interpretation, and importance of the Voting Rights Act of 1965.

John LeJeune, assistant professor of political science at Georgia Southwestern State University, tackles the thorny issue of partisan gerrymandering, noting that efforts to weaken or eliminate the practice will likely continue, but only through state action.

G. Terry Madonna, director of the Center for Politics and Public Affairs at Franklin & Marshall College, and John McLarnon, associate professor of history at Millersville University, evaluate the merits of major reform proposals for the Electoral College.

Ron Hayduk, professor of political science at San Francisco State University, offers moral and practical reasons for restoring noncitizen voting, a common practice until the 1920s.

Pete Martin, founder and CEO of Votem, makes the case for online voting, suggesting that it will make voting more accessible, secure, and verifiable.

Finally, Americans' view on voting rights is the subject of an essay by Natalie Jackson, director of research at the Public Religion Research Institute.

The Supreme Court's Decisions on Representation: An Unfinished Revolution
Donald Grier Stephenson Jr.

The American polity embodies a tension between at least two fundamental principles: popular sovereignty and limited government. Popular sovereignty, or government by the "consent of the governed," as the Declaration of Independence avowed, is institutionalized at all levels of the political system, from city councils and state legislatures to Congress. In his address at the Gettysburg battlefield in 1863, President Abraham Lincoln called this principle "government by the people." Essential to popular sovereignty is a system of representation which in turn shapes the allocation of power. Juxtaposed to popular sovereignty is the principle of limited government that resides in the nature of a constitution itself. Ironically, the Constitution is at once both the proud assertion of popular sovereignty ("We the People . . .," as the Preamble declares) and the embodiment of limits on what the people may do. The Constitution is therefore much more than a blueprint of the structure of the national government that calls for a bicameral legislature, a separately elected president, and a Supreme Court. The Constitution imposes constraints on those who occupy the offices it creates and on state lawmakers and other officials too.

From the earliest years of the Republic, the Supreme Court has closely identified itself with constitutional limitations with the result that the Court matters as much as it does in American politics today because it has been accepted as the unique guardian of the restraints the Constitution imposes. Without the presence of the judiciary as an umpire of the political system, limited government would perhaps be more form than substance.

Ironically, the Court's decisions during the 1960s on districting and representation vividly illustrated how the two principles could be both in conflict and mutually supporting. While the Constitution mandated equal representation for the states in the Senate, it called for representation in the House of Representatives to be allocated proportionally, with each state guaranteed one delegate and the rest of the House membership apportioned among the states based on numbers from the most recent decennial census. Thus, a state's population determines its influence in the House but not in the Senate. These contrasting models of representation—numerically based in the House and geographically based in the Senate—in turn influenced how most state legislatures set up their own districting plans.

An act of Congress in 1842 required each state with more than one representative to employ single-member districts composed of contiguous territory, and statutes in 1901 and 1911 mandated compact congressional districts, but the Apportionment Act of 1929 left out any requirements for compact, contiguous, or equally populated districts. As the years went by, populations of House districts across the nation grew increasingly imbalanced, as did the populations of the hundreds of state legislative districts. The result was a distortion in representation that overweighted rural areas at the expense of population centers, making some people's votes worth more than others.

The Supreme Court initially was hesitant to intervene. In *Colegrove* v. *Green* (1946), voters seeking relief from Illinois's numerically skewed congressional districts were told to turn to their state legislature or to Congress, not to the Court for relief. Courts were not to enter what Justice Felix Frankfurter called a "political thicket." The defect in Frankfurter's thinking about the proper remedy for unfairness in districting, however, was that legislators holding power were unlikely either to reduce their own influence or, in effect, to vote themselves out of office. They were more problem than solution.

After the Court in *Baker* v. *Carr* (1962) abandoned that hands-off policy, a series of decisions followed within the span of only two years that vastly changed electoral politics in the United States. *Baker* itself had been flawed in that, while concluding that federal courts could provide relief for numerically imbalanced districts, it failed to provide guidelines to distinguish an acceptable from an unacceptable districting plan. That missing piece came in 1963 in *Gray* v. *Sanders* (1963), where the Court, applying what came to be called the one-person-one-vote principle, invalidated the infamous Georgia county unit system of primary elections for statewide offices that greatly disfavored urban counties. A candidate could win the popular vote by a wide margin but lose the election. A year later, *Wesberry* v. *Sanders* (1964) extended the equality principle to congressional districts, with the climactic conclusion of the process that had been set in motion by *Baker* v. *Carr*, coming only four months later in *Reynolds* v. *Sims* (1964). By applying the now familiar principle of one-person-one-vote, the justices challenged the legitimacy of at least forty state legislatures by mandating numerically equal districts for both legislative chambers.

Was the Court correct in its decisions to reform representation in the United States? Many people thought the Court had gone too far. As Justice John Harlan II insisted in his dissent in *Reynolds*, it was a mistake to believe that every social ill in the country could find a cure in the Constitution or in the judiciary, and it was equally mistaken to think that the Court's job was to initiate reform when other parts of the government fail to act. Other critics claimed that the Court was behaving like a continuing constitutional convention, adding requirements to the Constitution that the framers had not. Calling the Court's position draconian and an uncritical, simplistic, and heavy-handed application of sixth-grade arithmetic, Justice Potter Stewart advocated a flexible standard, so that the Constitution would be satisfied provided that (1) a districting plan was rational and (2) the plan did not permit the systematic frustration of the will of a majority of the electorate.

Would Stewart's proposal have been preferable to the Court's? To answer that question, consider that the obvious advantage of the one-person-one-vote rule: its simplicity. Once the Court in later decisions indicated how much variation from the norm would be acceptable (hardly any for congressional districts, a bit more for state legislative districts in accommodating such considerations as geographical features and municipal boundaries), it became relatively easy to spot a districting plan that was constitutionally problematic. Stewart's alternative would have injected flexibility but at the cost of greater ambiguity.

This series of districting cases from long ago demonstrated that skewed systems of representation had caused a breakdown in popular sovereignty. To the rescue came an unelected and unrepresentative group of judges applying the principle of limited government to save popular sovereignty from itself. Once implementation of the decisions was complete by the late 1960s—no easy feat in itself—a monumental shift in political power became a reality.

Yet, by highlighting the complexities of representation, those same decisions also revealed the distortions that could be caused by gerrymandering. As old as the republic itself, this practice in its classic form has entailed the drawing of district lines to boost or reduce the influence of a political party in a legislative body. Since 1960 (*Gomillion* v. *Lightfoot*), the Supreme Court has prohibited racial gerrymandering, but with partisan gerrymandering, the effect can be similar by *packing* one party's adherents into a few districts (thus reducing their strength elsewhere) or by *cracking* adherents among several districts (and so fracturing their influence). Thus, even though districts may be equal in population (and thereby satisfy the one-person-one-vote rule), the effect of a single vote can be increased or reduced.

While the Supreme Court as early as 1986 (*Davis* v. *Bandemer*) held that federal courts could hear cases involving districts that might be gerrymandered, the Court was unable then to agree on a clear definition of a gerrymander. Left in doubt was the kind of evidence and the period of time required to prove an unconstitutional gerrymander—a particularly troubling consideration in light of the fact that redistricting occurs in every state after each decennial census. Such uncertainties led the Court nearly to overrule *Bandemer* in *Vieth* v. *Jubelirer* (2004), where four justices were prepared to hold that partisan gerrymandering was nonjusticiable (inappropriate for judges to decide). This position then commanded a majority in 2019

(*Rucho* v. *Common Cause*). The contrast with the redistricting cases from the 1960s could not be sharper. Without a definition of an unconstitutional gerrymander that could attract the votes of five justices, this aspect of districting now remains entirely in the hands of those legislators who hold a majority and seek partisan advantage. Consequently, there remains unfinished what could have been a more complete revolution in representation.

Donald Grier Stephenson Jr. is Charles A. Dana Professor of Government, Emeritus, at Franklin and Marshall College where he taught from 1970 until 2017. Reared on a farm near Covington, Georgia, he is a graduate of Davidson College (1964), and received MA and PhD degrees from Princeton University in 1966 and 1967, respectively. Between 1968 and 1970, he was in the United States Army, completing his duty at the rank of captain. He is author of Campaigns and the Court: The U.S. Supreme Court in Presidential Elections *(1999),* The Waite Court *(2003), and* The Right to Vote *(2004), and is coauthor of* American Constitutional Law *(17th ed., 2018) and* Introduction to American Government *(9th ed., 2017). He writes "The Judicial Bookshelf" for* The Journal of Supreme Court History.

Felon Disenfranchisement
Kara E. Stooksbury

An estimated six million Americans are denied the right to vote because they have been convicted of a felony. The United States is the only democratic country that imposes this type of punishment. Felons who have completed their sentences should not be prohibited from voting because these policies are racially discriminatory and antithetical to democratic principles.

Although suffrage exclusions for criminal offenses date to the early national period, their modern iterations are largely a vestige of post–Civil War policies designed to thwart the guarantees of the Fifteenth Amendment. States implemented these policies contemporaneously with other methods of disenfranchising blacks, including poll taxes, literacy tests, and grandfather clauses, all of which have been eliminated. Interestingly, the states that disenfranchised felons in the late nineteenth century also had the highest numbers of blacks. When Alabama broadened its existing disenfranchisement laws in 1901 to exclude individuals convicted of crimes involving "moral turpitude," the state legislator who sponsored the statute stated that, "The crime of wife beating alone would disqualify 60 percent of the Negroes" (Staples 2014). Given that history, it is unsurprising that today Alabama has one of the highest rates of felon disenfranchisement in the country. According to The Sentencing Project, eligible black American voters across the country are four times more likely to lose their voting rights for felony convictions than the rest of the eligible voting population (Chung 2019). Nationally, 13 percent of black men have lost their voting rights due to felon disenfranchisement policies.

While these policies are facially neutral, blacks are disproportionately affected by felon disenfranchisement laws due to racial disparities in the criminal justice system. Blacks are more likely than whites to be arrested and charged with criminal offenses, and they also receive harsher sentences ("Report to the United Nations" 2018). Additionally, black defendants do not fare as well as white defendants in plea bargaining: White defendants are 25 percent more likely than black defendants to have their most serious initial charge dropped or reduced to a lesser charge. When charged with a felony, white defendants are more likely to be convicted of a misdemeanor instead (Berdejó 2018, 1191).

Aside from Maine and Vermont, which allow even incarcerated felons to vote, states have various procedures for reinstating voting rights. The complexity of the requirements creates significant obstacles for felons who have completed their sentences. In Tennessee, for example, state law establishes conditions by which some felons may regain their voting rights. The manner of restoration is dependent upon the crime committed and the year of the conviction. Individuals convicted prior to January 15, 1973, retain the right to vote unless convicted of any of twenty-one crimes, including horse stealing and incest. Persons convicted between January 15, 1973, and May 17, 1981, automatically have their voting rights restored following completion of their sentences. And those convicted after May 17, 1981, must meet several requirements to have their voting rights restored. First, they must receive a pardon, complete the maximum sentence for the crime, or be granted release from parole supervision. Second, they must pay any outstanding court-ordered restitution or fees and be current on any child support payments. And third, they must obtain a court order or a Certificate of Restoration before they can register to vote. Those convicted (after May 17, 1981) of voter fraud, treason, murder, or rape, however, may never have their voting rights restored ("Restoration of Voting Rights" 2019).

The Brennan Center for Justice found that even election officials were confused about their state's requirements for allowing previously incarcerated felons to vote (Wood and Bloom 2008). In a survey of Tennessee election officials in 2007, none of the ninety-five election commissioners could name the requirements for obtaining a Certificate of Restoration. The uncertainty concerning felon voting rights extends to lesser crimes as well. In Ohio, for example, which allows individuals convicted of a misdemeanor to vote, 30 percent of election officials did not know or were unsure whether those individuals could vote. In the five states that allow individuals on probation, but not parole, to vote, confusion also existed. In Colorado, half of local election officials did not know that people on probation could vote. Generally, individuals on probation have committed misdemeanors or low-grade felonies, but are often mistakenly told by election officials that they cannot vote (Wood and Bloom 2008).

Adding to this confusion, voting rights for felons in some states are in flux. Consider the situation in Kentucky: In November 2015, Governor Steve Beshear, a Democrat, restored voting rights to nonviolent felons who had been released from prison and met other criteria. In December 2015, however, the new Kentucky governor, Matt Bevin, a Republican, rescinded that executive order and replaced it with one requiring felons to apply to the governor on an individual basis to have their voting rights restored. Yet, in December 2019, on just his third day as governor, Andy Beshear, a Democrat and son of the former governor, restored voting rights to felons who had completed their prison sentences along with the terms of their probation or parole ("Voting Rights Restoration" 2019). Perhaps it is no surprise that felons in Kentucky do not know whether they are eligible to vote from one election to the next.

The suppression of felon votes has altered election outcomes. According to a statistical analysis of close presidential and congressional elections, had felons been allowed to vote, the result would have been different in a number of contests. Two scholars even conclude that, in the especially close 2000 presidential election, Al Gore would have won Florida if felons had not been disenfranchised (Manza and Uggen 2006, 203). Prior to the election, Florida election officials purged the names of felons from voting rolls. In doing so, some eligible voters who had no criminal records were confused with felons who had similar names and were mistakenly removed from the rolls. Eligible voters were also mistakenly removed for other reasons. Even an election supervisor's name was on the initial purge list. Also of note, the individuals mistaken for felons or removed for other reasons were disproportionately black (Berman 2015, 208–210).

In states that restore voting rights, voter turnout among felons is between 10 and 20 percent in presidential elections, which is considerably lower than the average voter turnout of 50–55 percent (Stockman 2018). Many of these individuals are deterred by confusion over whether they are eligible to vote and fears that they will be prosecuted for voting illegally. The penalties for voting illegally range from fines in some states to prison sentences in others.

Those who support criminal disqualification often argue that because felons have broken the law, they should be prohibited from participating in the lawmaking process. The conservative Heritage Foundation argues that the ballot box should be off limits to felons until they can prove they have been rehabilitated (Stockman 2018). The ability to participate fully in civic life, however, is part of that process. Some have posited that incarceration, even for a short period of time, affects turnout by altering the felons' perceptions of their place in society (White 2019). Those who have been incarcerated often think that they are still perceived by government and society as criminals, rather than full citizens who have paid their debts for their misdeeds. Additionally, those who have served time in prison often lose their jobs or face other economic hardships, both of which decrease the likelihood of voting.

Most modern felon disenfranchisement laws were intended to prevent blacks from voting. Unfortunately, many of those policies still have that effect. Individuals who have paid their debt to society are often subjected to a maze of bureaucratic red tape and the whims of politicians in attempting to regain their right to participate fully in electoral politics. Reinstating voting rights to those who have completed their sentences facilitates their reintegration into society and ensures representational equality, a critical component of a democracy.

Kara E. Stooksbury is chair of the Department of History, Political Science and Sociology and associate professor of political science at Carson-Newman University, where she teaches undergraduate courses in constitutional law, privacy law, law in American society, and sex-based discrimination. Stooksbury received her MA and PhD in political science from the University of Tennessee, Knoxville. She is the coeditor of Encyclopedia of American Civil Rights and Liberties: Revised and Expanded Edition *(ABC-CLIO, 2017).*

References

Berdejó, Carlos. 2018. "Criminalizing Race: Racial Disparities in Plea Bargaining." *Boston College Law Review*, 59 (4): 1189–1249. https://lawdigitalcommons.bc.edu/cgi /viewcontent.cgi?article=3659&context=bclr

Berman, Ari. 2015. *Give Us the Ballot: The Modern Struggle for Voting Rights in America*. New York: Farrar, Straus, and Giroux.

Chung, Jean. 2019. "Felony Disenfranchisement: A Primer." The Sentencing Project, 27 June. https://www .sentencingproject.org/publications/felony -disenfranchisement-a-primer/

Manza, Jeff, and Christopher Uggen. 2006. *Locked Out: Felon Disenfranchisement and American Democracy*. New York: Oxford University Press.

"Report to the United Nations on Racial Disparities in the U.S. Criminal Justice System." 2018. The Sentencing Project. https://www.sentencingproject.org/publications /un-report-on-racial-disparities/

"Restoration of Voting Rights." 2019. Tennessee Secretary of State. https://sos.tn.gov/products/elections/restoration -voting-rights

Staples, Brent. 2014. "The Racist Origins of Felon Disenfranchisement." *New York Times*, 18 November. https://www.nytimes.com/2014/11/19/opinion/the-racist -origins-of-felon-disenfranchisement.html

Stockman, Farah. 2018. "They Served Their Time. Now They're Fighting for Other Ex-Felons to Vote." *New York Times*, 11 May. https://www.nytimes.com/2018/05/11/us /voting-rights-felons.html

"Voting Rights Restoration in Kentucky." 2019. Brennan Center for Justice, 12 December. https://www .brennancenter.org/our-work/research-reports /voting-rights-restoration-efforts-kentucky

White, Ariel. 2019. "Perspective: Even Very Short Jail Sentences Drive People Away from Voting." *Washington Post*, 28 March. https://www.washingtonpost.com /outlook/2019/03/28/even-very-short-jail-sentences-drive -people-away-from-voting

Wood, Erika, and Rachel Bloom. 2008. "De Facto Disenfranchisement." Brennan Center for Justice, August. https://www.brennancenter.org/sites/default/files/2019-08 /Report_DeFactoDisenfranchisement.pdf

Voter Fraud: Real or Imagined?
Adam B. Lawrence

The U.S. Constitution is the world's oldest and most celebrated blueprint for Republican government. Yet, at its adoption, the document did not grant anyone the right to vote. And at its birth, the United States was far from a democratic nation. The founding generation believed, as James Wilson attested, that voting was a "privilege of free men" that should be extended only "as far as considerations of safety and order" would permit (Hall 1997, 108–109). Most political leaders believed that only property owners possessed the economic independence necessary to participate in public affairs; and that those who did not own property were economically dependent and too easily subjected to manipulation or control by others. Even Thomas Jefferson, perhaps the most democratic statesman of the era, supported property qualifications. Additionally, the founders feared what might happen should the property requirement be abandoned. As John Adams warned, "There would be no end of it. New claims will arise; women will demand the right to vote; lads from twelve to twenty-one will think their rights not enough attended to; and every man who has not a farthing, will demand an equal voice with any other" (Taylor 1979, 208–213).

The current generation is not similarly alarmed. The franchise today is far more inclusive—and the electoral process far more democratic—than anyone in 1787 envisioned. But many remain concerned about voter fraud, the specter of which has often been invoked as a justification for restrictions on voting rights. Opponents of those restrictions contend that such measures do little to address the problem and suppress the right of lawful voters to cast ballots. The objective of this essay is not to take sides in that debate, but rather to address the question: Is voter fraud real or imagined?

Voter Fraud in the Twenty-First Century

Following the disputed 2000 presidential election, in which George Bush won Florida—and ultimately the presidency—by a few hundred popular votes in that state, both political parties expressed greater interest in electoral integrity and voter legitimacy. In 2004, Republican election officials in Florida purged its voter rolls of convicted felons, though as it turned out, the list of felons used by the officials was mistaken, including voters who had been lawfully reinstated. Additionally, the list was racially skewed in a way that appeared partisan: It included twenty-two thousand blacks (most of whom vote Democratic) and just sixty-one Latinos (who tend to vote Republican). That same year, in apparent violation of the Help America Vote Act of 2002, the Ohio Secretary of State, a Republican, ordered election officials not to offer provisional ballots to people they did not personally recognize or to people who claimed they did not receive an absentee ballot (U.S. Election Assistance Commission 2010, 155–165). These and other actions convinced Democrats that Republicans wanted to prevent lawful voters from casting ballots.

Similarly, Republicans suspected Democrats of voter fraud, most notably by encouraging noncitizens to vote and ignoring risks associated with early and absentee voting. In 2005, the Senate Republican Policy Committee concluded that "voter fraud continues to plague our nation's federal elections, diluting and canceling out the lawful votes of the vast majority of

Americans" ("Putting an End to Voting Fraud" 2005, 1). In 2008, the Republican Party accused ACORN, a liberal activist group, of engaging in voter registration fraud. ACORN admitted that it submitted thousands of fraudulent forms with phony names. The leaders of ACORN said they flagged the problematic forms themselves, but submitted them nonetheless, believing that the law required it. Allegations of ACORN's activities were repeated by the 2008 Republican nominee, John McCain, in a nationally televised presidential debate when he said that ACORN was "on the verge of maybe perpetrating one of the greatest frauds in voter history, maybe destroying the fabric of democracy" (Seelye 2008).

Public Opinion of Voter Fraud

A review of the evidence awaits, but most Americans have made up their minds. A 2016 *Washington Post*–ABC poll found that 46 percent believed voter fraud occurs very or somewhat often; another 50 percent said it happens occasionally or rarely. Among Donald Trump supporters, 69 percent said it happened very or somewhat often; among Hillary Clinton supporters, just 28 percent believed so (Guskin and Clement 2016).

The Case against Widespread Voter Fraud

Although there are numerous instances of attempted or actual voter fraud—the Miami mayoral race in 1997 (Navarro 1998), the ACORN voter registration fiasco in 2008 (Friess 2009), and the ninth congressional district in North Carolina in 2018 (Graham 2019), for example—there are no studies documenting widespread voter fraud (Ingraham 2017). In 2006, a five-year investigation conducted by the administration of President George W. Bush found no evidence of an organized effort to illegally influence federal elections. The investigation produced eighty-six criminal convictions, but many were the result of people misunderstanding eligibility rules or filling out paperwork incorrectly (Lipton and Urbina 2007).

In 2012, researchers at Arizona State University asked all fifty states to send information for every case of fraudulent activity involving registration fraud, absentee ballot fraud, vote buying, false election counts, campaign fraud, ineligible votes, voting twice, voter impersonation, and intimidation. They found ten cases of voter impersonation, 491 cases of absentee ballot fraud, and 401 cases of voter registration fraud—all over a period of twelve years and more than 620 million votes cast. Of the allegations whose resolution could be determined, 46 percent resulted in acquittals, dropped charges, or decisions not to bring charges.

As of 2016, thirty-three states had adopted voter ID requirements, passed mostly by Republican-controlled state legislatures whose leaders claimed that cheating at the ballot box was a routine occurrence. But academic studies show, and most election law experts agree, that the kind of voter fraud voter ID laws are designed to prevent—voter impersonation—is extraordinarily rare.

In 2014, Justin Levitt conducted one of the most comprehensive investigations of voter impersonation. His examination of more than one billion ballots cast in national elections from 2000 to 2014 uncovered a total of thirty-one credible cases of voter impersonation (Levitt 2014).

In 2016, a *Washington Post* analysis of news reports of voter fraud in the 2016 presidential election found four cases out of 136 million votes cast. Two cases involved Trump voters trying to vote twice: one a Republican judge who attempted to fill out a ballot on behalf of her dead husband and another a poll worker completing an absentee ballot for a mayoral candidate in Florida (Bump 2016).

In 2017, the Heritage Foundation compiled a database of 749 instances of voter fraud over the past four decades. These include 105 instances from the previous five years, 488 from the previous ten years, ten involving voter impersonation, and forty-one cases of noncitizens voting ("A Sampling of

Election Fraud" 2017). This is striking in light of Trump's claim that he won the popular vote "if you deduct the millions of people who voted illegally" (Gajanan 2016). It is also worth noting that the database covers a period of time in which over three billion votes were cast. Even if all 749 cases of voter fraud are valid, we are left to conclude that voter fraud accounted for 0.0000002 percent of all votes cast. In other words, more people are struck by lightning each year than commit in-person voter fraud (Kertscher 2016).

Adam B. Lawrence is associate professor of government and political affairs and director of the Walker Center for Civic Responsibility and Leadership at Millersville University.

References

Bump, Philip. 2016. "There Have Been Just Four Cases of Documented Cases of Voter Fraud in the 2016 Election." *Washington Post*, 1 December. https://www.washingtonpost.com/news/the-fix/wp/2016/12/01/0-000002-percent-of-all-the-ballots-cast-in-the-2016-election-were-fraudulent/

Friess, Steve. 2009. "Acorn Charged in Voter Registration Fraud Case in Nevada." *New York Times*, 5 May. https://www.nytimes.com/2009/05/05/us/05acorn.html

Gajanan, Mahita. 2016. "Without Evidence Donald Trump Says Millions Voted 'Illegally' in the Election He Won." *Time*, 26 November. https://time.com/4582868/donald-trump-people-illegally-voted-election/

Graham, David A. 2019. "North Carolina Had No Choice: A House Election Gets Its Inevitable Do-Over." *The Atlantic*, 22 February. https://www.theatlantic.com/politics/archive/2019/02/north-carolina-9th-fraud-board-orders-new-election/583369/

Guskin, Emily, and Scott Clement. 2016. "Poll: Nearly Half of Americans Say Voter Fraud Occurs Often." *Washington Post*, 15 September. https://www.washingtonpost .com/news/the-fix/wp/2016/09/15/poll-nearly-half-of -americans-say-voter-fraud-occurs-often/

Hall, Mark. 1997. *The Political and Legal Philosophies of James Wilson, 1972–1798*. Columbia, MO: University of Missouri Press.

Ingraham, Christopher. 2017. "Here are Nine Investigations on Voter Fraud That Found Virtually Nothing." *Washington Post*, 25 June. https://www.washingtonpost.com/news /wonk/wp/2017/01/25/here-are-nine-major-investigations -on-voter-fraud-that-found-virtually-nothing/

Kertscher, Tom. 2016. "Which Happens More: People Struck by Lightning or People Committing Voter Fraud by Impersonation?" *Politifact*, 17 April. https://www.politifact .com/wisconsin/statements/2016/apr/07/mark-pocan /which-happens-more-people-struck-lightning-or-peop/

Levitt, Justin. 2014. "A Comprehensive Investigation of Voter Impersonation Finds 31 Credible Incidents Out of One Billion Ballots Cast." *Washington Post*, 6 August. https:// www.washingtonpost.com/news/wonk/wp/2014/08/06/a -comprehensive-investigation-of-voter-impersonation -finds-31-credible-incidents-out-of-one-billion -ballots-cast/

Lipton, Eric, and Ian Urbina. 2007. "In 5-Year Effort, Scant Evidence of Voter Fraud." *New York Times*, 12 April. https://www.nytimes.com/2007/04/12/washington /12fraud.html

Navarro, Mireya. 1998. "Fraud Ruling Invalidates Miami Mayoral Election." *New York Times*, 5 March. https://www .nytimes.com/1998/03/05/us/fraud-ruling-invalidates -miami-mayoral-election.html

"Putting an End to Voting Fraud." 2005. U.S. Senate Republican Policy Committee. http://www.votelaw.com

/blog/blogdocs/Voter%20Fraud%20Paper%20(no%20sig)
.pdf

"A Sampling of Election Fraud Cases from across the
Country." 2017. The Heritage Foundation. https://www
.heritage.org/sites/default/files/voterfraud_download
/VoterFraudCases_5.pdf

Seelye, Katharine. 2008. "McCain's Warning about Voter
Fraud Stokes a Fiery Campaign Even Further." *New York
Times*, 26 October. https://www.nytimes.com/2008/10/27
/us/politics/27vote.html

Taylor, Robert J., ed. 1979. *The Adams Papers, Papers of John
Adams*. Vol. 4. Cambridge, MA: Harvard University Press.

U.S. Election Assistance Commission. 2010. https://www.eac
.gov/assets/1/6/EMG_chapt_16_august_26_2010.pdf

Voter ID
Howard C. Ellis

"My father voted Republican till the day he died. Then he
started voting Democratic."

—Anonymous old joke

The right to vote is fundamental. No citizen entitled to vote
should be prevented from doing so because authorities have
imposed undue burdens on his or her ability to vote. Equally
important is the principle that no person not entitled to vote
should be able to do so. Either possibility could change the
outcome of a close election. Either possibility can cause the
public to lose faith in the validity of the democratic processes. Polls show that about half the voting public has no
faith that votes are counted properly. The most often heard
claim is that minority-group votes are suppressed (Lithwick
2019).

One issue that raises both of these possibilities is voter ID,
that is, a proposed legal requirement, already on the books in
some states, that a would-be voter who shows up in person

at the polls—as opposed to voting by absentee ballot—must show identification sufficient to prove he or she is, namely, a person who is registered to vote in that district and who has not already voted in that election (Specht 2018). Requiring voter ID is intended to prevent an impostor from voting in the name of some other person who is entitled to vote. But, is the benefit of preventing voter fraud that the voter ID requirement might provide worth the burden on some voters of acquiring a voter ID that might keep them from voting at all?

This issue divides the public virtually entirely on party lines (Bialik 2018). While many Republican-controlled state legislatures have adopted voter ID requirements, only one Democratic-controlled legislature, Rhode Island, has (Woodman 2016). Democrats claim that voter ID is a Republican scheme to suppress Democratic votes among the poor, minorities, and the elderly. Republicans see Democratic opposition to voter ID as intended to facilitate fraudulent voting, which the Republicans believe Democrats regularly engage in (Lithwick 2019).

Perhaps the answer to the debate lies in doing an actual count of the respective numbers of fraudulent votes without voter ID compared to the number of votes suppressed by voter ID.

In *Crawford* v. *Marion County Election Board* (2008), the Supreme Court held that an Indiana law requiring voters to identify themselves at the polls was constitutional. Six justices agreed that the state's interest in avoiding in-person fraudulent voting was important. The majority also agreed that the requirement to obtain a free picture ID by going to the local Department of Motor Vehicles (DMV) was not sufficiently onerous to constitute a substantial burden on citizens who currently lacked an ID. The majority further recognized that there may be a small number of citizens for whom the burden will be enough to prevent them from voting, but that was not sufficient reason to invalidate the general requirement of a picture ID.

Three justices, however, saw the balance between the state's interest in deterring in-person voter fraud and the burden of obtaining a picture ID differently. On the one hand, the dissenters focused on the exceedingly rare occurrence of persons caught committing in-person voter fraud (no such cases were found to have occurred in Indiana), rendering the state's supposed interest insignificant. On the other hand, the dissenters pointed out that there may be tens of thousands of persons who currently lacked a picture ID, and for the very poor, the elderly, and the disabled, it can be extremely difficult to obtain the requisite ID, even if the ID were provided free of charge. They might not have the ability to get to the DMV on their own. They might not possess the necessary documents, such as a birth certificate. They might not be able to afford the price of obtaining such documents. That hardly seems fair.

One reason that the threat of in-person voter fraud arguably seems significant is that the voter rolls in most states are loaded with the names of persons who are no longer eligible to vote. They may have died, or moved away, or been convicted of felonies. Without a picture ID requirement, it would seem to be easy enough for an impostor to show up claiming to be one such person and vote in that person's name. To voter ID supporters, the lack of criminal convictions for in-person voter fraud is not proof that it is not happening, because it is so easy to get away with it. If I show up at my late brother's polling place and try to vote in his name, will I be caught? I know his basic information. I know what his signature looks like. Chances are, since he lived in a big city, that the poll workers will not know him or me by sight. If it turns out that his name has been removed from the list I can just say, "I must be in the wrong place. I'll figure it out. Sorry for the inconvenience."

Opponents of voter ID cite the severe penalties associated with fraudulent voting (up to five years in prison) compared to the vanishingly small benefit derived by the fraudster as elections are virtually never decided by one or two votes. Thus, opponents claim, there is no real incentive to commit in-person voter fraud, and that is why there are so few convictions for it. The risk of being caught, however, is also vanishingly small. One wonders, though, if a conspiracy to cast a few hundred fraudulent votes in a big city is plausible. That many votes could decide a close election. In 2008, Al Franken won the Minnesota senate election by 312 votes out of 2.8 million votes cast (Roff 2010). Were there four hundred fraudulent votes? Who knows? Voter ID in Minnesota was not the law in 2008 and was rejected in 2012 (Melillo 2012).

Not all voter ID requirements are the same. Some states have a strict requirement, meaning that only specific photo IDs will suffice, that only very narrow categories of persons are exempted, such as the disabled in nursing homes, or persons with a religious objection to being photographed. In such states, someone appearing at the polls without the requisite ID can cast a provisional ballot but that ballot will not be counted unless the voter appears at the election office, typically within ten days, to show his ID (Specht 2018). Other states are more lenient. They allow student IDs, credit cards, and other forms of ID that do not have a photo. They often allow for provisional ballots to be counted if the voter's signature matches one on file, or if a poll worker recognizes the voter and can vouch for him or her (Underhill 2019).

Some studies show that voter ID laws can reduce voter turnout. According to these studies, most of the reduced turnout tends to be among poor and minority voters, who, as it happens, tend to vote for Democrats. Other studies show that voter ID laws create virtually no effect on voter turnout (Specht 2018).

So what is the best solution?

I suggest that requiring a photo voter ID is best, with the following provisos: First, the ID must be free of any cost to the indigent voter. This includes the further proviso that, if a birth certificate is required, it too must be provided to indigent applicants free of charge. Second, the ID must be made available in easily reachable locations, or by mail, or online. Third, for people who, because of disability or age, are not going to be able to obtain an ID on their own, the state must commit to aid them, even if it means providing state employees to drive them to the DMV.

Why require the voter ID at all? Besides the need to assure the public that voter fraud is not easy to commit, incentivizing people who do not have a photo ID to get one provides them with a host of nonvoting related benefits. A photo ID is required to get on an airplane, to cash a check, to apply for credit, to apply for public benefits, to go to a doctor or hospital, to purchase alcohol or cigarettes, and more. In fact, not having an ID is an impediment to ordinary living. So instead of allowing people to vote without a photo ID, why not do everything feasible to ensure that everyone has one, and thereby allow all citizens to enjoy what everyone else takes for granted, namely, full membership in ordinary society, while also eliminating the potential for in-person voter fraud. Everyone who is entitled to vote can vote, and it will be much more difficult for the nonentitled to vote. It is a win-win.

Howard C. Ellis is professor emeritus of business administration at Millersville University of Pennsylvania.

References

Bialik, Kristen. 2018. "How Americans View Some of the Voting Policies Approved at the Ballot Box." Pew Research Center. https://www.pewresearch.org/fact-tank/2018 /11/15/how-americans-view-some-of-the-voting-policies -approved-at-the-ballot-box/

Lithwick, Dahlia. 2019. "The Most Important Question Facing Americans Today Who Counts?" *Slate*. https://slate .com/news-and-politics/2019/09/the-most-important -question-who-counts.html

Melillo, Amanda. 2012. "How Minnesota's Voter ID Amendment Was Defeated." Brennan Center for Justice. https://www.brennancenter.org/our-work/analysis-opinion /how-minnesotas-voter-id-amendment-was-defeated

Roff, Peter. 2010. "Al Franken May Have Won His Senate Seat through Voter Fraud." *US News*. https://www.usnews.com/opinion/blogs/peter-roff/2010/07/20/al-franken-may-have-won-his-senate-seat-through-voter-fraud

Specht, Paul. 2018. "States with Voter ID Laws Have Seen 'Zero Decrease' in Turnout, NC Republican says." *Politifact*. https://www.politifact.com/north-carolina/statements/2018/jun/20/tim-moore/states-voter-id-laws-have-seen-zero-decrease-turno/

Underhill, Wendy. 2019. "Voter Identification Requirements | Voter ID Laws." National Conference of State Legislatures. http://www.ncsl.org/research/elections-and-campaigns/voter-id.aspx

Woodman, Spencer. 2016. "The Strange Case of Rhode Island's Voter-ID Law." *Vice*. https://www.vice.com/en_us/article/qbx7j5/the-strange-case-of-rhode-islands-voter-id-law

The Voting Rights Act of 1965
Lori Maxwell

The Voting Rights Act (VRA) of 1965 was one of the two cornerstones of civil rights legislation President Lyndon Johnson pushed through Congress after the tragic assassination of President John F. Kennedy in 1963. The first was the Civil Rights Act of 1964, which prohibited discrimination in places of public accommodation on account of race, color, religion, sex, or national origin. The other major piece of social legislation that fundamentally changed American life was the VRA, which sought to remedy the discrimination exposed by a 1961 U.S. Commission on Civil Rights document demonstrating prohibitive voting barriers in the deep south (Stephens, Scheb, and Glennon 2015, 539). This essay examines briefly the history of electoral discrimination, the background of the VRA, the specific provisions of the VRA, and the reauthorizations of the VRA, concluding with a call to continue reauthorizations.

Attempts at electoral disenfranchisement on the basis of race have a long and complicated history in Southern politics. States imposed literacy tests (tests of literacy or comprehension, often exempting whites; now illegal); adopted poll taxes (fees to vote; outlawed by the Twenty-Fourth Amendment); enacted grandfather clauses (excusing persons from certain voting requirements if they, or their ancestors, had been eligible to vote prior to a certain date, always a year in which most blacks had not been eligible to vote; now unconstitutional); and required or allowed white primaries (the law or practice between 1870 and 1944 of restricting participation in the Democratic primary to whites, thus ensuring that blacks would not be able to help select the party's nominee for the general election; now violative of the Fifteenth Amendment). Much of this disenfranchisement, of course, is synonymous with the post-Reconstruction decades of the late eighteenth and early nineteenth centuries.

The aforementioned 1961 U.S. Commission on Civil Rights report, however, provided more recent, but equally dismal, electoral practices. Less than 10 percent of eligible blacks in at least 129 counties in the deep South were even registered to vote. Even worse, in those counties where blacks comprised a majority of the population, the average percentage of their electoral registration was only 3 percent (Stephens, Scheb, and Glennon 2015, 539). On March 7, 1965, in what came to be known as "Bloody Sunday," blacks and other civil rights protestors in Selma, Alabama, marched across the Edmund Pettus Bridge to highlight the racially discriminatory practices that were preventing their attempts to register blacks to vote. The marchers were met on the other side of the bridge by state troopers and a civilian mob, who proceeded to beat the peacefully marching men, women, and children. The beatings were broadcast on national television. Five months after the events in Selma, on August 6, President Lyndon Johnson signed into law the VRA of 1965, the most significant piece of voting legislation in American history.

The effect of the VRA is hard to overstate. The specific provisions eliminated literacy tests in voting. The VRA did not specifically eliminate poll taxes, but directed the U.S. attorney general to challenge the use of the poll tax. After several such challenges, the Twenty-Fourth Amendment eliminated poll taxes in federal elections. Enforcement provisions were also included in the VRA as federal registrars were sent to maintain voting rolls in some instances. Also, several key states in the deep South that had been most resistant to black enfranchisement—Alabama, Georgia, Louisiana, Mississippi, South Carolina, and Virginia—were required, under Section 5, to obtain "preclearance" from the federal government before making any changes to their electoral procedures or systems. The logic for this preclearance was simple: It was not enough to prohibit only those means of disenfranchisement currently used by Southern states; the authors of the VRA knew that, without preclearance from a federal authority, Southern states would find other ways to disenfranchise blacks.

On March 7, 1966, the one-year anniversary of Bloody Sunday, the Supreme Court ruled, in *South Carolina* v. *Katzenbach*, that the VRA was an extreme, yet constitutional, exercise of legislative power. Chief Justice Earl Warren predicted correctly: "Hopefully, millions of non-white Americans will now be able to participate for the first time on an equal basis in the government under which they live." Indeed, the VRA has enfranchised 1.5 million blacks since 1965, and that does not even account for other minority groups that have benefited (Berman 2015). Moreover, the initial rise in voter registration in the years immediately after the passage of the VRA was clearly indicative of its success. In Mississippi, voter registration among blacks increased from 6.7 percent before the VRA to 59.8 percent by 1967. In Alabama, black voter registration grew from 24 to 57 percent in the same time period.

The VRA was reauthorized and strengthened by Congress in 1970, 1975, 1982, 1992, and 2006—most often in a bipartisan manner. More specifically, in 1975, the VRA was expanded to allow protections for "language minorities" so that registration and voting materials be provided in voters' native languages. The 1982 amendments extended provisions for twenty-five years and made it easier for individual voters to bring a lawsuit against discriminatory practices. The 2006 amendments extended provisions of the VRA for another twenty-five years. Though not scheduled to expire until 2031, as of 2020, another bipartisan legislative reauthorization awaits in the Republican-controlled Senate.

While the Congress and presidency have historically supported the VRA and its reauthorizations in a bipartisan manner, the judicial branch has recently been more circumspect with respect to its application. In 2013, in *Shelby County* v. *Holder*, for example, the justices struck down the provision of the VRA that contained the coverage formula for determining which states and localities were subjected to the preclearance requirement based on their longstanding histories with voter discrimination. The narrow majority held that the forty-year-old coverage formula was outdated and no longer reflective of current conditions or responsive to current needs. To be clear, the Court did not declare the preclearance requirement unconstitutional. Without a coverage formula, though, no jurisdiction would be subject to preclearance. In short, the justices gutted the preclearance requirement without declaring it unconstitutional. Unless Congress enacts a new coverage formula—highly unlikely in these hyperpartisan times—no state or locality, irrespective of its history with racial discrimination, will be required to obtain permission prior to changing its electoral rules and practices. Perhaps coincidentally, the years since *Shelby County* was decided have witnessed the closing of polling places, disproportionately in predominately black counties and neighborhoods; reductions in early voting;

purges of voter rolls, again disproportionately affecting blacks and other minorities; and the imposition of strict voter ID laws.

The Court has also invalidated state efforts to remain compliant with Section 2 of the VRA by creating majority-minority electoral districts. Starting in 1993—in *Shaw* v. *Reno*—the Court declared that majority-minority districts would be subject to strict judicial scrutiny. (To survive strict judicial scrutiny, a state must demonstrate that its actions have a compelling interest, be narrowly tailored to achieve that interest, and not be accomplishable by other less restrictive measures.) More recently, in *Abbott* v. *Perez* (2018), the Court tackled the inherent tension between the race-neutral requirement of the Equal Protection Clause of the Fourteenth Amendment and the requirement in Section 2 of the VRA that encourages states to consider race when drawing electoral districts. In *Abbott*, the justices sided with Texas in a challenge asserting that its legislative districts were drawn in violation of Section 2. According to the majority, even if a state had a history of racial discrimination in drawing legislative districts, that state was still entitled to the presumption that it acted properly in drawing later redistricting plans. In practice, this means that plaintiffs alleging a dilution of minority voting strength in a redistricting plan must demonstrate that the state legislature intended to discriminate when it enacted its plan.

In these and related cases, conservative justices have repeatedly criticized the use of race in legislative redistricting and cast doubt upon the constitutionality of majority-minority districts. The result: States are now reluctant to employ race in redistricting or create majority-minority districts, in spite of the commands of the VRA.

The Constitution, however, must not, in every instance, be "colorblind." For evidence, we need only look at the hundreds of thousands of enfranchised citizens that have a vote and voice as a result of the VRA of 1965, legislation that President Johnson described as "[a] triumph for freedom as huge as any ever won on the battlefield."

Lori Maxwell is professor of political science at Tennessee Tech University where she also serves as chair of sociology and political science. She teaches constitutional law and presidency courses and her research interests include the overlap between political culture and popular culture.

References

Berman, Ari. 2015. "Give Us The Ballot: The 1975 Expansion of the Voting Rights Act." *The Atlantic*, 5 August. https://www.theatlantic.com/politics/archive/2015/08/give-us-the-ballot-expanding-the-voting-rights-act/399128/

Stephens, Otis, John M. Scheb, II, and Colin Glennon. 2015. *American Constitutional Law: Civil Rights and Liberties.* Stamford, CT: Cengage.

Partisan Gerrymandering
John LeJeune

"Gerrymandering" is drawing electoral districts with the paramount aim of maximizing one's own electoral interests. A partisan gerrymander is "the formation of election districts, on another basis than that of single and homogenous political units as they existed previous to the apportionment, with boundaries arranged for partisan advantage" (Griffith 1907, 21). The term "gerrymandering" derives from an 1812 law, signed by Governor Elbridge Gerry, whereby a Democratic majority in the Massachusetts Legislature sought to strengthen its grip on the state senate by drawing district lines in which "counties were divided in the most arbitrary and partisan manner" (Griffith 1907, 63). The tactic worked: In the ensuing election, twenty-nine Democratic senators were elected by 50,164 votes, while a Federalist majority of 51,766 votes garnered only eleven seats (Griffith 1907, 73).

Debates over political gerrymandering are complicated by constitutional and legislative history. Though the practice has existed in America since the colonial period, Article I, Section 4, Clause 1, of the Constitution—"The Times, Places and Manner of holding Elections for Senators and Representatives, shall be prescribed in each State by the Legislature thereof"—lays the groundwork for gerrymandering today. Majority parties in state legislatures (also relying on Tenth Amendment reserved powers) have subsequently used their line-drawing authority to gerrymander state legislative and congressional districts. The tactic involves either "packing" opposition voters into a single district to eliminate their effect elsewhere, or "cracking" the opposition by spreading supporters thinly throughout multiple districts.

But notably, the same Elections Clause also grants that "Congress may at any time by Law make or alter such Regulations, except as to the Places of chusing Senators." This gives Congress authority to regulate congressional elections and override state rules in that context. For example, the Apportionment Act of 1842 bound all states to adopt single-member district elections to the House of Representatives. The Elections Clause does not grant Congress explicit authority to regulate state and local elections. Nevertheless, "Congress has the authority, under a number of constitutional amendments, to enforce prohibitions against specific discriminatory practices in all elections, including federal, state and local elections" (Gamboa 2001, 2). Accordingly, the VRA of 1965 outlawed discriminatory voting practices in federal and state elections and, as amended in 1982, prohibited "any state practice 'which results in' members of a racial or language minority having 'less opportunity than other members of the electorate to participate in the political process and to elect representatives of their choice,'" provided "[t]hat nothing in this section establishes a right to have members of a protected class elected in numbers equal to their proportion in the population" (Shapiro 1984, 190).

In this constitutional and legal context, from the 1960s onward, the Supreme Court has regularly entertained challenges to gerrymandered districts on a range of constitutional grounds. In the early 1960s, cases like *Wesberry* v. *Sanders* (1964) and

Reynolds v. *Sims* (1964) solidified the "one person, one vote" principle requiring equal population in congressional and state legislative districts, often relying on the Fourteenth Amendment's Equal Protection Clause to establish the unconstitutionality of the "dilution and undervaluation" of individual votes. While some consistently described these decisions as judicial overreach in an area traditionally reserved for state legislatures, the principle of equal population was a manageable standard for courts to implement.

The same cannot be said for later gerrymandering challenges. Finding a "judicially discoverable and manageable standard" for resolving racial and partisan gerrymandering complaints has perennially challenged the Court, although the Supreme Court has been more willing to articulate and enforce imprecise standards in racial gerrymandering cases. One reason for this difference is the Court's strong mandate to address equal protection claims that involve racial discrimination. This mandate stems both from the Equal Protection Clause's manifest intent, and is buttressed by congressional legislation derived from the Fourteenth, Fifteenth, and other rights-protecting amendments.

Partisan gerrymandering lacks such clarity. One problem with partisan gerrymandering claims is that "they involve *political* groups, which are neither as durable or cohesive as racial or ethnic groups," and this renders the link between partisan identity, equal protection claims, and the Court's affirmative mandate to intervene difficult to sustain (Rush 1994, 683). Not coincidentally, in partisan contexts, both plaintiffs and sympathetic justices have pivoted away from equal protection arguments and toward First Amendment claims grounded in the right to effective speech and association. Congressional action has also not encouraged judicial intervention. Congress's adoption of congressional single-member districts as a rule in 1842 rendered "asymmetric" electoral outcomes practically inevitable in Washington; and its explicit rejection of mandated proportional representation in the amended Civil Rights Act of 1982, where some form of proportional mandate might have been most expected, further undercuts claims that disproportionate electoral outcomes are legally problematic.

Most recently, plaintiffs in *Rucho* v. *Common Cause* (2019) claimed that party-gerrymandered congressional districts in North Carolina (and Maryland) violated the First Amendment, the Equal Protection Clause, the Elections Clause, and Article I, Section 2, of the Constitution. The Supreme Court ultimately decided against them on grounds that, first, the Court lacked "limited and precise standards that are clear, manageable, and politically neutral" to identify unconstitutional partisan gerrymanders and address subsequent claims; and second, that "[t]he only provision in the Constitution that specifically addresses the matter assigns it to the political branches." Leaning on the Elections Clause, the Court left responsibility for tackling gerrymandering to Congress and local state governments.

Writing for a narrow majority, Chief Justice John Roberts argued at length about the difficulty of establishing manageable and politically neutral standards for the Court to address the inequities of partisan gerrymandering. In dissent, Justice Elena Kagan argued that "[the majority] could have used the lower courts' general standard—focusing on 'predominant' purpose and 'substantial' effects—without fear of indeterminacy. I do not take even the majority to claim that courts are incapable of investigating whether legislators mainly intended to seek partisan advantage." Doing so would have notably placed the Court on similar terrain as racial gerrymandering, and specifically *Miller* v. *Johnson* (1995), which determined that where race is a "predominant, overriding" factor in district line-drawing, the state's plan is subject to strict scrutiny, and must be narrowly tailored to advance a compelling state interest.

This raises an important question: If the "predominant intent" standard in *Miller* was manageable for race, then why not also adopt it in the context of partisan gerrymandering? As Kagan continued in *Rucho*: "Although purpose inquiries carry certain hazards . . . they are a common form of analysis in constitutional cases. . . . Those inquiries would be no harder here than in other contexts." Responding to that claim, Roberts maintained that whereas "[i]n racial gerrymandering cases, we rely on a 'predominant intent' inquiry . . . because 'race-based decisionmaking is inherently suspect,'" in partisan contexts, "[a] permissible intent—securing partisan advantage—does not become constitutionally impermissible, like racial discrimination, when that permissible intent 'predominates.'" Thus, "[t]he 'central problem' is not determining whether a jurisdiction has engaged in partisan gerrymandering. It is 'determining when political gerrymandering has gone too far,'" since "[t]o hold that legislators cannot take partisan interests into account when drawing district lines would essentially countermand the Framers' decision to entrust districting to political entities."

In sum, adopting a "predominant intent" test for partisanship fails because the redistricting process, when conducted by partisan legislators, is by its very nature inherently partisan. In other words, where state legislators have *any* discretion at all to choose between one district line or another, predominant partisan intent would be the *de facto* assumption.

One might argue, however, that juxtaposing racial and partisan gerrymandering in this way skews the question fundamentally, for even in racial contexts, the "predominant intent" test does not end the game, but merely triggers a strict scrutiny analysis to determine whether the state's interests in the law are compelling, and its methods narrowly tailored. Viewed in this light, the necessary step for justiciability is not establishing a politically neutral *test* to determine when partisan gerrymandering is "too much"; it is, rather, to identify a *trigger*—like a distinct and assignable First Amendment violation—that compels the Court to review claims against partisan gerrymanders under some level of heightened scrutiny.

Nevertheless, while partisan gerrymandering claims will not be heard by federal courts post-*Rucho*, efforts to weaken or eliminate the practice of partisan gerrymandering will likely continue, through state legislative action—which may include the creation of independent redistricting commissions—and state courts applying state constitutional provisions.

Dr. John LeJeune is an assistant professor of political science at Georgia Southwestern State University in Americus, Georgia.

References

Gamboa, Anthony. 2001. *Report to the Congress: The Scope of Congressional Authority in Election Administration.* Washington, DC: United States General Accounting Office.

Griffith, Elmer C. 1907. *The Rise and Development of the Gerrymander* (Dissertation). Chicago, IL: Scott, Foresman and Company.

Rush, Mark E. 1994. "Gerrymandering: Out of the Political Thicket and into the Quagmire." *PS: Political Science and Politics*, 27 (4): 682–685.

Shapiro, Howard M. 1984. "Geometry and Geography: Racial Gerrymandering and the Voting Rights Act." *Yale Law Journal*, 94 (1): 189–208.

Electoral College Reform
G. Terry Madonna and John McLarnon

No exact count has been made about the number of proposals to supplant or reshape the Electoral College. One scholar suggests that over seven hundred bills have been introduced in Congress to replace or reform the Electoral College. Between 1947 and 1968 alone, more than 265 constitutional amendments to that effect were proposed in Congress. In fact, there have been more proposed amendments to abolish or alter the Electoral College than any other proposed constitutional amendment (Hardaway 1994, 6).

These numbers do not include proposals introduced in state legislatures, which have the constitutional authority to determine how electors within their respective states are apportioned and selected. In the first three presidential elections, state legislatures picked the electors. In 1800, state legislatures chose electors in ten states, while the voters picked them directly in six. By 1828, however, South Carolina was the only state not choosing electors by popular vote (Brinkley 2009, 215). Today, all states choose electors by popular vote.

Some reform proposals have generated more interest than others, a few have come close to passage, and one is slowly approaching sufficient support. The most persistent proposal is direct popular election of the president. Another is proportional distribution of electoral votes. A third is known as the congressional districting plan. And a fourth is the National Popular Vote Interstate Compact (NPVIC).

Direct Popular Election

Delegates at the Constitutional Convention had serious misgivings about electing the president by direct popular vote. Many believed that voters could be easily misled by political leaders and were incapable of making informed judgments. Furthermore, there was concern that under popular vote, aspects of monarchial rule could return to the continent. Over the years, popular vote proposals have awarded the presidency to the candidate with the largest number of nationwide votes, and some have required that the popular vote leader earn at least 40 percent of the vote or face a runoff election. Popular vote proposals typically occur following close national vote contests and also after the five presidential elections in which the popular vote victor was not elected president.

While direct popular election is the most democratic reform and finds high levels of support among the populace, it is also the least likely to happen. Because direct popular election is not a reform, but rather an abolishment, of the Electoral College, it can only be accomplished directly by constitutional amendment, which requires a two-thirds vote in each chamber of Congress, followed by ratification from three-fourths of the states. Even assuming that support for such a proposal could be found in the House of Representatives (the institution that represents the *people*), the proposal would almost certainly be defeated in the Senate (the institution that represents the *states*). In the Senate, every state is entitled to equal representation, regardless of its population. The near forty million persons who live in California have two seats in the Senate; the 577,000 folks who live in Wyoming also have two senators. So, even though California has almost seventy times more people than Wyoming, the two states are equals in the Senate. Thus, even if forty million Californians wanted to abolish the Electoral College, their political influence in the Senate could be offset by the half million or so residents of Wyoming.

As a general rule, large states are more supportive of direct popular election because it would enhance their electoral influence. And small states tend to prefer the Electoral College because it grants them disproportionate electoral influence. (To recall, Article II, Section 1, of the Constitution grants to each state the number of electoral votes equal to whole number of representatives and senators to which the state is entitled in Congress. California has fifty-three representatives and two senators, thus fifty-five electoral votes. Wyoming has one representative and two senators, thus three electoral votes.) Wyoming has approximately 0.0018 percent of the U.S. population, but has 0.0055 percent of the electoral votes. By contrast, California has roughly 12.2 percent of population, but only 10.2 percent of the electoral votes. Wyoming (like other small states) is overrepresented in the Electoral College, and California (like other large states) is underrepresented.

And even if a proposed constitutional amendment were to make it out of the Senate, it would still need to be ratified by thirty-eight of the states. That means any thirteen states— even the smallest thirteen (with a combined population of only one-third of California's population)—could prevent ratification.

Although the Electoral College is likely here to stay, that does not preclude other reforms. The Constitution leaves to the states the question of how to apportion electors. Currently, forty-eight states use the "winner-take-all" method, in which the candidate with the most popular votes receives all of the state's electors. But that method is not required by the Constitution. States may choose to apportion electors by other means.

Proportional Distribution

Proportional distribution calls for the electoral votes of a state to be awarded between or among the candidates roughly by the same percentage as the popular vote in that state. That is, if a candidate were to earn 30 percent of the popular vote, he or she would receive 30 percent of the state's electoral vote. (Mathematical exactitude is not possible, of course, but a formula could be developed well in advance of the election to govern the distribution of the electoral votes.) One major advantage of this distribution would be a more accurate reflection of each state's, and thus the national, political will.

Proportional distribution plans were first introduced in Congress in the late nineteenth century. The latest major effort to implement the plan came in the 1950s when Senator Henry Cabot Lodge and Representative Ed Gossett proposed a constitutional amendment. The proposal passed the Senate but failed in the House (Longley and Braun 1972, 49–56; Hardaway 1994, 145). It is worth noting, however, that a state can of its own accord adopt proportional distribution of electoral votes, as state legislatures (and not Congress) direct the appointment of electors. No constitutional amendment would be required for these changes, as the Electoral College remains intact.

Proportional distribution also incentivizes individuals to vote. Every vote for a candidate helps secure a larger share of the state's electoral votes. Under the "winner-take-all" method, a Republican in California or a Democrat in Oklahoma has little motivation to vote, knowing that her or his candidate has only a slim chance to win. Proportional distribution would also affect campaign strategy. No longer could candidates ignore "safe states." And no longer would national elections be decided by just a few "swing states."

Congressional Districting

A third proposed reform is the congressional districting plan. Instead of choosing delegates to the Electoral College in state-wide contests, electors would be selected out of congressional districts. Each candidate would receive one electoral vote for each congressional district won, and the winner of the overall popular vote in the state would get the two "bonus" electoral votes. (Remember: A state has the number of electoral votes equal to its number of congressional districts plus two.)

In the nineteenth century, eight states selected their electors in congressional districts. Currently only two states—Maine and Nebraska—use this process. Generally speaking, the district selection would lead to more campaigning in states with the most competitive congressional districts, further politicize congressional redistricting by inviting greater gerrymandering, and encourage third parties to select certain districts to win elections as opposed to winning electors statewide (Longley and Braun 1972, 57–64).

The congressional districting plan can be achieved without a constitutional amendment. As was true with proportional distribution, any state that wants to so divide its electoral votes need only enact legislation to this effect.

National Popular Vote Interstate Compact

The most recent efforts to modify the election of the president is the NPVIC (https://www.nationalpopularvote.com). The purpose of the compact is to ensure that the national popular vote winner is elected president. Under the compact, a state would pledge its electoral votes to the candidate with the greatest number of popular votes nationwide, regardless of the outcome in that state. Because no state wants to make such a promise by itself, the NPVIC would not go into effect until jurisdictions (states and the District of Columbia) with a total of 270 electoral votes—a majority of electoral votes—agreed to support its provisions. As of this writing, sixteen states, with 196 of the 270 electoral votes necessary to elect a president, have agreed to join the compact.

The NPVIC does not tinker with the Electoral College. And it leaves the power to decide how electors are chosen to the states. As such, it would not necessitate a constitutional amendment.

At Franklin and Marshall College, Dr. G. Terry Madonna is director of the Center for Politics and Public Affairs, professor of public affairs, and director of the Franklin and Marshall College Poll. He joined F&M in May 2004.

John McLarnon is the chair of the History Department at Millersville University in Pennsylvania.

References

Brinkley, Alan. 2009. *The Unfinished Nation: A Concise History of the American People*. New York: McGraw Hill.

Hardaway, Robert M. 1994. *The Electoral College and the Constitution: The Case for Preserving Federalism*. Westport, CT: Praeger.

Longley, Lawrence D., and Alan G. Braun. 1972. *The Politics of Electoral College Reform*. New Haven, CT: Yale University Press.

Noncitizen Voting
Ron Hayduk

The acquisition of political rights—including voting rights—has been a vital tool for every disempowered group in American history to achieve economic, social, and civil rights. Why not for immigrants too? Given significant anti-immigrant sentiment, the notion of allowing noncitizens to vote might appear outlandish. Upon examination, however, one encounters a more complex history, set of issues, and contemporary practices. A few basics to begin.

(1) Noncitizen voting (NCV) is not prohibited by the U.S. Constitution.

(2) Noncitizens enjoyed voting rights from the founding until the 1920s, participating in local, state, and federal elections in forty states.

(3) NCV is rational. There are compelling moral and practical reasons for restoring NCV, including notions of equality, as well as benefits that accrue to all members of a society.

(4) NCV is feasible. Currently, noncitizens can legally vote in thirteen jurisdictions in the United States. Globally, at least forty-five countries on nearly every continent allow NCV (Ferris et al. 2019, 9).

The Rise and Fall of Noncitizen Voting

Early in American history, NCV was a logical democratic practice tied to notions of "inhabitants" and difficult to challenge. NCV became contentious during the antebellum period and westward expansion. The War of 1812 reversed the spread of alien suffrage, in part by raising the specter of foreign "enemies." Between 1812 and 1821, nine states made U.S. citizenship, instead of residency, a requirement for voting. Southern states had additional incentive to limit the franchise as many newcomers, particularly the Irish, were hostile to slavery.

By the mid-1800s, the need for new labor prompted Congress and many new states and territories to permit NCV as an incentive to attract settlers to the West and to encourage naturalization and U.S. citizenship. The general practice was to require residency for a period of time, ranging from six months to two years, before granting voting rights. In 1848, Wisconsin extended full voting rights to alien declarants (persons who had declared their intention to become citizens). Wisconsin's model proved popular: Congress enacted similar provisions for the Territories of Oregon, Minnesota, Washington, Kansas, Nebraska, Nevada, Dakota, Wyoming, and Oklahoma. After achieving statehood, many of these jurisdictions retained this practice. NCV was practiced to its greatest extent during the 1870s and 1880s (Hayduk 2006, 25). As table 3.1 shows, by the close of the nineteenth century, most states had some, and many much, history with NCV (Aylsworth 1931, 114; Hayduk 2006).

Table 3.1   Noncitizen Voting in Selected States and Territories, 1848–1926

State	Years
Alabama	1868–1901
Arkansas	1874–1926
Colorado	1876–1902
Florida	1868–1894
Georgia	1868–1877
Idaho	1863–1890
Indiana	1851–1921
Kansas	1854–1918
Michigan	1835–1894
Minnesota	1849–1896
Missouri	1865–1921
Montana	1864–1889
Nebraska	1854–1918
North Dakota	1861–1909
Oklahoma	1850–1907
Oregon	1848–1914
South Dakota	1850–1918
Texas	1869–1921
Wisconsin	1848–1908
Wyoming	1850–1899

But with the massive increase of darker-skinned and politically suspect immigrants from Southern and Eastern Europe between 1880 and 1920, antialien passions flourished and reversed these practices. As the number of immigrants grew, the power of the immigrant vote grew, particularly in the cities and states where immigrants were concentrated. This contributed to the formation of "political machines," the rise of mass social movements, and the creation of third political parties, all of which posed a threat to the dominant political and social order. The anti-immigrant backlash at the turn of the twentieth century and hysteria during World War I led to the elimination of this longstanding practice in 1926, when Arkansas rolled back NCV.

The loss of NCV, coupled with the malapportionment of cities where most immigrants resided, came at the same time when the population of urban America rivaled the population in rural and suburban parts of the country. Immigrant disenfranchisement—which occurred simultaneously with the disenfranchisement of other poor and minority groups— produced a sharp decline in voter participation, particularly of low-income people, limiting more democratic politics and progressive possibilities for years to come (Hayduk 2006, 30).

The Revival of NCV

Contemporary advocates of NCV draw heavily on its history to disrupt the "common sense" thinking that links voting rights to citizenship. The Civil Rights movement, which swept away some historical barriers to voting, also helped usher in a revival of NCV. New York City was the first to restore NCV in 1968 in school board elections, though the practice ended in 2002 when school boards were eliminated. Chicago followed suit in 1988 (Ryan et al. 1997, 1). Eleven municipalities in Maryland allow residents to vote in local elections, regardless of citizenship or immigration status. In the 2000s, four towns in Massachusetts voted to restore NCV, although they still need state-enabling legislation to implement these laws. In 2016, voters in San Francisco passed a ballot proposal allowing NCV in school board elections. Another dozen jurisdictions have considered restoring NCV rights. Some campaigns sought voting rights for all residents—both documented ("legal") and undocumented ("illegal") immigrants—while others wanted to enfranchise only legal permanent residents. Some campaigns were waged via ballot proposals, while others employed legislative processes. At present, Los Angeles (for school board elections) and New York City (for local elections) are considering NCV, but formal proposals have not been introduced. Table 3.2 summarizes the contemporary uses of noncitizen voting (Hayduk and Coll 2018).

In each campaign, several characteristics stand out. First, demographic shifts propelled immigrant mobilization. Second, proponents of NCV voting engaged in grassroots organizing, coalition building, lobbying of elected officials, and media relations. Third, representatives of immigrant and minority backgrounds supported legislation. And fourth, opponents raised objections to, or blocked, immigrant voting rights campaigns; nearly every campaign has witnessed contention.

Immigrants and their allies argue for inclusion by claiming they are, like other residents, legitimate stakeholders. They generally make three basic arguments: (1) voting rights are embodied in the social contract; (2) voting helps guard against discrimination and bias; and (3) increased voter participation can produce mutual benefits for all community members of a polity (Hayduk and Coll 2018, 10–12).

The number of noncitizen immigrants in the United States— approximately twenty-three million—is staggering. In states and localities where immigrants are concentrated, their numbers can reach a quarter to a half of the total population. For example, one of every four residents in California is foreign born, with more than a half of the foreign-born noncitizens. In seven California counties—including Santa Clara, San Francisco, and Los Angeles—one in three residents is an immigrant.

Table 3.2   Contemporary NCV Laws and Campaigns

Jurisdiction	Type	Year(s)	Coverage	Outcome(s)
Chicago, IL	Local Statute	1989	School elections	Implemented
Massachusetts	4 Local Statutes	1990-2016	LPRs	Passed*
Maryland	11 Local Statutes	1990-2018	All residents	Implemented
Washington, DC	Local Statutes	1991-2014	LPRs	Failed
Texas	State Statute	1995	LPRs	Failed
Connecticut	State Statute	2003	LPRs, with property	Failed
New York, NY	Local Statute	2005; 2013	LPRs	Failed
Minnesota	State Statute	2007	LPRs	Failed
Portland, ME	Ballot Proposal	2010	LPRs	Failed
New York	State Statute	2014	All residents	Failed
San Francisco, CA	Ballot Proposal	2016	School elections	Implemented
Burlington, VT	Ballot Proposal	2018	LPRs	Passed*
Montpelier, VT	Ballot Proposal	2018	LPRs	Passed*

*Still needs state approval.

In New York City, noncitizens comprise more than 20 percent of the total population in nearly half the city council districts, and more than 40 percent in some districts. Similar proportions can be found in "new immigrant destinations" in the United States.

What do these conditions mean for such basic democratic principles as "consent of the governed," "no taxation without representation," and "one person, one vote"? Contemporary immigrant political exclusion challenges the ideals of a modern democracy, cutting to the heart of our political practice.

Immigrants' cumulative lack of political power—from fewer votes to fewer representatives—translates into fewer pathways to opportunity, poor socioeconomic conditions, and government policies that slight them. Although hardly homogeneous, immigrants as a group tend to score low on many social indicators of wellbeing, including income, poverty, housing, hunger, and education (Card and Raphael 2013, 1–23). Such outcomes often result from immigrant political exclusion, which in many places now approximates that of blacks, women, and youth before constitutional amendments or laws were adopted in 1870, 1920, 1965, and 1971. (Parallels also exist for the five million residents in U.S. territories who cannot vote in federal elections and over four million felons disenfranchised by state laws.)

A prominent slogan in immigrant rights protests during 2006 was, "Today we march. Tomorrow we vote." Why not let immigrants vote? Campaigns to restore immigrant voting are part of the broader set of movements in American history and contemporary practice that seek full inclusion, equal rights, and social justice. Campaigns for NCV are most effective to produce community empowerment when led by immigrants and their allies, particularly in the current climate of increased enforcement (Hayduk and Coll 2018, 15).

Ron Hayduk, a professor of political science at San Francisco State University (SFSU), is the author of Democracy for All: Restoring Immigrant Voting Rights in the United States.

References

Aylsworth, Leon E. 1931. "The Passing of Alien Suffrage." *American Political Science Review*, 25 (1): 114–116.

Card, David, and Steven Raphael. 2013. *Immigration, Poverty, and Socioeconomic Inequality*. New York: Russell Sage.

Ferris, Dan, Ron Hayduk, Alyscia Richards, Emma Schubert, and Mary Acri. 2019. "Noncitizen Voting Rights in the Global Era: A Literature Review and Analysis." *Journal of International Migration and Integration*, 20: 1–23.

Hayduk, Ron. 2006. *Democracy for All: Restoring Immigrant Voting Rights in the United States.* New York: Routledge.

Hayduk, Ron, and Kathleen Coll. 2018. "Urban Citizenship: Campaigns to Restore Immigrant Voting Rights in the U.S." *New Political Science*, 40 (2): 336–352.

Ryan, Susan, Anthony S. Bryk, Gudelia Lopez, Kimberly P. Williams, Kathleen Hall, and Stuart Luppescu. 1997. *Charting Reform: Local School Councils—Local Leadership at Work.* Chicago, IL: Consortium on Chicago School Research.

Online Voting
Pete Martin

"Nobody will ever deprive the American people of the right to vote except the American people themselves, and the only way they could do this is by not voting."
—Franklin Delano Roosevelt

Online voting (via mobile device or computer) enhances voters' rights and enfranchises voters by making voting more accessible, more secure, and more verifiable. It will also help increase voter turnout by making it easier to vote.

The right to vote in free and fair elections is a basic right and one on which other rights depend. Interestingly, the unamended Constitution did not mention the right to vote. Several amendments, however, have conferred the right to vote; and federal laws have eased the registration or voting process. Nevertheless, voting rights in the United States have progressed at a slower pace than everything else—technology, information, commerce, and communication. And access to the ballot has not been realized equally by everyone.

The high mark for voter turnout in a presidential election was in 1960, when 63 percent of qualified voters cast ballots. Turnout has averaged about 55 percent since, though most other democratic countries consistently experience turnouts of 70 percent or higher. While survey data suggest that many people intend to vote, a large percentage of voters fail to do so. According to a survey of nonvoters, a busy schedule was the primary reason why people did not vote ("Voting and Registration" 2015). Respondents also noted being out of town for work, illness, transportation problems, and other inconveniences for failing to vote.

Military and overseas voters continue to experience obstacles to voting. The 2018 turnout for military personnel serving overseas was only 7 percent ("DOD Releases Study" 2018). In those states that do not permit web-based balloting for military and overseas personnel, voters must request an absentee ballot, wait for it to arrive at the military location, physically complete the ballot, and mail it back. The average elapsed time is forty-three days. Furthermore, even if someone commits to undertake this process, there is no guarantee that the ballot will arrive and be counted in time. In 2018, 6,670 ballots in Florida alone were not counted because they were not returned by election day (Fineout 2018).

Those with limited physical abilities also face difficulties with voting. In 2016, the National Federation for the Blind (NFB) sued several states, arguing that the absentee voting process was not compliant with the Americans with Disabilities Act (ADA) of 1990. The NFB filed federal lawsuits against election offices in Maryland, Ohio, New York, and California, alleging that blind and visually impaired voters were being discriminated against at the ballot box. Many of the group's lawsuits were successful.

Online and mobile voting alleviate a problem often cited for why eligible people do not vote. Mobile voting makes voting easier and more accessible for a significant proportion of the population, thereby increasing voter engagement. One recent academic study suggested that mobile voting could increase voter turnout by three to five percentage points. It also concluded that the effects of mobile voting are greater than those from most other electoral reforms, such as early voting, vote-by-mail, and election-day registration (Fowler 2019, 3–4).

Even for those with limited abilities, mobile voting technology can integrate with assistive devices, allowing ballot contents to be read aloud privately, then be used to securely mark their ballot.

For online voting to work, certain technical elements need to be in place—most notably an internet connection and a hardware device—that may be less accessible to rural, low-income, disadvantaged, and elderly populations. This "digital divide" is closing rapidly, however, thanks to the efforts of Microsoft, Google, and other technology companies.

According to Pew Research, mobile technology use among rural adults has risen, with the share of those owning smartphones and tablets increasing sharply since 2011, while ownership of desktop or laptop computers, by contrast, has only risen slightly (Perrin 2019). Also, smartphones are increasingly becoming the on-ramp to the internet as a replacement for home broadband services (Anderson and Kumar 2019).

One of the key challenges to online voting is how to authenticate the identity of would-be voters. This challenge is not unique to online voting; it is also true of any form of remote voting, including vote-by-mail and absentee voting. Thirty-five million ballots were cast remotely in the 2018 midterm election.

While authenticating voters is challenging, methods to accomplish this are available. Through biometrics and by matching faces to voter IDs, voters to utility bills, and using signature and fingerprint matching techniques, technology can provide a level of verification that exceeds any other form of remote voting. Unfortunately, most laws across the United States prohibit this form of voter authentication; many progressive jurisdictions, however, are working on it.

One significant criticism of online voting is the potential for voter fraud. While voter fraud concerns are legitimate, voter fraud is not unique to online voting. Voter fraud can occur with paper ballots as well, and some paper ballot irregularities can be fixed with online voting. For example, undervoting, overvoting, damaged paper ballots, and stray markings that lead to questions of voter intent are avoidable with online voting.

Online voting can also enforce good voting behavior, ensuring that ballots are counted properly. Trust in government and the belief that an individual vote will matter is at an all-time low. According to the Center for American Progress, those who feel most unrepresented do not believe that things will improve even if they cast a vote; therefore, they do not participate. By not voting, their needs do not get addressed by those in power. This is especially true in local elections, where the winners have a far greater influence on the day-to-day lives of their constituents—which potholes get filled and control over public school operations, for example—than do the victors in elections at the national level. In local elections, turnout trends toward single-digit percentages, though the outcomes matter greatly.

Online voting can also reduce election expenses. The average cost for a single vote in an in-person election ranges from ten to twenty-five dollars per vote cast, depending on the country and voter turnout. The European Parliament claims that online voting in Estonia, which is widely recognized as a leader in national online voting, is 2.5 times cheaper than the paper alternative ("Report on the IMCO Mission" 2017). Online voting can have a profound effect on lowering the costs of elections—especially local elections where the cost per vote can be even higher than in national elections.

To regain the public's trust in elections, the single most important step is to allow the voter to prove that their vote was cast properly and counted as intended. This is nearly impossible with paper ballots as counting and processing are done outside the public eye.

Most voters have a balanced view of mobile and online voting. Voters want the convenience and accessibility of online voting, and they understand the potential security vulnerabilities it presents. In other words, they would prefer the convenience of online or mobile voting but want to be confident that it is safe and immune from hacking and compromise. Organizations like Votem (www.votem.org) suggest that mobile voting—supported by blockchain technology (an innovative approach to making systems more resilient and difficult to hack)—can improve the voting process through better access for all people, allowing voters to verify individually and instantaneously that their vote was counted as cast, and providing a safer, more transparent and verifiable process.

Through these improvements, voter turnout will increase and elections will be less contested.

Pete Martin is the founder and CEO of Votem, a blockchain-based mobile voting company, and he is the author of the upcoming book Sparking a Mobile Revolution: How Mobile Voting Will Change the World as We Know It. *Previously, he was the founder and CEO of Kompliant Software, a trade compliance software firm, and co-founder and CEO of EntryPoint Consulting, an SAP Systems Integration Company, which was sold to KPMG. Martin has spent his career in technology-related businesses, including as EVP of worldwide operations for Marketswitch Corp, vice president at SAP America, and sales positions with IBM. Involved with blockchain technology since 2015, he is a sought-after speaker on topics related to the use of blockchain technology in various use cases, including corporate and political governance.*

References

Anderson, Monica, and Madhumitha Kumar. 2019. "Digital Divide Persists Even as Lower-Income Americans Make Gains in Tech Adoption." Pew Research Center. https://www.pewresearch.org/fact-tank/2019/05/07/digital-divide-persists-even-as-lower-income-americans-make-gains-in-tech-adoption/

"DOD Releases Study of U.S. Voters Abroad." 2018. Federal Voting Assistance Program. https://www.fvap.gov/info

/news/2018/9/12/dod-releases-biennial-study-of-us-voters-abroad

Fineout, Gary. 2018. "Thousands of Mailed Ballots in Florida Were Not Counted." *AP News*, 10 December. https://apnews.com/8488a401807045fcb642ea2cdf81fc29

Fowler, Anthony. 2019. "Promises and Perils of Mobile Voting." Paper presented at the Annual Meeting of the Election Sciences, Reform and Administration Conference, Philadelphia, PA, July.

Perrin, Andrew. 2019. "Digital Gap between Rural and Nonrural American Persist." Pew Research Center. https://www.pewresearch.org/fact-tank/2019/05/31/digital-gap-between-rural-and-nonrural-america-persists/

"Report on the IMCO Mission to Tallinn, Estonia." 2017. European Parliament, Committee on the Internal Market and Consumer Protection. http://europarl.europa.eu/doceo/document/IMCO-CM-605929_EN.pdf?redirect

"Voting and Registration in the Election of November 2014." 2015. U.S. Census Bureau. https://www.census.gov/data/tables/time-series/demo/voting-and-registration/p20-577.html

Americans' Views on Voting Rights
Natalie Jackson

The phrase "voting rights" typically refers to issues surrounding enfranchisement (ability to vote) and disenfranchisement (inability to vote) and protecting the right to vote for those who are eligible. Because the unamended Constitution offered no uniform rule on voting rights, states retained the authority to determine who could participate. Seven constitutional amendments, however, either make the franchise more inclusive or the electoral process more democratic. Most notable among these are the Fifteenth, Nineteenth, and Twenty-Sixth

Amendments. The Fifteenth prohibits a state from denying a citizen the right to vote based on "race, color, or previous condition of servitude." The Nineteenth precludes a state from abridging that right based on sex. And the Twenty-sixth forbids any state from withholding the right to vote to any citizen, who is eighteen years of age or older, on account of age. Beyond these (and a few other) constitutional restrictions—and a handful of federal laws—states are responsible for legislating eligibility and rules for voting. Local jurisdictions determine where polling places are located and how many polling places are set up. Any potential impediments to voting, particularly those that target or disproportionately affect specific groups, become "voting rights" issues.

How Americans Think about Voting

Nearly two-thirds (64 percent) of Americans think voting is the most effective thing they can do to bring about change on the issues they care about—far more than, say, volunteering for a cause (12 percent), contacting an elected official (9 percent), being active on social media about the cause (5 percent), or participating in rallies or donating money (3 percent each) (Jones et al. 2018). Only about 50–60 percent of eligible voters, however, have voted in recent presidential elections. Turnout in midterms and other state and local elections is generally under 50 percent. Most Americans think that is a problem: 67 percent say "too few people voting" is a major problem, an additional 21 percent say it is a minor problem, and only 9 percent say it is not a problem (Jones et al. 2018). At the same time, 60 percent say "too many uninformed people voting" is a major problem. This tension between wanting more people to vote and preventing uninformed or ineligible voting carries through all voting rights issues. In general, Democrats worry more about making sure everyone can vote, and Republicans worry more about preventing ineligible voting. Nonwhite Americans, who have historically been targeted by voting restrictions, are more concerned with ensuring access to voting than are white Americans.

Voting Access and Barriers to Voting

Two major voting rights issues that remain particularly salient are registration requirements—registering in advance before an election and automatic registration—and criminal disqualification. A few states allow voters to register and vote on election day, while others require registration in advance—sometimes long in advance. Despite the variance, 61 percent of Americans agree that "all citizens should be allowed to register and vote on the same day" (Jones et al. 2018). Nearly three-fourths (74 percent) of Democrats, compared to 42 percent of Republicans, agree everyone should be able to register and vote on the same day. Majorities of all races support same-day registration, but Hispanic Americans (71 percent) are more likely to agree than white (58 percent) and black (59 percent) Americans.

Another common voter registration practice among states is so-called "Motor Voter" laws, which allow eligible citizens to register to vote when they do business with the state's DMV or certain other state agencies. Two-thirds (67 percent) of Americans agree that "all citizens should be automatically registered to vote" under these conditions (Jones et al. 2018). Again, Democrats (83 percent) are more supportive of this provision than Republicans (52 percent). Blacks (76 percent) and Hispanics (73 percent) are more likely to agree with automatic registration than their white counterparts (63 percent).

As for disenfranchisement, some states have historically barred convicted felons from voting even after serving their sentences. Many of these restrictions have been overturned in recent years, and public opinion shows broad support for restoring felons' voting rights. More than seven in ten (71 percent) Americans are in favor of allowing convicted felons to vote after they have served their sentence, including 85 percent of Democrats and 63 percent of Republicans (Jones and Najle

2019). More than seven in ten whites (71 percent) and Hispanics (73 percent) agree, and eight in ten (80 percent) blacks agree.

Why Any Restrictions at All?

The popularity of provisions encouraging voting masks the fact that many Americans worry about ineligible voters voting, which creates tension with those who worry about eligible voters being denied the right to vote. More than one-third (36 percent) say "people casting votes who are not eligible to vote" is a major problem, and an additional 31 percent think it is a minor problem (Jones et al. 2018). Twenty-nine percent say it is not a problem. The partisan differences are fairly large—a majority (52 percent) of Republicans say this is a major problem, compared to 31 percent of Democrats. Whites (34 percent) and blacks (33 percent) hover near the one-third mark saying it is a major problem, while Hispanics (44 percent) are more likely to say ineligible voters voting is a major problem.

On the other hand, 38 percent of Americans say that "eligible voters being denied the right to vote" is a major problem, with another 29 percent thinking it is a minor problem, and 29 percent believing it is not a problem (Jones et al. 2018). Party and race differences are much larger on this question: Only 19 percent of Republicans say this is a major problem, compared to 56 percent of Democrats. Similarly, 27 percent of whites think eligible voters being denied the right to vote is a major problem compared to 60 percent of Hispanics and 62 percent of blacks. Nonwhite Americans have historically—and currently—been more at risk of being systematically denied the right to vote, and these numbers show that concern remains salient for these groups.

When asked to choose which problem is bigger—ineligible voters voting or eligible voters being prevented from voting—Republicans and Democrats are on opposite sides, as are whites and nonwhites. Republicans (68 percent) are much more likely to say ineligible voters is the bigger problem, while Democrats (62 percent) say eligible voters prevented from voting is the bigger problem. A plurality of white Americans (44 percent) say ineligible voters voting is the bigger problem, while majorities of blacks (66 percent) and Hispanics (52 percent) say the bigger issue is preventing eligible voters from exercising their right.

The higher concern about preventing eligible voters from voting among nonwhites is reflected in their reports of experiencing problems while trying to vote. Nonwhites are more likely than whites to report a variety of problems at the polls, including waiting in long lines (20 vs. 10 percent), being harassed while trying to vote (8 vs. 1 percent), being told they are not registered when they are (7 vs. 2 percent), and being told they do not have the correct identification (6 vs. 2 percent) (Jones and Najle 2019).

Who Would Benefit If More People Voted?

Democrats' strong support for protecting voting rights and increasing access are partially explained by the fact that they believe they would benefit most from more people voting. Two-thirds (68 percent) of Democrats say their party would benefit more if everyone votes, and only 2 percent say the Republican Party would benefit more (Jones et al. 2018). One in five (20 percent) Democrats say both parties would equally benefit, and 8 percent say neither party would benefit. Comparatively, 41 percent of Republicans think their party would benefit most, 14 percent say Democrats would benefit most, 35 percent say both parties would equally benefit, and 9 percent say neither party would benefit. Most Republicans do not think Democrats would benefit from more voters voting, but the majority also do not think their own party would benefit most. This pattern could help explain the lower support for policies that encourage voting among Republicans.

The patterns of stronger support for increasing voting access among nonwhite Americans compared to white Americans are most likely attributable to both their experiences, as noted above, and the history of denying access to nonwhite, and particularly black, Americans. Even with a constitutional amendment prohibiting denial of the franchise based on race or color, whites continued to prevent blacks from voting. Many of those barriers were not removed until the 1960s, and voter suppression efforts remain unfortunately common in some areas.

Natalie Jackson is research director at the Washington, D.C., nonprofit survey research firm PRRI. Natalie received her PhD in political science from the University of Oklahoma and was a postdoctoral associate at the Duke University Initiative on Survey Methodology. Her work has appeared in peer-reviewed journals Electoral Studies *and* Social Science Quarterly, *as well as in several edited volumes.*

References

Jones, Robert P., Daniel Cox, Rob Griffin, Maxine Najle, Molly Fisch-Friedman, and Alex Vandermaas-Peeler. 2018. "American Democracy in Crisis: Civic Engagement, Young Adult Activism, and the 2018 Midterm Elections." Public Religion Research Institute (PRRI). https://www.prri.org/research/american-democracy-in-crisis-civic-engagement-young-adult-activism and-the-2018-midterm-elections

Jones, Robert P., and Maxine Najle. 2019. "American Democracy in Crisis: The Fate of Pluralism in a Divided Nation." Public Religion Research Institute (PRRI). https://www.prri.org/research/american-democracy-in-crisis-the-fate-of-pluralism-in-a-divided-nation/

DO YOU WANT TO VOT
REGISTER HERE
THIS DATE APRIL 1 1948 FROM 10.30 AM 5
CO-SPONSORED BY ALPHA PHI ALPHA FRAT & NAACP

4 Profiles

Introduction

The individuals and organizations profiled in this chapter have made contributions to voting, voting rights, or elections in America.

Two were political leaders—*James Madison* and *Abraham Lincoln*—who, though they occupy hallowed space in the American experience, have views on voting rights that have often been overlooked. Given Madison's centrality to the Constitutional Convention and our understanding of the document it produced and Lincoln's role in the nation's "new birth of freedom," their views on suffrage merit greater attention.

Some—the *suffragettes* and the *National Association of Colored Persons* (NAACP)—were instrumental in securing the right to vote for women and blacks, respectively. Others—the *Know-Nothings*, *Francis Parkman*, and the *Texas Democratic Party*—worked hard to deny the right to vote to certain segments of the population.

Three—the *Waite Court*, *Ruth Bader Ginsburg*, and *John Roberts*—played critical roles in interpreting constitutional and statutory provisions pertaining to voting rights. And the *U.S. Department of Justice* is responsible for enforcing federal laws.

Black citizens wait in line to register to vote in 1948. It was only after 1940 that blacks began to reclaim that which was promised in 1870 with ratification of the Fifteenth Amendment. Grassroots political activism, congressional action, presidential leadership, and judicial engagement finally ended a century of discriminatory practices. (Library of Congress)

Others—the *American Civil Liberties Union* (ACLU), the *League of Women Voters*, and *Rock the Vote*—have sought to make the franchise more accessible and to increase voter education and turnout.

Finally, *Richard Hasen* is a leading academic on voting rights and election law; his scholarship informs decision-makers and educates the general public.

The profiles appear alphabetically.

American Civil Liberties Union (ACLU)

The American Civil Liberties Union (ACLU) was founded in 1920 to defend and preserve the individual rights and liberties guaranteed by the U.S. Constitution and the laws of the United States. The ACLU was created in response to the post–World War I Palmer Raids of 1919–1920, when U.S. Attorney General Mitchell Palmer directed the Federal Bureau of Investigation (FBI) to conduct warrantless searches and seizures of the homes and businesses of suspected communist radicals, to arrest the agitators, and to deport suspected communist sympathizers.

The ACLU has traditionally been a staunch defender of the civil liberties protected by the Bill of Rights, the first ten amendments to the U.S. Constitution. It has been active as a litigant, filing lawsuits on behalf of individuals whose rights were threatened or encroached by government action. While the ACLU has been most vocal in the areas of free speech, freedom from religion, and the rights of criminal defendants, starting in 1965, the organization launched the Voting Rights Project (VRP) to support and defend voting rights.

The ACLU maintains that voting is a right, not a privilege. Following the passage of the Voting Rights Act (VRA) in 1965, the ACLU had a two-fold strategy. First, it lobbied for reauthorization of the VRA each year it was before Congress, believing that the Act helped blacks register to vote and participate in elections and democratic governance. Second, the ACLU supported lawsuits that sought to extend voting rights beyond a formal individual right to opportunities of blacks and other minorities to elect individuals who would best represent the political interest of their racial group. As such, the ACLU encouraged states to create legislative districts that were composed of a majority of minority voters to enhance black and minority representation in Congress.

As the Supreme Court interpreted the Equal Protection Clause of the Fourteenth Amendment to discourage the creation of majority-minority legislative districts, the ACLU's overall legal strategy to protect and advance voting rights changed. In recent years, the ACLU has worked to promote access to the ballot, encouraging states to pass online voter registration, same-day voter registration, and early voting. In addition to legislative advocacy, the ACLU has litigated in many voting rights areas, including challenging various forms of voter suppression and encouraging states to restore voting rights to felons.

In 2012, the ACLU joined the Inter Tribal Council of Arizona in challenging an Arizona law that required individuals to provide documentary evidence of citizenship when registering to vote, and directed voter registration officials to reject any application for registration that was not accompanied by such evidence. The ACLU argued that the law stood in conflict with the National Voter Registration Act (NVRA) of 1993, which required states to "accept and use" a uniform federal form to register voters for federal elections. The ACLU was victorious when, in *Arizona* v. *Inter Tribal Council of Arizona, Inc.* (2013), the Supreme Court ruled that the Arizona law was preempted by the NVRA's requirement that states accept the federal form as proof of citizenship.

The ACLU has also been active in fighting voter ID laws, aggressive voter purging efforts, and other election laws the organization deems discriminatory. For example, in 2018, the ACLU filed a suit in Pennsylvania, asserting that the state's absentee ballot law, the most restrictive in the country, was unnecessarily disenfranchising voters. Under Pennsylvania law, an individual can apply for an absentee ballot up to one week before election day, but all absentee ballots must be returned before 5:00 p.m. on the Friday before the election. The ACLU argued that the state has not offered any compelling reason for requiring absentee ballots to be returned prior to election day.

The ACLU has also challenged a New Hampshire law that requires all voters to follow the same procedures as in-state residents. Because all in-state residents must obtain a driver's license or register their vehicles in the state, the ACLU argued that the law was intended to suppress the voting rights of college students, who were less likely to possess a New Hampshire driver's license or vehicle registration. The ACLU has maintained that many state voting laws that appear to be neutral and harmless are actually motivated by a desire to suppress the voting rights of particular individuals.

In addition to challenging state laws that suppress voting rights, the ACLU has also been vigilant in trying to *restore* the voting rights of ex-felons. After Florida voters approved Amendment 4 in 2018 to restore the voting rights of felons who had finished their prison sentences, the state legislature limited the amendment's effect by requiring ex-felons to pay all court fees and fines prior to having their voting rights restored. In a challenge to the law, the ACLU maintained that Florida imposed an unconstitutional poll tax. The ACLU has also challenged felon disenfranchisement laws in other states.

Lastly, consistent with its position that the meaning or weight of one's vote might be just as important as the formal right to vote, the ACLU has been instrumental in challenging instances of partisan gerrymandering and encouraging the Supreme Court to agree on a standard to apply in those cases.

Ruth Bader Ginsburg (1933–)

Ruth Bader Ginsburg is perhaps best-known for her work fighting for women's equality in her roles as the cofounder and general counsel for the Women's Rights Project at the American Civil Liberties Union (ACLU) in the 1970s. As an associate justice on the U.S. Supreme Court (1993–), however, Ginsburg's views on voting rights, primarily articulated in her dissent in *Shelby County* v. *Holder* (2013), have earned her significant attention.

When Ginsburg joined the Court in 1993, the Court was at the beginning of what proved to be a lengthy debate on whether, or to what degree, state legislatures could use race as a factor in gerrymandering decisions, and what role courts should play, if any, in protecting minority voting rights. In her second term, Ginsburg wrote a dissenting opinion in *Miller* v. *Johnson* (1995), in which she voiced concerns with the majority's pronouncement that, when drawing legislative districts, race cannot be the "predominant factor" in the analysis.

In a spirited dissent, Ginsburg argued that the legality of gerrymandering practices to protect or assist minority voters should be evaluated in the appropriate historical context. While the majority interpreted the Equal Protection Clause of the Fourteenth Amendment to require that government treat white and minority voters equally, Ginsburg noted that the Court had previously interpreted the Clause to ensure that apportionment plans did not dilute minority voting strength. The reason the Court had allowed race to be used in gerrymandering practices to advance minority voting rights was because, historically, the "franchise has not been enjoyed equally by black citizens and white voters." For Ginsburg, one role of the courts was to ensure that members of racial minorities enjoyed the same voting rights that whites had experienced for much longer periods of time.

Ginsburg further noted that one way courts could protect black voting rights is by respecting Congress's decision that racial minorities could challenge vote dilution claims under Section 2 of the Voting Rights Act (VRA) of 1965. According to Ginsburg, the VRA signified a monumental shift for black voting rights because it not only provided a legislative solution to voting rights discrimination but ensured that the federal courts would play a role in preserving those same rights.

Ginsburg's dissent foreshadowed the (William) Rehnquist and (John) Roberts Courts unwillingness to use their institutional power to interpret key terms of the VRA in ways to expand black voting power.

In 2013, the Court was asked to decide the constitutionality of Section 5 of the VRA. Section 5 required that "covered jurisdictions" receive preclearance from the U.S. attorney general or the U.S. District Court for the District of Columbia before making changes to their election law. Rather than directly addressing the preclearance issue, *Shelby County* struck down Section 4's criteria for determining which governmental entities were required to seek preclearance prior to making any change in election law.

In dissent, Ginsburg lauded the successes of the VRA in helping to secure voting rights for black Americans, maintaining that the Act's accomplishments were noteworthy because no other previous federal action was able to protect black voting rights to the same degree. While the Fourteenth and Fifteenth Amendments were intended to grant blacks the political power they were missing under the unamended Constitution, private and state efforts—mostly in the South—to restrict black voting rights remained as effective as ever. The VRA ensured that black voting rights would be guaranteed by giving blacks the right to hold governments accountable for diluting their voting power (Section 2) and by requiring an extra level of oversight for blacks residing in those "covered jurisdictions" (Section 5).

Under the VRA, black voter registration and participation had significantly increased. While the VRA's achievements were interpreted by the majority to be the reason for why the Act was no longer needed, Ginsburg argued that if "covered jurisdictions" were no longer required to seek preclearance for election law changes, discrimination against black voters would increase in the form of "second-generation" barriers—like voter ID requirements, voter roll purging, and vote dilution efforts. For Ginsburg, our nation's pervasive history of discrimination against black voters called for extraordinary

measures to ameliorate the damages associated with denying
blacks the right to vote. To declare the VRA no longer necessary because of its accomplishments, Ginsburg argued, "is like
throwing away your umbrella in a rainstorm because you are
not getting wet."

Ginsburg has been a powerful advocate for minority voting rights and for preserving the protections afforded in the
VRA. While she has been a dissenting voice in most voting
rights cases, she believes that the VRA grants minority voters
numerous procedural and substantive voting rights, and that it
is the federal courts' responsibility to ensure that those rights
are protected.

Richard L. Hasen (1964–)

Richard L. Hasen is Chancellor's Professor of Law and Political
Science at the University of California at Irvine (UCI) and a
leading thinker and prolific scholar on voting rights and election law. More than any other academic, Hasen has sought to
develop election law as its own field of study.

In *The Supreme Court and Election Law* (2003), Hasen evaluated the Court's intrusion into the political process, starting
with *Baker* v. *Carr* (1962), in which the Court declared that
challenges to state apportionment plans could be heard by
federal courts. He (2003, 75) argued that the Court should
play a role when governments seek to violate "core equality
principles" (basic rights that Americans agree on) but that the
Court should defer to legislative bodies when asked to decide
contested equality claims. This book provides a useful framework for understanding the Court's entrance into the "political
thicket" of apportionment.

In *The Voting Wars: From Florida 2000 to the Next Election
Meltdown* (2012), Hasen suggested that the politically divisive
and judicially resolved 2000 presidential election exposed two
major problems in our elections. First, it uncovered the hyper-
decentralized nature of American elections and the significant

procedural problems with how states and local governments administer elections. Second, it exposed rifts between political factions regarding what was important in ensuring fair elections—Republicans concerned about voter fraud; Democrats fearful of disenfranchising eligible voters. The "confluence" of these two problems created the potential for a major crisis. Hasen offered several recommendations to prevent that crisis by modernizing elections—nonpartisan, professional election administration; an independent national election czar; uniform standards for all ballots; national and lifetime registration, with unique identification numbers; and government-approved voting machine hardware and software—though acknowledging (prophetically it turns out) that none was likely to happen. Eight years later, Hasen remains pessimistic about the ability of our current election administration to handle another close election with professionalism and integrity.

In an article published in the *William and Mary Bill of Rights Journal*, Hasen offered a gloomy assessment of the voting wars in the 2016 presidential election: Election law litigation increased; and in our hyperpartisan atmosphere, distrust of political opponents got worse, not better. He (2018, 65) argued that the amplification of misinformation and propaganda through social media, combined with the decline of "mediating institutions" like political parties and the mainstream media, have made voting wars more problematic, which have contributed to the decline in American democracy.

Hasen has been censorious of state election laws that create different classes of individuals. He believes that strict voter ID laws create unique hardships for people who face difficulty in obtaining proper identification. Hasen has thus been critical of the Court's decision in *Crawford* v. *Marion County Election Board* (2008) that Indiana's voter ID law was constitutional in light of the state's interest in combating actual or perceived voter fraud.

Hasen has also argued that litigation designed to "soften" the effect of voter ID laws has been largely unsuccessful. To mollify each side in the voter ID debate, judges have often "split the difference" by allowing voter ID laws to go into effect but yet weakening many of the harsher elements of the law. Hasen (2016) suggested that rather than using a "softening" strategy, litigant opponents of voter ID laws need to demonstrate effectively the real-world effect of the law on *individuals* and encourage judges to require states to demonstrate, with empirical evidence, that voter fraud is real.

Those in academia have long been accused of developing and exchanging ideas with other academics outside the public domain. A standard argument is that professors remain significantly insular, only writing books and articles for other academics; in short, their scholarship never reaches a larger audience. One of Hasen's lasting contributions to the field of voting rights and election law is the influence that his ideas have had on the national debate. Those ideas have largely been disseminated in three ways. First, he founded and runs the Election Law Blog (https://www.electionblog.org), which has earned him numerous awards by the American Bar Association. Hasen's blog is read not just by academics but by journalists, politicians, and practitioners in the field. Second, along with Dan Lowenstein, Hasen cocreated an Election Law Internet Discussion Group that facilitates near-daily discussion among those interested in voting rights and election law. Third, because of his expertise, journalists and national news organizations often call on Hasen to explain voting rights and election law controversies.

Hasen has been an instrumental figure in the creation of the election law and voting rights discipline. He is a leading expert on voting rights, gerrymandering, voter ID, campaign finance, and many other election law issues. Furthermore, his scholarship is accessible to scholars and the general public alike.

Know-Nothings

The American Party, more commonly known as the "Know-Nothings," was a nativist political party in the mid-nineteenth century that arose in response to social, political, and economic developments. The party was hostile toward immigrants and Catholics and sought to restrict the political power of both groups by championing lengthy residency requirements, tough voter registration laws, and stringent literacy tests. Though short lived, the Know-Nothings rivaled the major political parties in the 1850s.

Private nativist societies, motivated by bigotry and fear, had long existed in the United States. For the most part, those societies were small and apolitical. The 1830s and 1840s witnessed the arrival of large numbers of immigrants, most notably Irish and German Catholics, to American shores. Religious differences, economic competition between the native and foreign born, and disdain toward the alleged social evils that immigrants embraced—drunkenness, pauperism, and crime—led to calls for political reform, especially in the cities where foreigners were concentrated. As early as 1843, anti-immigration and anti-Catholicism emerged in New York politics under the banner of the American Republican Party, which pledged to bar immigrant voting and remove the Catholic influence from public schools. In 1849, Charles Allen founded a secret patriotic fraternal organization in New York City known as the Order of the Star-Spangled Banner. Its mission was to arrest the rise of immigration and Catholicism. Immigrants, the order claimed, drank too much, had loose morals, and were inclined to criminal behavior; Catholics wanted to establish Papal control in the United States; and neither group possessed "old-stock" American values. Membership in the order was restricted to native-born Protestants, all of whom had to take an oath of allegiance to the cause. When questioned about the order, members claimed, "I know nothing," prompting Horace Greeley, founder and editor of *The New York Tribune*, to label them, "Know-Nothings." By 1854, the order had lodges in every Northern state and some Southern states. While it is nearly impossible to calculate membership in a secret organization, estimates range from 800,000 to 1,500,000 members.

That same year, the order entered politics, running and supporting candidates who would defend "traditional" political and religious values. The Know-Nothings wanted to restrict officeholders to native-born Protestants and limit the franchise to citizens. To make citizenship more difficult to attain, they favored lengthening the naturalization period for aliens. The message resonated. In Massachusetts, the Know-Nothings won the governorship, an overwhelming majority in the state legislature, the state's entire congressional delegation, and the mayoralty in Boston. Upon assuming power, the Massachusetts' Know-Nothings attempted to restrict the political strength of the Irish community in Boston through legislative redistricting, patronage appointments, and franchise-narrowing constitutional amendments and legislation, such as cumbersome registration systems and literacy tests. (They also criminalized gambling and drinking, two "favorite" Irish pastimes.) The Know-Nothings went after Catholics, too, banning public aid to parochial schools, requiring public schools to read daily from the King James (Protestant) version of the Bible, and appointing a committee to investigate sexual immorality in Catholic convents. The order also had electoral successes in California, Connecticut, New Jersey, New York, Pennsylvania, and Rhode Island. Those successes—coupled with the demise of the Whig Party, brought about by the politics of the Kansas-Nebraska Act—led to the creation of a new formal political party, first under the name Native American Party and later simply American Party.

Not all scholars agree on the factors that gave rise to Know-Nothingism. Most point to the economic impoverishment of native-born laborers and their resulting resentment of immigration competition, paired with fear of a "Romanist" conspiracy (Holt 1978; Gienapp 1987; Fogel 1994; Bennett 1998; Holt 1999). Others discount economic factors and downplay nativism and anti-Catholicism, stressing on the Know-Nothing's adamant antislavery sentiment instead (Annbinder 1992). Regardless of the reasons for its rise, Know-Nothingism was an epidemic following the election of 1854. In many parts of the country, the American Party was the fastest growing party, winning disillusioned Democrats and Whigs. In 1855, the party swept elections in Kentucky, Maryland, and Texas, and controlled state legislatures in all of New England, save Maine and Vermont. Additionally, at least fifty members of Congress, including Nathaniel Banks, speaker of the House of Representatives, claimed membership in the party. One study suggests that as many as 124 House members were, or had been, affiliated with the Know-Nothings (Annbinder 1992, 197, n. 8). (The secretive nature of membership in the party precludes precise accounting.)

While nativism had found a vast following, some were unpersuaded and unimpressed. In a letter to a friend in 1855, Abraham Lincoln, an emerging Republican leader, wrote:

> I am not a Know-Nothing. That is certain. How could I be? How could any one who abhors the oppression of negroes, be in favor of degrading classes of white people? Our progress in degeneracy appears to me to be pretty rapid. As a nation, we began by declaring that *"all men are created equal."* We now practically read it "all men are created equal, *except negroes.*" When the Know-Nothings get control, it will read "all men are created equal, except negroes, *and foreigners, and Catholics."* When it comes to this I should prefer emigrating to some country where they make no pretence of loving liberty—to Russia, for instance, where despotism can be taken pure, and without the base alloy of hypocracy. (Lincoln 1953, II, 323)

Essayist Ralph Waldo Emerson wrote that the Know-Nothings represented an "abdication of reason . . . an immense joke" (Bennett 1988, 131).

The Know-Nothings time on the national stage was brief. When the National Council of the American Party convened in Philadelphia in 1855, its platform restated nativist themes, concluding with the grand pronouncement: "America must be ruled by Americans." But Southern delegations insisted that the antislavery agitation stop. When the Southerners prevailed, northern delegations walked out. Like the Whigs before them, the Know-Nothings could not handle the issue of slavery. Antislavery Know-Nothings joined the Republican Party emerging from the remains of the Whig and Free Soil parties, while proslavery Know-Nothings found a home in the Democratic Party. The party nominated former Whig president and half-hearted Know-Nothing, Millard Fillmore, in the presidential election in 1856. He won one state, Maryland, and garnered only 22 percent of the popular vote nationwide. By 1857, the Know-Nothings were gone.

The League of Women Voters

The League of Women Voters (LWV), founded in 1920 by Carrie Chapman Catt, is a nonpartisan civic organization devoted to educating voters about important issues, increasing voter turnout, and strengthening American democracy through popular involvement. In its early years, the LWV existed primarily to help women exercise their right to vote in an educated fashion, but was also known for supporting female candidates, championing female political empowerment, and even endorsing protective legislation. While the LWV has maintained its nonpartisan status, the organization has evolved from a feminist advocacy organization into a more mainstream organization devoted to educating all voters, regardless of sex.

The mainstreaming began in the 1940s when, at the request of President Harry Truman, the LWV developed a strong relationship with the United Nations Charter Conference. In this capacity, the LWV has consistently urged the United States to work closely with the United Nations on foreign policy. The LWV's interests now encompass nearly all political issues, both domestic and international.

As the LWV ceded its electoral mobilization function to political parties and its female-only focus to other groups, like the National Organization of Women (NOW), it reinvented itself as an organization committed to educating citizens on a wide range of issues related to voting rights. For example, in the 1960s, the LWV worked on expanding voting rights for the citizens of the District of Columbia. The League worked to support passage of the Twenty-Third Amendment, ratified in 1961, which granted district residents Electoral College representation. The LWV has also supported granting D.C. residents representation in the House of Representatives and the Senate, which then evolved into advocating statehood for the district.

Two major legislative victories for the LWV were the National Voter Registration Act (NVRA) of 1993 and the Help America Vote Act (HAVA) of 2002. The League has long supported making voting registration easier. The NVRA, more commonly known as the "Motor Voter" law, was designed to ease the registration process by making forms and assistance more widely available to citizens wishing to register to vote. Under the law, states are required to make voter registration forms available where people register their cars, at welfare agencies and other public offices, and by mail. After passage of the NVRA, the LWV sought to minimize the problems that states faced when implementing the law.

The LWV has also worked to make the act of voting easier. After the 2000 election demonstrated serious voting irregularities, most notably in Florida, the LWV supported passage of the HAVA, which, among other things, created the Election Assistance Commission (EAC), an independent agency to assist states by providing the resources and information needed for election reforms.

More recently, the League has focused much of its efforts in challenging excessive partisan gerrymanders as unconstitutional. The LWV maintains that partisan gerrymandering practices make elections unfair by diluting the power of certain voters, which reduces voter participation. For example, the

LWV filed an *amicus curiae* ("friend of the court") brief in the Supreme Court case *Gill* v. *Whitford* (2018), which dealt with a partisan gerrymander from Wisconsin.

Before the Court, Wisconsin (on behalf of Beverly Gill, chairperson of the state Elections Commission) argued that states should be entitled to a "safe harbor" if they followed traditional redistricting principles, such as compactness, contiguity, and respecting political subdivisions. In other words, a state's fealty to traditional redistricting principles immunized it from partisan gerrymandering claims. The LWV encouraged the justices to reject that assertion and to authorize federal courts to adjudicate partisan gerrymandering claims. In the end, the Court dismissed *Gill* as nonjusticiable, holding that the citizens who originally filed the lawsuit had not demonstrated standing to do so.

When the justices took up another partisan gerrymandering case the following year in *Rucho* v. *Common Cause* (2019), the LWV of North Carolina filed a similar brief. For the LWV, partisan gerrymanders infringe on voting rights because they dilute the voting power of some voters, which thereby discourages citizens from voting. While the Court ultimately rejected the LWV's partisan gerrymandering arguments, we are likely to see the LWV and other groups challenge partisan gerrymanders in state courts, alleging them to be violative of state constitutional provisions.

Over the past century, the LWV has evolved from an organization of women designed to help other women exercise their right to vote and achieve political equality to an organization composed of men and women interested in advancing voting rights and developing an educated electorate. The LWV has been a powerful force in the debate over how best to protect and expand voting rights for all Americans. The League has been influential in expanding the electorate by increasing voter registration, supporting get-out-the-vote drives, and opposing policies that have the potential to decrease voter turnout.

Abraham Lincoln (1809–1865)

The sixteenth president of the United States (1861–1865), Abraham Lincoln was born in a one-room log cabin near Hodgenville, Kentucky. In 1835, after a brief stint in the Illinois Legislature as a member of the Whig Party, Lincoln determined to become a lawyer. Though he had less than one year of formal schooling, Lincoln learned the profession by "reading law" and clerking in the law office of John Todd Stuart. For the next two decades, save for one term in the U.S. House of Representatives, Lincoln practiced law in Springfield, the state capital. He returned to politics in the mid-1850s as a Republican, seeking the U.S. Senate seat from Illinois in 1858. During that campaign, Lincoln gained national attention for a series of debates with Stephen Douglas, the Democratic candidate. Though Lincoln lost that campaign, in 1860 he was elected president. Lincoln's entire presidency was bracketed by war. Less than six weeks after Lincoln's inauguration, the South Carolina militia fired upon Fort Sumter, precipitating the Civil War. Four years later, following Lincoln's reelection, the war concluded. Five days hence, Lincoln was assassinated.

Lincoln's views on slavery and suffrage defy easy interpretation. Early in his career, though opposed to slavery in principle, Lincoln did not perceive the peculiar institution particularly important or divisive, and concluded that nothing could be done about it in the states where it existed. He was thus antislavery and antiabolition. Lincoln supported the efforts of the American Colonialization Society to return blacks to Africa, and persisted in this advocacy until well into his presidency (Donald 1995, 167). Even as a national political figure, Lincoln assured a Cincinnati audience in 1859 that he had no purpose to interfere with slavery. As president, Lincoln made clear in a "public letter" to Horace Greeley that the original motive for resisting Southern secession was not emancipation: "My paramount object in this struggle is to save the Union. If I could save the Union without freeing any slaves, I would do it, and if I could save it by freeing all the slaves I would do it; and if I could save it by freeing some and leaving others alone I would also do that" (White 2009, 504). In the first year of the war, Lincoln resisted abolition, fearing that it might cause the border states to secede. On January 1, 1863, Lincoln issued the Emancipation Proclamation, freeing the slaves "within the rebellious states," but justified it not on egalitarian principles but as a war measure intended to cripple the Confederacy. Later that year, Lincoln delivered the Gettysburg Address, which mentioned neither slavery nor emancipation, instead focusing on the preservation of self-government. When Congress first considered an antislavery amendment in early 1864, Lincoln remained silent. Following his reelection in November 1864—which also generated a stronger Republican majority in Congress—Lincoln lobbied Democratic and border-state congressmen to support the Thirteenth Amendment.

If Lincoln were slow to abolition, he was even slower to universal suffrage. His first known statements on suffrage came in the mid-1830s. Like most Whigs, Lincoln believed that property ownership ought to be prerequisite for voting, favoring "all sharing the privileges of the government, who assist in bearing its burthens." When pressed, he explained, that meant "admitting all whites to the right of suffrage, who pay taxes or bear arms." But then he added, "by no means excluding females." This statement led some to conclude that Lincoln was an early supporter of voting rights for women. (In the twentieth century, women's rights organizations invoked this comment as evidence that Lincoln thought women should be allowed to vote.) One historian refers to this as a "tongue-in-cheek joke," everyone, including Lincoln, knowing that under Illinois law women neither paid taxes nor served in the militia (Donald 1995, 59). Lincoln's early comments—"admitting all whites to the right of suffrage"—also reveal that he did not support black suffrage.

As his speeches throughout the 1850s make clear, Lincoln considered blacks to be morally and socially inferior to whites. To be antislavery was not to be in favor of black equality, black advancement, black citizenship, or black suffrage. In the Lincoln-Douglas debates in 1858, Lincoln expressed unmistakably his opposition to black equality:

> I am not, nor ever have been in favor of making [jurors] of the negroes . . . or qualifying them to hold office, or having them to marry with white people. I will say in addition, that there is a physical difference between the white and black races, which I suppose, will forever forbid the two races living together upon terms of social and political equality, and inasmuch, as they cannot so live, that while they do remain together, there must be the position of superior and inferior, that I as much as any other man am in favor of the superior position being assigned to the white man. (Holzer 1993, 189)

He was equally adamant in his opposition to black suffrage: "I am not nor ever have been in favor of [it]." In 1860, *The New York Times* commented about Lincoln: "He declares his opposition to negro suffrage, and to everything looking toward placing negroes upon a footing of political and social equality with the whites" (Foner 2019, 7).

During the Civil War, however, Lincoln's views on race evolved as he was exposed to black people, such as Frederick Douglass, whom he considered "one of the most meritorious men in America"; black soldiers, many of whom fought gallantly in the Union army; and black slaves, for whom he exhibited deep compassion. On April 11, 1865, Lincoln publicly declared his support for extending the elective franchise to "the very intelligent" blacks and those who "serve our cause as soldiers" (Donald 1995, 585). Lincoln's support for limited black suffrage enraged a young actor who happened to be in attendance that day. "That means nigger citizenship," said John Wilkes Booth. "Now by God, I'll put him through. That is the last speech he will ever make." Three days later, Booth shot Lincoln, who died the following morning.

Lincoln was succeeded by Andrew Johnson, a Tennessee Democrat, who opposed the Civil Rights Act of 1866, the Fourteenth Amendment (1868), and other attempts to bestow political and civil rights on blacks. Many historians lay the failure of Reconstruction at his feet.

James Madison (1751–1836)

"Father of the Constitution," coauthor of *The Federalist Papers*, and fourth president of the United States (1809–1817), James Madison was born in Port Conway, Virginia, and educated at the College of New Jersey (now Princeton University). He was elected a delegate from the state of Virginia to the Constitutional Convention of 1787. Though not the official secretary of the Convention—William Jackson was charged with that task—Madison's notes of the proceedings comprise the most detailed observations ever published on the Convention, thus earning him the title "Father of the Constitution." (To protect his fellow conventioners from partisan warfare, Madison steadfastly refused to allow publication of his notes until after his death. Nevertheless, much of what historians know today about the Convention derives from his meticulous commentary.)

The ten-month struggle for ratification of the proposed Constitution produced several worthwhile pieces of literature, the most important of which was a series of articles known as *The Federalist Papers*, of which Madison wrote twenty-nine. *The Federalist Papers* remains one of the great treatises on the American constitutional system.

Given Madison's centrality to the Constitutional Convention and his contribution to our understanding of the Constitution, his views on property and suffrage merit a brief discussion. Madison believed that the two cardinal objects of government were the rights of persons and the rights of property. Consequently, "the most either can claim is such a structure of [government] as will leave a reasonable security for the other. . . . The most difficult of all political arrangements is that of so adjusting the claims of the two classes as to give security to each and to promote the welfare of all" (Elliot 1859, IV, 21).

The problem with protecting both persons and property was a practical one: How to secure both, given economic inequalities between those with and those without property? Either side, given the opportunity, would encroach upon the rights of the other. "Give all power to property, and the indigent will be oppressed. Give it to the latter and the effect may be transposed" (Madison 1865, I, 187). Nonetheless, Madison maintained that in a republic the rights of property would be more vulnerable than the rights of persons. This was for two reasons. First, the propertied class would always be the minority. And second, because holders of property also shared all the other rights common to those without property, the former would be more restrained from infringing the rights of the latter.

Balancing these two classes of persons—to protect the rights of both—was made more difficult by republican principles. Madison accepted "the fundamental principle that men cannot be justly bound by laws in making of which they have no part." Even so, he feared that if suffrage were extended equally to all, government would be controlled by a majority "not interested in the rights of property." Those without property, or the hope thereof, could not be expected to sympathize with its rights. Madison knew that in future times the great majority of citizens would be without property. He predicted that those without property would "combine under the influence of their common situation" to threaten the rights of property. Having thus determined that the only way to secure property rights was to place some restrictions on the franchise, Madison concluded that property owners—the "more capable set of men"—would be the "safest depositories of Republican liberty" (Mason and Leach 1959, 125). One observer summarized it this way:

> In principle, suffrage was the right of all; but in practice, if political rights were given equally to all, the rights of persons and the rights of property would not be equally

protected. . . . At the time of the convention, Madison was prepared to risk the rights of persons and restrict the political rights of a future majority in order to protect property; with a reluctant afterthought about republican principles, he concluded that freehold suffrage would be best. (Nedelsky 1990, 19)

Madison, of course, was unable to persuade the delegates to lay down a constitutional prescription in regard to suffrage and property. The Convention finally entrusted the election of members of the House of Representatives to "the People of the several States," with the only stipulation that the electors in each state should have the same qualifications as the electors for the "most numerous Branch of the State Legislature." The Constitution thus gave authority for determining elector qualifications for the House of Representatives—whose members were the only national officers elected directly by the people—to the states.

Perhaps, not surprisingly, when the proposed Constitution was laid before the states (and the people) for ratification, its supporters, Madison included, boasted about the right of suffrage being the fundamental article of republican government. Three of *The Federalist Papers*—Nos. 52, 54, and 57—deal with suffrage. In *The Federalist*, No. 57, Madison, writing under the pseudonym "Publius," noted, "Who are to be the electors of the federal representatives? Not the rich, more than the poor; not the learned, more than the ignorant; not the haughty heirs of distinguished names, more than the humble sons of obscure and unpropitious fortune. The electors are to be the great body of the people of the United States" (Hamilton, Madison, and Jay 1961, 319).

Decades later, Madison commented on the dilemma of republican government: "In a just and free government, . . . the right both of property and of persons ought to be effectively guarded. Will the former be so in case of universal and equal suffrage? Will the latter be so in case of a suffrage confined to the holders of property?" (Elliot 1859, V, 581). Those remain fair questions.

National Association for the Advancement of Colored People (NAACP)

The National Association for the Advancement of Colored People (NAACP) is the oldest and largest civil rights organization in the United States. Formed in response to anti-black violence, the NAACP was founded in 1909 in New York City by an interracial group of activists, including W. E. B. Du Bois, Henry Moskowitz, Mary White Ovington, Moorfield Storey, Mary Church Terrell, Oswald Garrison Villard, William English Walling, and Ida B. Wells-Barnett. The first charter, adopted in 1911, listed among the NAACP's goals, "to advance the interests of colored citizens; to secure for them impartial suffrage; and to increase their opportunities for securing justice in the courts, education for their children, employment according to their ability, and complete equality before law." The organization largely eschewed direct methods of protest, instead advocating legislative reform and filing legal challenges to discriminatory laws. In the early decades, the Association focused on an antilynching campaign. By midcentury, the NAACP's Legal Defense and Educational Fund (LDF), formerly the "Legal Bureau," had won major civil rights legal victories, most notably *Smith* v. *Allwright* (1944), which invalidated the "white primary," and *Brown* v. *Board of Education*, which declared racial segregation in public schools violative of the Equal Protection Clause of the Fourteenth Amendment. Today, the organization is headquartered in Baltimore, Maryland, with more than two thousand branches and a half-million members worldwide. Its mission is "to secure the political, educational, social, and economic equality of rights in order to eliminate race-based discrimination and ensure the health and well-being of all persons."

With respect to voting rights, the first legal challenge supported by the NAACP was against the so-called "grandfather clauses." The Fifteenth Amendment forbade states from excluding any person from the exercise of the franchise on account of race. Nevertheless, Southern opposition led to the adoption of constitutional or legislative provisions whose admitted purpose was to disenfranchise as many blacks as possible while retaining the ballot for whites. The grandfather clauses excused citizens from certain voting requirements if they, or their ancestors, had been eligible to vote prior to a certain date. The date chosen, of course, was always a year in which most blacks had not been eligible to vote. Oklahoma's law limited the franchise to those who could read and write any section of the state constitution, but exempted from that requirement those persons (and lineal descendants of those persons) who were, on January 1, 1866, or any time prior thereto, entitled to vote under any form of government. When a challenge to that law reached the Supreme Court, in *Guinn* v. *United States* (1915), Storey, a leading lawyer, former president of the American Bar Association, and first president of the NAACP, filed an *amicus curiae* brief on behalf of the NAACP. The NAACP's position proved persuasive: The justices effectively outlawed grandfather clauses.

In the interwar period, the El Paso, Texas, branch of the NAACP mobilized in support of L. A. Herndon, who successfully challenged first a state law that prohibited blacks from voting in the Democratic Party primary; and then a state law that authorized the Democratic Party to exclude blacks from its primaries. While the Supreme Court struck down both laws, neither decision compelled the Democratic Party to admit blacks or let them participate in primaries. The Houston branch assisted R. R. Grovey in his unsuccessful challenge to the Democratic Party's exclusion of blacks when adopted by party convention. The LDF's first major victory came in *Smith*. The petitioner, Lonnie Smith, was represented by the chief legal counsel of the LDF (and future associate justice of the Supreme Court), Thurgood Marshall. In his brief to the Court, Marshall argued that the legal consequence of a state law that made primaries an integral part of the procedure of choice was that the right to vote in primaries was secured by the Fifteenth Amendment. The justices accepted Marshall's argument, invalidating the white primary. *Smith* was a watershed ruling. It also rekindled and mobilized opposition from Southern whites. As one NAACP branch official from Louisiana reported, "[T]he White South is sturred [sic] up . . . and you may expect more of us to be killed down here than ever due to the . . . decision of the Supreme Court" (Klarman 2004, 246). While voter registration had increased significantly by 1952, to 20 percent, the NAACP's work was far from finished. More was required before most Southern blacks could vote. Marshall later referred to *Smith* as the NAACP's most important victory (high praise for a man and an Association that would later win *Brown*, the more famous school desegregation case).

Following World War II, the NAACP assisted hundreds of blacks in lawsuits demanding the nondiscriminatory administration of voting requirements. Following the arrest of NAACP-member Rosa Parks, for whom the Association provided lawyers and paid legal costs, and the successful conclusion of the Montgomery bus boycott, which the Association supported, other more direct-action protest organizations emerged. The NAACP was slow to support most direct-action protests, preferring instead its comparatively passive and largely successful, even if time-consuming, litigation strategy.

In 1962, with the endorsement of President John F. Kennedy, the NAACP partnered with other organizations to launch the Voter Education Project to promote voter registration efforts, particularly in the South. A similar coalition of civil rights organizations, including the NAACP, supported "Freedom Summer," a 1964 initiative to register as many black voters as possible in Mississippi that resulted in murder, widespread violence, and national media attention. In the months preceding the Selma-to-Montgomery March in 1965, the LDF represented scores of blacks who attempted to register to vote in Alabama. Following "Bloody Sunday"—on which peaceful activists began their march to Montgomery to draw attention to black voter registration and were viciously assaulted by state law enforcement officers, the march and beatings broadcast on national television—the NAACP urged Congress and President Lyndon Johnson to pass a federal Voting Rights Act. The Voting Rights Act of 1965 became the single most important suffrage law in American history.

Francis Parkman (1823–1893)

American historian, critic of democracy, and outspoken opponent of universal suffrage, Francis Parkman was born in Boston, Massachusetts, into a family of wealth and privilege. While a student at Harvard College, Parkman traveled widely, first on a six-month grand tour of Europe, where he found himself briefly attracted to the idea of Catholicism; and later throughout Maine, Massachusetts, and New Hampshire. In 1846, after graduating from Harvard Law School, Parkman set out on a Western expedition, a six-month, near two-thousand-mile journey over the Oregon Trail.

This excursion formed the basis for Parkman's best-known work, *The Oregon Trail*, and epic saga of the American frontier. It was also during this trip that Parkman encountered for the first time Native Americans.

Parkman's nineteen-day stay with a band of Oglala Sioux Indians near Laramie (in the Wyoming Territory) convinced him that Native Americans were "some of the vilest outcasts in the country," "thorough savages," and a "troublesome and dangerous species of wild beast" (Parkman 2008, 11; 102; 237). They were impatient, intolerant, undisciplined, barbaric, ungovernable, and irredeemable. Their subjugation to white men and displacement represented progress, the superiority of civilization to savagery. Parkman's dehumanizing views on Native Americans were rooted in part on his misunderstanding of the significance of biological differences among groups of people. Nevertheless, similar views were not uncommon in the mid-nineteenth century. It is therefore not surprising that Native Americans were largely denied the right to vote. Conferring suffrage upon "uncivilized" persons made no sense.

By the 1870s, the growth of industry, the rise of cities, and the influx of immigrants spurred some to question universal manhood suffrage. Concentrated in the large cities in the Northeast, most notably New York and Boston, these middle- to upper-class intellectuals, academics, capitalists, and professional elite feared the economic and social changes that came with—and the "political machines" that accompanied—densely populated cities with largely unskilled foreign-born factory workers. They were particularly concerned with what these tens of thousands of unpropertied "restless workmen" might be able to accomplish, if organized effectively, at the ballot box. To limit this threat to property rights and American values, these Gilded Age reformers advocated a variety of limitations on the franchise. It was during this post–Civil War period that Parkman, E. L. Godkin, Charles Francis Adams, II, and others sharpened their critiques of democracy.

In an article entitled "The Failure of Universal Suffrage," published in the widely read journal, *The North American Review*, Parkman called universal suffrage a "questionable blessing." A careful read, however, reveals that "questionable" may have been too generous. The idyllic New England Protestant village of olden days, which was safely and well governed by the votes of every man, had grown into a teeming city, marked by factories, workshops, and acres of tenement-houses; and chockfull of foreigners, "to whom liberty means license and politics means plunder, to whom the public good is nothing and their own trivial interests everything, who love the country for what they can get out of it" (Parkman 1878, 7). Left unsaid, but well-known, was that many of these foreigners were Catholic. Parkman criticized political parties for imposing universal suffrage on the country and promoting it as a sacred principle, when it derived from contending parties bidding against each other for votes of people who care not "a farthing for the general good." Self-government only worked among those people "who by character and training are prepared for it." Parkman then turned his attention to the spoils system, which eliminated the most qualified men for public office in the interest of party. He called for young men of promise to return to public office and affairs, and suggested that they begin with the cities, where "the diseases of the body politic are gathered to a head," the need for attacking them "most urgent," the dangerous classes "most numerous and strong," and the effects of flinging suffrage to the many "most disastrous" (Parkman, 1878, 20). While the essay clearly evidenced Parkman's prejudice against immigrants and the uneducated, it also heralded many of the franchise-narrowing initiatives and good-government reforms later adopted in states and major American cities.

Having tasted battle, Parkman pressed ahead with piece on "The Woman Question," published in 1879. The nineteen-page essay succinctly presented the case against women's suffrage. It can be summarized thus: First, men and women were fundamentally different, the former made for conflict, business, and politics, the latter unfit for each (though with other "high and priceless qualities" important in the home). Parkman talked about the failure that historically accompanied female political rule (and credited male statesmen for those rare instances of successful female political rule). He noted that vast majority of women were incapable of fighting, and emphasized the association between the right of voting and the duty of fighting. It was folly, Parkman concluded, to counteract the laws of God and nature though "political and social quackery." Second, most women were opposed to suffrage. It would be a "cruel and intolerable burden" to impose political duties on those who did not want to assume them. Third, it was a danger to popular government to give an equal voice to "the most impulsive and excitable half of humanity." Like Delilah "spreading her snares for the Congressional Samson," women would use their feminine charms and arts to gain an unfair advantage and corrupt the political process.

Parkman's views prompted a point-by-point rebuttal, published in the next issue of *The North American Review*, from five of the most prominent suffragists, including Julia Ward Howe,

Elizabeth Cady Stanton, and Lucy Stone (Howe, et al. 1879). His opposition to female suffrage well established, Parkman, in a sequel article, nevertheless conceded that if women wanted suffrage, they would certainly get it: "A more than readiness to conform to the wishes of the other sex is a national trait in America" (Parkman 1880, 20). Those wishes became a formal reality with adoption of the Nineteenth Amendment in 1920.

John G. Roberts (1955–)

When John Roberts was nominated to replace William Rehnquist as the Chief Justice of the United States in 2005 by President George W. Bush, he noted in his confirmation testimony that a judge's responsibility was to act as an umpire and "call balls and strikes," not to promote an established political agenda. With respect to voting rights and the Voting Rights Act (VRA) of 1965, most agree that Roberts learned how to call balls and strikes from serving as a clerk to then Associate Justice Rehnquist in the October 1980 term and from working as a special assistant to the U.S. attorney general in the early 1980s. In those positions, Roberts exhibited deep skepticism about the reach of the VRA, the role of the federal courts in advancing minority voting rights, and the prospects for proportional representation in American elections.

The Supreme Court fundamentally changed the reach of the VRA in *Mobile* v. *Bolden* (1980) when it held that a challenge to racial discrimination under Section 2 had to demonstrate that the government acted with intentional discrimination; showing discriminatory *effect* alone was insufficient. The following year, Rehnquist hired Roberts as a clerk. Rehnquist was a strong supporter of states' rights and federalism, which led him to question the VRA's reach into traditional state authority. Roberts followed suit.

In his next post—as a special assistant to the U.S. attorney general—Roberts wrote over twenty memos urging Congress not to override *Mobile* by allowing people to challenge state voting practices that only had a racially discriminatory *effect* (Berman 2015, 149–150). Roberts was particularly concerned that an effects test would lead jurisdictions to replace at-large voting districts with proportional representation in order for minority voters to gain the representation they felt they deserved. In amending the language of Section 2 in 1982, Congress rejected Roberts's position. Nevertheless, his nomination to chief justice in 2005 helped shape the Court's voting rights doctrine and repudiation of key provisions of the VRA.

The Court first grappled with the legality of the Section 5 "preclearance requirement" in *Northwest Austin Municipal Utility District, Number One* v. *Holder* (2009). In that case, the Court refused to address whether Section 5 was unconstitutional, opting to decide the case on the narrow statutory question of whether NAMUDNO was entitled to a preclearance bailout. By passing on the constitutional question, the Roberts Court effectively put Congress on notice that if it did not amend the law to clarify which jurisdictions needed to preclear election law changes with the federal government, the Court was poised to strike it down.

Roberts's views on the VRA finally were made explicit in *Shelby County* v. *Holder* (2013). Surprising many, the Court declared Section 4's coverage formula (determining which states and political subdivisions were subject to the "preclearance requirement") unconstitutional because Congress had failed to update the formula in light of current empirical realities. Requiring only some governments to receive permission from the federal government before making changes to their election law imposed "substantial federalism costs." For Roberts, the "preclearance requirement" violated the equal sovereignty of the states.

Roberts's belief that the Constitution does not mandate any proportional representational scheme also appeared in his majority opinion in the partisan gerrymandering case, *Rucho* v. *Common Cause* (2019). For decades, the Court had been wrestling with whether federal courts were the proper institution to check state legislative efforts to gerrymander legislative districts for excessive partisan benefit. In *Rucho*, the Court ruled that "partisan gerrymandering claims present political questions beyond the reach of the federal courts." Roberts opined that the federal courts were ill-equipped to create and enforce a fair and manageable standard to adjudicate partisan gerrymandering disputes. He was clearly concerned that when searching for a standard to apply in partisan gerrymandering cases, advocates and judges might reach for proportional representation as a solution to a party's inability to translate political support into political power. Citing *Mobile*, Roberts noted that the Court's cases "clearly foreclose any claim that the Constitution requires proportional representation or that legislatures in reapportioning must draw district lines to come as near as possible to what their anticipated statewide vote will be."

In addition to deciding major VRA and partisan gerrymandering cases, the Roberts Court has been active in other voting rights issues. In *Crawford* v. *Marion County Election Board* (2008), the Court upheld Indiana's voter ID law, and in *Husted* v. *A. Philip Randolph Institute* (2018), the justices upheld Ohio's strict voter roll purging practices. In both, Roberts was in the majority. For him, reasonable state efforts to protect the integrity of the ballot have been paramount to any concerns that those restrictive practices might disproportionately impact minority voters.

Rock the Vote

One well-established law in political science research is that the older you get, the more likely you are to vote. The youngest voting bloc (eighteen to twenty-four-year-olds) historically has the lowest voting rates. To rectify the problem of lower rates of political participation, Rock the Vote was founded in 1990 by entertainment executive Jeff Ayeroff as a nonpartisan, nonprofit organization devoted to increasing the voting power of young Americans. Initially formed in response to a censorship campaign against musicians, Rock the Vote realized that its power and influence was best channeled into increasing voter participation of young Americans.

In its early years, the organization employed celebrities in public service announcements to extol the virtues of voting and encourage young adults to "rock the vote," that is, to show up at the polling stations on election day. In 1996, Rock the Vote began using e-mail and the internet to remind young adults to get out and vote. More recently, in the age of social media, the organization has used targeted advertisements on Facebook, Twitter, and other platforms to appeal to young voters.

Rock the Vote has also expanded its educational work. Rock the Vote believes that the key to growing the electorate is to educate young Americans on the issues facing their generations and why voting and political participation are in their best interests. For example, to help prepare high school students for voting, Rock the Vote created teaching resources called "Democracy Class" that combine lesson plans, teacher resources, and mock elections. School districts across the country have used "Democracy Class" as a way to educate teenagers about the importance of elections, registering to vote, and participating in American democracy.

A key question associated with Rock the Vote is whether its efforts have been successful. One thing is certain, regardless: The youngest voting bloc has historically voted at lower rates than their older counterparts. According to the U.S. Census Bureau, in 1988, the last presidential election before Rock the Vote, youth voting rates were 36.2 percent. In 1992, the first presidential election after Rock the Vote, voting rates increased to 42.8 percent. While research has been unable to attribute the increase in youth voting in 1992 to Rock the Vote specifically, at least the group's goal of increasing youth voter turnout occurred in the first presidential election after its get-out-the-vote efforts originated. That increase, however, has not been sustained. The 1996 and 2000 elections witnessed all-time lows of 32.4 and 32.3, respectively, for the youngest voting bloc. The percentages for the last four presidential elections are as follows: 41.9 (2004), 44.3 (2008), 38.0 (2012), and 39.4 (2106). In short, youth voting rates have fluctuated between 32.4 and 44.3 percent in the seven elections since Rock the Vote, with an average of 38.7 percent. In the five presidential elections between 1972 (the first after ratification of the Twenty-Sixth Amendment) and 1988 (the last pre-Rock the Vote), youth voting rates fluctuated between 36.2 and 49.6 percent, with an average of 41.7 percent ("Reported Voting and Registration by Race, Hispanic Origin, Sex, and Age Groups: November 1964 to 2018" 2018).

By these numbers, Rock the Vote appears to have had limited success in driving youth voter turnout.

The Suffragettes

What began in the Wesleyan Chapel in a small village in upstate New York in July 1848 morphed into the largest mass movement for suffrage in American history and culminated in the formal removal of sex as a qualification for voting in 1920. Though many contributed to the effort, and not all women, among the more notable suffragettes were Lucretia Mott (1793–1880), Elizabeth Cady Stanton (1815–1902), Lucy Stone (1818–1893), Susan B. Anthony (1820–1906), and Carrie Chapman Catt (1859–1947).

The most senior women's rights activist of the nineteenth century was born Lucretia Coffin in Nantucket, Massachusetts, and raised a Quaker. She and her husband, James Mott, settled in Philadelphia, where they were active in antislavery causes. In 1840, Mott was refused participation in the World Anti-Slavery Convention in London on account of her sex, the convention leaders not wanting women's rights to detract from abolition. It was at this convention, however, that Mott met Stanton. Their partnership led to the Seneca Falls Convention, where Mott helped draft the Declaration of Sentiments, which provided examples of discrimination against women, including denial of the franchise, and called for the "immediate admission" of women to all the rights and privileges of citizenship. In 1866, Mott was elected president of the American Equal Rights Association (AERA), which supported equal rights, including suffrage, for blacks and women.

Born Elizabeth Cady in Johnstown, New York, Stanton most clearly represented "in one individual what the movement was all about" (Gurko 1974, 57). The daughter of a distinguished lawyer and state judge, young Stanton read law books and debated politics, becoming at an early age aware of the discriminatory effect of the law upon women. She attended the coeducational Johnstown Academy. Denied the opportunity to study at Union College because of her sex, Stanton enrolled in a female seminary in Troy. In 1840, she married the abolitionist Henry Stanton; eight years later, she co-organized the Seneca Falls Convention. From that point, her engagement with the cause of women's rights never waned (Stanton 1898). In comparison to other suffragettes, Stanton embraced a broader women's right agenda, including property ownership, marital rights, divorce laws, and birth control. In 1866, Stanton ran for Congress, not expecting to win but hoping to draw attention to the illogic of voting limitations: Though she was prohibited from voting under New York law, she was not restricted from holding political office. She garnered only twenty-four votes, but received far more publicity. In 1869, Stanton cofounded the National Woman Suffrage Association (NWSA), serving as its president for twenty-one years; and the president of its successor, the National American Woman Suffrage Association (NAWSA), for two years. In 1888, Stanton appeared at a New Jersey polling booth on election day and asserted her right to vote as a property owner and taxpayer in the state. The election inspector wrapped his arms around the ballot box and held one had over the slot, denying Stanton the opportunity to vote.

Lucy Stone was born in West Brookfield, Massachusetts, and raised on a farm. Her first object lesson in the mistreatment of women came from her authoritarian father, who made clear that her lot in life was predetermined by tradition and Biblical injunction. At the age of twenty-five and with $70 to her name, Stone matriculated at Oberlin College, the only school in the country that offered degrees to women. She became a powerful public orator in defense of abolition and women's rights. When Stone married Henry Blackwell in 1855, the couple included in their vows a protest against coverture, a legal doctrine whereby women lost their legal existence upon marriage. She further defied custom by keeping her last name. Disagreement over the Fifteenth Amendment—Stanton and Anthony opposed it because it did not secure female suffrage; Stone supported it, "thankful" to see anyone earn the franchise—led to a split in the women's rights movement: In 1869, Stanton, Anthony, and others formed the NWSA, while Stone, Julia Ward Howe, and their allies organized themselves into the American Woman Suffrage Association (AWSA).

Susan B. Anthony is the most well-known suffragette. Born in western Massachusetts and raised a Quaker in New York, Anthony turned to teaching to assist her family's dire financial situation following the Panic of 1837, in which the family lost almost everything. She experienced the legal disabilities against women when her maternal grandparents died. Though they left a share of their estate to Anthony's mother, by law that inheritance had to be transferred to Anthony's father (and then would have been claimed by her father's creditors). The family was rescued from financial ruin by Anthony's maternal uncle. Her entrance into political activism came with temperance. Upon learning that male teachers earned four times what she earned, Anthony's attention turned to equal pay for equal work. Suffrage limitations bothered her little until the mid-1850s and did not become her raison d'être until after the Civil War when she joined the national suffrage movement. In 1872, in her most public act of civil disobedience, Anthony cast an illegal ballot in a presidential election in New York, for which she was convicted at trial and fined $100. "I shall never pay a dollar of your unjust penalty," Anthony informed the judge.

Nor did she. The judge did not press the issue, thus foreclosing Anthony's opportunity to appeal. (A century later, the U.S. Mint began issuing the Susan B. Anthony dollar coin, the first legal tender to honor a female citizen.) When the two national woman suffrage organizations merged in 1890, Anthony became the dominant figure in the new NAWSA for its first decade.

Anthony was replaced as president of NAWSA by Carrie Chapman Catt. Born Carrie Lee, this "second-generation" suffragette and skilled political strategist guided the organization during much of the final two decades of the campaign for women's suffrage. She retired from the NAWSA after adoption of the Nineteenth Amendment but went on to found the League of Women Voters, whose mission was to help women carry out their new responsibilities as voters.

Texas Democratic Party

The Democratic Party was the dominant political party in the state of Texas from the 1840s until the mid-1900s. Between 1848 and 1948, the state's electoral votes were cast for the Democratic nominee in every presidential election, save for 1928. During the Civil War, the party supported secession and aligned itself with the proslavery wing of the national party. Following Reconstruction, the party pursued a variety of strategies to prevent blacks from voting. The Fifteenth Amendment precluded race as a criterion for voting. Nevertheless, the Texas Legislature, controlled by Democrats, maintained the traditional white franchise by adopting race-neutral laws that had the effect of disqualifying blacks from voting. The most effective of these preserved the "white primary."

The final choice in any political contest is made by voters in a general election, which is typically a race between candidates from opposing parties. Those candidates, however, are usually chosen in primaries, in which voters select the person to represent the party in the election. But what if one party were so dominant in a state (as the Democrats were in Texas between Reconstruction and 1848) that the winner of the primary was virtually guaranteed to win the election? In that situation, any meaningful political choice by voters would be made not in the election but rather in the primary. In 1903, the Texas Legislature conferred upon the state's parties the legal privilege of determining their membership and, therefore, deciding who could participate in their primaries. The Texas Democratic Party promptly denied membership to blacks. So blacks could vote in elections, but not in primaries. Of course, in Texas, the election often only had one name on the ballot—the winner of the Democratic primary.

In *Newberry* v. *United States* (1921), which involved allegations of electoral fraud in a Republican primary in Michigan, the Supreme Court held that the Fifteenth Amendment—"The right of citizens of the United States to vote shall not be denied or abridged by the United States or by any State on account of race, color, or previous condition of servitude"—did not apply to primaries, which were "in no real sense part of the manner of holding [an] election." Accordingly, primaries were exempt from the Constitution's prohibition on racial discrimination in voting. Consequently, the Texas Legislature clarified its election law: "[I]n no event shall a negro be eligible to participate in a Democratic Party primary election held in the State of Texas, and should a negro vote in a Democratic primary election, such ballot shall be void and election officials are herein directed to throw out such ballot and not count the same." (The fact that the legislation did not even mention Republican primaries is illustrative of the dominance of the Democratic Party in Texas politics during this time.) After L. A. Nixon, a black physician from El Paso, was refused a ballot in a Democratic primary, he challenged the law as violative of the Fourteenth—"No State shall . . . deny to any person within its jurisdiction the equal protection of the laws"—and Fifteenth Amendments. In *Nixon* v. *Herndon* (1927), a unanimous Court found it unnecessary to consider the Fifteenth Amendment claim because the law was a "direct and obvious infringement" of the Equal Protection Clause, which had a "special intent" to protect blacks from discrimination: "[C]olor cannot be made the basis for a statutory classification affecting the right set up in this case."

This case did not mark the death knell of the "white primary." The Texas Legislature responded, with the intent to provide a legal means to prevent blacks from primary voting, by amending the law thus: "Every political party in this State shall . . . have the power to prescribe the qualifications of its own members and shall in its own way determine who shall be qualified to vote or otherwise participate in such political party." Pursuant to this law, the Texas Democratic Party resolved that "all white Democrats . . . be allowed to participate in the primary elections." After Nixon was (again) denied suffrage in the Democratic primary, he (again) alleged violations of the Fourteenth and Fifteenth Amendments. The Court (again) struck down the law because the party's authority to enact the rule could be traced to the power conferred upon it by the state legislature. Since the party exercised only delegated powers, and since no authority to prescribe qualifications for primary voters was ever delegated by the membership to the party, the party acted under the authority of the statute as "delegates of the state." But the Court refused either to affirm or deny that a political party had inherent power without restraint by any law to determine its own membership.

That caveat provided an opening for the Texas Democratic Party, which, in the absence of any state legislation, limited participation in its primaries to "white citizens." When challenged in *Grovey* v. *Townsend* (1935), a unanimous Court upheld that party resolution, in spite of its blatant racial discrimination, on the grounds that the Fourteenth and Fifteenth Amendments restricted state action only. Private organizations, to include political parties, were entirely free to engage in discriminatory practices. The Texas Democratic Party had stumbled upon a constitutionally acceptable method to deprive blacks of meaningful electoral participation.

This method was shortlived. In *Smith* v. *Allwright* (1944), the Court invalidated the "white primary" as violative of the Fifteenth Amendment. Because the selection of candidates for public office whose names were to be placed on the election ballot was entrusted by an act of the state legislature to parties, those parties were, when conducting primaries, acting as agents of the state.

Undeterred and determined to keep blacks disenfranchised, the Texas Democratic Party created "Jaybird Associations" throughout the state. These county associations, which excluded blacks from membership, conducted "preprimaries" in which candidates for Democratic primaries were chosen. More often than not, the victor in the Jaybird "preprimary" was the perfunctory choice of the voters in the Democratic primary and thus the election. In *Terry* v. *Adams* (1953), the Court extended the ruling in *Smith* to these unofficial primaries, concluding that these preprimaries, like the Democratic primaries, had become "an integral part, indeed the only effective part, of the elective process that determines who shall rule and govern."

U.S. Department of Justice

Political life for blacks changed fundamentally on August 6, 1965, when President Lyndon Johnson signed the Voting Rights Act (VRA) into law. The U.S. Department of Justice (DOJ) was given responsibility for enforcing the terms of the Act. Its meaning and enforcement, however, fluctuated over time as different presidential administrations responded to political circumstances.

The task for the DOJ was monumental. In a substantive sense, the DOJ was responsible for enforcing a major piece of social legislation that called for significant intrusion into traditional state practices. Section 2 applied to the entire country and prohibited any "State or political subdivision" from imposing any "voting qualification or prerequisite to voting" on "account of race or color." Section 3 outlined procedures for how and when "Federal examiners" could be sent into states to assist blacks in securing the right to vote. Section 4 guaranteed that "no citizen shall be denied the right to vote in any Federal, State, or local election because of his failure to comply with any test or device in any State," and it outlined a "coverage formula" for determining which states and political subdivisions would be subject to Section 5's "preclearance requirement," which required various jurisdictions—mostly in the South—to obtain preapproval for any change in their election law.

Limited resources meant that the DOJ had to make choices regarding which provisions to emphasize in its enforcement authority. In the years immediately following passage, the Johnson Administration focused its efforts on registering black voters in the jurisdictions with the worst voting records, but even with those efforts, federal examiners were not assigned to nearly two hundred counties in covered states with African American registration rates below 50 percent (Rhodes 2017, 44).

The DOJ's Section 5 preclearance responsibilities were noticeably lacking. The DOJ dealt with the preclearance requests without any set of established procedures in place, and only 10 of the 260 proposed preclearance requests between 1965 and 1969 were rejected (Fuentes-Rohwer and Guy-Uriel 2007, 517). In short, in the early years, the VRA's successes were mixed, with some advancement in black voter registration but with concern that laws intending to discriminate against black voters were too easily approved by the attorney general due to a lack of rigorous, rules-based procedures in place for preclearance requests.

As Congress was debating the reauthorization of the VRA in 1970 and 1975, Presidents Richard Nixon and Gerald Ford were in the untenable position of privately opposing many of Act's key provisions but knowing that opposition to reauthorization was fraught with significant political consequences. While Nixon and Ford publicly supported the reauthorizations, the

DOJ's enforcement was less than robust. For instance, Nixon appointed his campaign manager, John N. Mitchell, to serve as attorney general, which signaled to the southern states that the "law and order" rhetoric of the 1968 campaign would be channeled to weakening key provisions of the VRA. In fact, the Civil Rights Division (CRD) of the DOJ failed to send additional examiners to southern counties that trailed in black voter registration and the DOJ "soft-pedal[ed] federal preclearance of changes in election rules and regulations in covered jurisdictions" (Rhodes 2017, 79). The Nixon Administration's signaling of lax VRA enforcement also resulted in many covered jurisdictions not even seeking preclearance of election law changes (Kousser 2008). Ford sought to improve the reputation of the DOJ by holding states accountable for implementing bilingual elections. Like the Nixon Administration, however, it failed to use its power to hold covered jurisdictions accountable for not seeking preclearance for new laws.

In 1982, during President Ronald Reagan's first term, Congress once again reauthorized the VRA, this time for twenty-five years. This reauthorization strengthened Section 2 by allowing lawsuits challenging voting laws that have a discriminatory *effect*, not just intent, and by ensuring that the federal government would continue its oversight of electoral arrangements in "covered jurisdictions." Though Reagan lost this legislative battle, he still shaped the efficacy of the law through appointments to the DOJ and other enforcement choices. Reagan implemented a centralized decision-making scheme that required DOJ attorney decisions be approved by political appointees in the Department. The DOJ also filed fewer enforcement lawsuits, limiting any meaningful litigation to be pursued through private legal action.

During the George H.W. Bush (Bush I) and Bill Clinton administrations, the DOJ had a much more active role in enforcing the VRA. The DOJ was initially forceful in encouraging states to create majority-minority districts to comply with Section 2. Those efforts were stymied, however, when the

Supreme Court, in *Shaw* v. *Reno* (1993), ruled that redistricting based solely on race would be met with judicial skepticism.

Although the Barack Obama Administration was expected to develop an aggressive enforcement of the VRA after the CRD hired dozens of new attorneys to help enforce its terms, much of the DOJ's enforcement power was taken away when the Court declared Section 4 unconstitutional in *Shelby County* v. *Holder* (2013). The DOJ's power then largely shifted to enforcement of Section 2.

Because opposing the VRA was politically dangerous, many of the fights over it devolved to the bureaucracy and DOJ. Generally, under Republican presidents, the DOJ worked to limit implementation in ways that provided states greater flexibility over its own laws. Under Democratic administrations, the DOJ was more forceful in its implementation strategy.

The Waite Court (1874–1888)

The Waite Court refers to the Supreme Court of the United States from March 4, 1874, to March 23, 1888, when Morrison Remick Waite was the seventh chief justice of the United States. That fourteen-year period was "as remarkable, exciting, and consequential as any in Supreme Court history" (Stephenson 2003, xi). Waite's chief justiceship followed that of Salmon P. Chase, which began in 1864, and preceded that of Melville Fuller, which lasted until 1910. Collectively, fourteen men sat on the Court during Waite's tenure, including four other highly regarded justices, Samuel F. Miller (1862–1890), Stephen J. Field (1863–1897), Joseph P. Bradley (1870–1892), and John Marshall Harlan I (1877–1911).

The Waite Court was largely characterized by its reluctance to overturn federal and state statutes. (A good example of this is *Minor* v. *Happersett*, where the Court in 1875 upheld a Missouri law that limited the franchise to men by declaring that citizenship under the Fourteenth Amendment did not confer the right of suffrage; instead, voting was a privilege granted by the states.) The one notable exception to this judicial restraint was federal civil rights laws. In interpreting the Reconstruction Amendments—and the extent of congressional powers under them—the Court rendered decisions that had far-reaching effects on Reconstruction, race relations, and voting rights.

To enforce the Fourteenth and Fifteenth Amendments, Congress enacted the Enforcement Act of 1870. Its wording was remarkably dense and poorly chosen. Section 2 made it a federal crime for state officials to discriminate on account of "race, color, or previous condition of servitude." Section 3 permitted any citizen who had been denied the right to vote "as aforesaid" to file an affidavit to that effect with federal election supervisors, the affidavit alone qualifying the citizen to vote; and criminalized refusal by state officials to accept the affidavit. Section 4 barred *any* person from obstructing another from voting "as aforesaid." And Section 6 forbade persons from conspiring to prevent or hinder any citizen from the exercise and enjoyment of rights and privileges granted by the Constitution. On its face, the Act appeared to be an "appropriate" exercise of Congress's authority to guarantee elections and other constitutional privileges free from racial discrimination.

United States v. *Reese* (1876), the first voting rights case to come before the Supreme Court, involved election officials indicted under Sections 3 and 4 of the Act for refusing to receive and count the vote of a black citizen. After clarifying that the Fifteenth Amendment did not confer the right to vote upon anyone but merely prohibited a state from denying suffrage on account of race, the Court turned its attention to the provisions of the Act. To be "appropriate," the Act could prohibit only that which the amendment prohibited. Though Sections 3 and 4 did not mention "race," the government argued that the phrase "as aforesaid," which appeared in both sections, was an obvious reference to "race." The Court was unpersuaded. Because Sections 3 and 4 omitted reference to race, they were inappropriate exercises of congressional authority under the amendment. In short, the amendment did not grant general protection of the right to vote; therefore, Congress could not either. The Court's reading of the amendment was not novel; to the contrary, it was the widely understood Republican position. But the Court's reading of the Act seemed implausible. How could one not see the obvious nexus between "race, color, or previous condition of servitude" in the second section and "as aforesaid" in the third and fourth sections?

A second case, *United States* v. *Cruikshank* (1876), involved indictments against private individuals under Section 6 of the Act. To bring an indictment within the operation of the Act, said the Waite Court, "it must appear that the right, the enjoyment of which the conspirators intended to hinder or prevent, was one granted or secured by the Constitution or laws of the United States." Here, the indictments read that the defendants had obstructed others in their rights peaceably to assemble and to bear arms. But because those rights existed long before the adoption of the U.S. Constitution, they fell outside the protection of the Fourteenth Amendment and the Act. For their protection and enjoyment, "the people must look to the States." Additionally, the justices drew a distinction between state and private action, noting that the amendment limited the former but "add[ed] nothing to the rights of one citizen as against another." Private action, on which the indictments were based, was beyond the purview of the Constitution and the protection of the Act.

The Waite Court reiterated this "state action" doctrine in *The Civil Rights Cases* (1883), striking down the federal Civil Rights Act of 1875, which criminalized racial discrimination in privately owned places of public accommodations, such as hotels, restaurants, theaters, and public transportation. The justices held that the Act exceeded Congress's authority under the Thirteenth and Fourteenth Amendments. Under the former, Congress could legislate against slavery and involuntary servitude, but "mere discriminations" on account of race were not "badges" of either.

The latter's prohibitions were "against state law and acts done under state authority"; accordingly, Congress had no authority to regulate private rights or prevent private discrimination.

A year later, the Waite Court mitigated some effects of *Reese* and *Cruikshank* in *Ex parte Yarbrough* (1884), in upholding the federal Enforcement Act of 1871 (also known as the Ku Klux Klan Act of 1871), which criminalized various forms of voter intimidation, but without reference to race. The unanimous opinion noted that the Fifteenth Amendment "substantially confer[s] on the negro the right to vote" and upheld Congress's authority to protect and enforce that right. Any other conclusion would leave the country "at the mercy of the combinations of those who respect no right but brute force." *Yarbrough* remains the only case in which the Waite Court upheld federal power to punish private obstruction of a citizen's voting rights.

Finally, five members of the Waite Court helped resolve the presidential election of 1876. Democrat Samuel J. Tilden won the popular vote over Republican Rutherford B. Hayes, but Republicans contested electoral votes in four states. After much debate, Congress authorized a special election commission—composed of seven Democrats, seven Republicans, and one independent—to rule on the disputed electoral votes. Five members were chosen from each chamber of Congress; of those ten, five were Democrats and five Republicans. The remaining seats were filled by justices: Nathan Clifford and Stephen Field were Democrats (the only two on the Court); Samuel Miller and William Strong were Republicans; and David Davis was independent. But Davis disqualified himself when the Illinois Legislature selected him as a U.S. Senator. Joseph Bradley, a Republican, replaced Davis, giving the commission seven Democrats and eight Republicans. After a series of backroom negotiations, the commission, divided along party lines, awarded all of the disputed electors to Hayes, thus delivering the presidency to him by a margin of one electoral vote. Among the first acts of the Hayes presidency was withdrawing federal troops from the South, returning the region to its native sons.

In interpreting narrowly the Reconstruction Amendments and congressional power to enforce them (and indirectly awarding the presidency to Hayes), the Waite Court sharply limiting federal authority to protect the civil rights of Americans (and effectively ended Reconstruction).

References

Annbinder, Tyler G. 1992. *Nativism and Slavery: The Northern Know Nothings and the Politics of the 1850s*. New York: Oxford University Press.

Bennett, David H. 1988. *The Party of Fear: From Nativist Movements to the New Right in American History*. Chapel Hill, NC: The University of North Carolina Press.

Berman, Ari. 2015. *Give Us the Ballot: The Modern Struggle for Voting Rights in America*. New York: Picador.

Donald, David Herbert. 1995. *Lincoln*. New York: Simon and Schuster.

Elliot, Jonathan. 1859. *Debates on the Adoption of the Federal Constitution, in the Convention held at Philadelphia, in 1787, with a diary of the debate of the Congress of the Confederacy; as reported by James Madison, a member, and deputy from Virginia*. 5 vols. Philadelphia, PA: J. B. Lippincott and Company.

Fogel, Robert William. 1994. *Without Consent or Contract: The Rise and Fall of American Slavery*. New York: W. W. Norton.

Foner, Eric. 2019. *The Second Founding: How the Civil War and Reconstruction Remade the Constitution*. New York: W. W. Norton.

Fuentes-Rohwer, Luis and Charles E. Guy-Uriel. 2007. "The Politics of Pre-clearance." *Michigan Journal of Race & Law*, 12 (4): 514–535.

Gienapp, William E. 1987. *Origins of the Republican Party: 1852–1856*. New York: Oxford University Press.

Gurko, Miriam. 1974. *The Ladies of Seneca Falls: The Birth of the Women's Rights Movement*. New York: Schocken Books, Inc.

Hamilton, Alexander, James Madison, and John Jay. [1787–1788] 1961. *The Federalist Papers*. Edited by Clinton Rossiter. New York: Mentor.

Hasen, Richard L. 2003. *The Supreme Court and Election Law: Judging Equality from* Baker *v.* Carr *to* Bush *v.* Gore. New York: New York University Press.

Hasen, Richard L. 2012. *The Voting Wars: From Florida 2000 to the Next Election Meltdown*. New Haven, CT: Yale University Press.

Hasen, Richard L. 2016. "Softening Voter ID Laws through Litigation? Is It Enough?" *Wisconsin Law Review Forward*, 1: 100–121.

Hasen, Richard L. 2018. "The 2016 U.S. Voting Wars: From Bad to Worse." *William and Mary Bill of Rights Journal*, 26: 629–655.

Holt, Michael F. 1978. *The Political Crisis of the 1850s*. New York: W. W. Norton.

Holt, Michael F. 1999. *The Rise and Fall of the American Whig Party: Jacksonian Politics and the Onset of the Civil War*. New York: Oxford University Press.

Holzer, Harold. 1993. *The Lincoln-Douglas Debates: The First Complete, Unexpurgated Text*. New York: Harper Collins.

Howe, Julia Ward, Lucy Stone, Thomas Wentworth Higginson, Elizabeth Cady Stanton, and Wendell Phillips. 1879. "The Other Side of the Woman Question." *The North American Review*, 129 (276): 413–446.

Klarman, Michael J. 2004. *From Jim Crow to Civil Rights: The Supreme Court and the Struggle for Racial Equality*. New York: Oxford University Press.

Kousser, J. Morgan. 2008. "The Strange, Ironic Career of Section 5 of the Voting Rights Act, 1965–2007." *Texas Law Review*, 86 (4): 667–775.

Lincoln, Abraham. 1953. *The Collected Works of Abraham Lincoln*. 9 vols. Edited by Roy P. Basler. New Brunswick, NJ: Rutgers University Press.

Madison, James. [1787] 2005. *The Debates in the Federal Convention of 1787: Which Framed the Constitution of the*

United States. Edited by Galliard Hunt and James Brown Scott Clark, NJ: The Lawbook Exchange, Ltd.

Mason, Alpheus Thomas and Richard H. Leach. 1959. *In Quest of Freedom: American Political Thought and Practice.* Englewood Cliffs, NJ: Prentice-Hall.

Nedelsky, Jennifer. 1990. *Private Property and the Limits of American Constitutionalism: The Madisonian Framework and Its Legacy.* Chicago, IL: The University of Chicago Press.

Parkman, Francis. 1878. "The Failure of Universal Suffrage." *The North American Review,* 127 (263): 1–20.

Parkman, Francis. 1879. "The Woman Question." *The North American Review,* 129 (275): 303–321.

Parkman, Francis. 1880. "The Woman Question Again." *The North American Review,* 130 (278): 16–30.

Parkman, Francis. [1849] 2008. *The Oregon Trail.* New York: Oxford University Press.

"Reported Voting and Registration by Race, Hispanic Origin, Sex, and Age Groups: November 1964 to 2018." 2018. U.S. Census Bureau. https://www.census.gov/data/tables /time-series/demo/voting-and-registration/voting-historical -time-series.html

Rhodes, Jesse H. 2017. *Ballot Blocked: The Political Erosion of the Voting Rights Act.* Stanford, CA: Stanford University Press.

Stanton, Elizabeth Cady. 1898. *Eighty Years and More: Reminiscences, 1815–1897.* New York: T. Fisher Unwin.

Stephenson, Donald Grier, Jr. 2003. *The Waite Court: Justices, Rulings, and Legacy.* Santa Barbara, CA: ABC-CLIO.

White, Ronald C., Jr. 2009. *A. Lincoln: A Biography.* New York: Random House.

Introduction

The first part of this chapter contains data on state felon disenfranchisement laws, state voter ID laws, national voter turnout by sex and age, and a comprehensive table on voter registration practices—registration deadlines, same-day registration, automatic registration, online registration, and mail-in voting—in all fifty states and the District of Columbia.

The second part consists of documents, or excerpts thereof, related to voting rights, including the relevant provisions of the U.S. Constitution; the Declaration of Sentiments from the first women's rights convention in Seneca Falls, New York, in 1848; the Supreme Court decision *Smith* v. *Allwright* (1944); President Lyndon B. Johnson's "We Shall Overcome" speech in 1965; and the Supreme Court decision *Shelby County* v. *Holder* (2013). The documents appear chronologically.

Each entry is preceded by a brief introduction.

Data

Figure 5.1. Felon Disenfranchisement by State

In two states—Maine and Vermont—felons never lose the right to vote. In sixteen states and the District of Columbia,

---

Election officials hand-count ballots in the election of 1924. Until the middle of the twentieth century, election officials typically hand-counted each ballot and tallied the results. Today, automated counting systems are the norm, though manual counting may still be used for audits and contested elections. (Library of Congress)

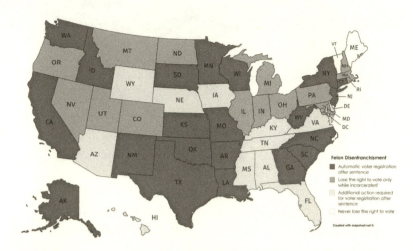

Figure 5.1.

Source: National Conference of State Legislatures. http://www.ncsl.org/research/elections-and-campaigns/felon-voting-rights.aspx

felons lose the franchise only while incarcerated; in these jurisdictions, felons who are on parole or probation are allowed to vote. In twenty-one states, felons lose the right to vote until the completion of their sentences, which includes any time on probation or parole. Finally, eleven states require additional action on the part of ex-felons to regain voting rights. Often, that additional action involves petitioning the governor, or some other designated authority, for reinstatement.

Figure 5.2. Type of Voter ID Law by State

Voter ID laws take many forms and are regularly changing. Nevertheless, the National Conference of State Legislatures (NCSL) categorizes voter ID laws as strict and nonstrict. Strict voter ID laws are those that allow citizens not in possession of ID to cast a provisional ballot, but require the voter to take additional steps after casting the ballot to verify their identity, all within a specified window of time. Nonstrict voter ID laws allow voters to cast a provisional ballot if not in possession of

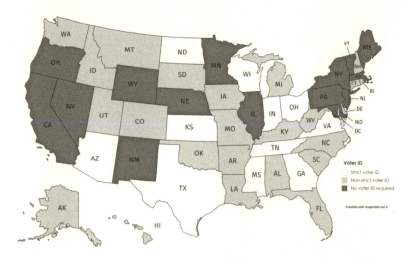

Figure 5.2.

Source: National Conference of State Legislatures (NCSL). http://www.ncsl.org
/research/elections-and-campaigns/voter-id.aspx#Details

proper ID, but election officials will determine, after the vote is
cast, whether the voter is a registered voter.

Table 5.1. Type of Voter ID Required by State

Another distinction is the type of ID the voter is required to present. Of the thirty-five states that mandate ID to vote, seventeen
require a photo ID, and eighteen accept a nonphoto ID. That
leaves fifteen states that do not require any form of ID to vote.

Table 5.1

	Photo ID	Non-photo ID
Strict	Georgia	Arizona
	Indiana	North Dakota
	Kansas	Ohio
	Texas	
	Mississippi	
	Tennessee	
	Virginia	
	Wisconsin	

(Continued)

Table 5.1   (Continued)

	Photo ID	Non-photo ID
Non-strict	Arkansas	Alaska
	Alabama	Colorado
	Florida	Connecticut
	Hawaii	Delaware
	Idaho	Iowa
	Louisiana	Kentucky
	Michigan	Missouri
	Rhode Island	Montana
	South Dakota	New Hampshire
		North Carolina
		Oklahoma
		South Carolina
		Utah
		Washington
		West Virginia

Source: National Conference of State Legislatures. https://www.ncsl.org/research/elections-and-campaigns/voter-id.aspx

Figure 5.3. Voter Turnout by Sex

Starting in 1980, the proportion of eligible female voters who voted in presidential elections exceeded the proportion of eligible male voters who voted. While a slightly higher percentage of women (61.9 percent) voted than men (61.5 percent) in 1980, the gap has increased to approximately four percentage points.

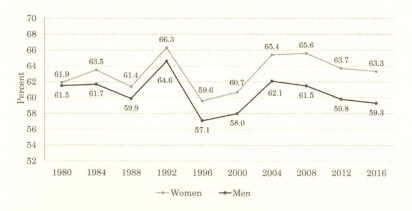

Figure 5.3.

Source: Center for American Women and Politics, Eagleton Institute of Politics, Rutgers University. https://cawp.rutgers.edu/sites/default/files/resources/genderdiff.pdf

In 2016, 63.3 percent of women reported voting while only 59.3 percent of men reported voting. This gap in voter turnout is also present in midterm elections.

Figure 5.4. Voter Turnout by Age

One enduring feature of American elections is that the older you are, the more likely you are to vote. In presidential elections, those sixty years and older vote at very high rates, 60 percent or above. Those eighteen to twenty-nine years of age vote at the lowest rate, often trailing older Americans by twenty to thirty percentage points. While overall voter turnout decreases significantly in midterm elections, voter turnout by age remains consistent.

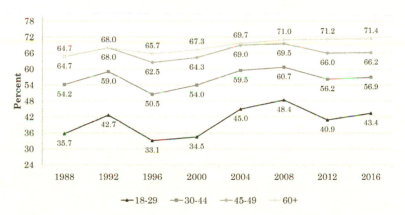

Figure 5.4.

Source: United States Election Project, Michael McDonald. http://www.electproject .org/home/voter-turnout/demographics

Table 5.2. Voter Registration Laws by State

As discussed in chapter 2, states have authority to determine particular voter registration requirements. Nineteen states provided for some form of automatic voter registration (AVR) and thirty-nine states allowed individuals to register to vote online.

Clear differences across the states with regard to registration deadlines are apparent. Currently, twelve states require voter registration materials to be submitted thirty days in advance of the election, at least in some form. On the other extreme, twenty-three states provide for some form of same-day registration. In those states, persons who fail to meet the voter registration deadline can still register on the day they vote.

As of mid-2020, twenty-one states provide for some form of mail-in voting. Four states—Colorado, Oregon, Washington, and Hawaii—use mail-in voting exclusively. (Hawaii began "postal voting" with the 2020 primary election.) The remaining states either permit certain elections to be conducted by mail or allow certain jurisdictions to adopt mail-in voting.

Table 5.2

State	Registration Deadline	Same-day Registration	Automatic Registration	Online Registration	Mail-in Voting
Alabama	15 days prior to election			Yes	
Alaska	30 days prior to election		Yes	Yes	Yes[3]
Arizona	29 days prior to election			Yes	Yes[3]
Arkansas	30 days prior to election				
California	15 days prior to election	Yes	Yes	Yes	Yes[2]
Colorado	8 days prior to election, if registering by mail or online; can pick up ballot if within 8 days of election	Yes	Yes	Yes	Yes[1]
Connecticut	7 days prior to general election; 5 days prior to primary election	Yes	Yes	Yes	
Delaware	4th Saturday prior to election			Yes	
District of Columbia	21 days prior to election	Yes	Yes	Yes	

Table 5.2 (Continued)

State	Registration Deadline	Same-day Registration	Automatic Registration	Online Registration	Mail-in Voting
Florida	29 days prior to election			Yes	Yes[3]
Georgia	28 days prior to election		Yes	Yes	
Hawaii	29 days prior to election	Yes		Yes	Yes[1]
Idaho	25 days prior to election	Yes		Yes	Yes[4]
Illinois	27 days prior to election; 16 days if registering online	Yes	Yes	Yes	
Indiana	28 days prior to election			Yes	
Iowa	10 days prior to general election; 11 days prior to any other election	Yes		Yes	
Kansas	21 days prior to election			Yes	Yes[3]
Kentucky	29 days prior to election			Yes	
Louisiana	30 days prior to election if in person; 20 days prior to election if online			Yes	
Maine	21 days prior to election if by mail	Yes	Yes		
Maryland	21 days prior to election	Yes	Yes	Yes	Yes[3]
Massachusetts	20 days prior to election		Yes	Yes	
Michigan	15 days prior to election; in-person up to election	Yes	Yes		
Minnesota	21 days prior to election	Yes		Yes	Yes[4]
Mississippi	30 days prior to election				

(Continued)

Table 5.2 *(Continued)*

State	Registration Deadline	Same-day Registration	Automatic Registration	Online Registration	Mail-in Voting
Missouri	4th Wednesday prior to election			Yes	Yes[3]
Montana	30 days prior to election; late-registration thereafter	Yes			Yes[3]
Nebraska	3rd Friday prior to election for mail-in registration; 2nd Friday prior to election for in-person registration; 10 days prior to election for online registration			Yes	Yes[2]
Nevada	30 days prior to election for mail-in and in-person registration	Yes	Yes	Yes	Yes[4]
New Hampshire	6 to 13 days prior to the election, depending on the town you live in	Yes			
New Jersey	21 days prior to election		Yes		Yes[4]
New Mexico	28 days prior to election	Yes	Yes	Yes	Yes[4]
New York	25 days prior to election			Yes	
North Carolina	25 days prior to election	Yes			
North Dakota	No voter registration requirements				Yes[2]
Ohio	30 days prior to election			Yes	
Oklahoma	24 days prior to election			Yes	
Oregon	21 days prior to election		Yes	Yes	Yes[1]
Pennsylvania	30 days prior to election			Yes	
Rhode Island	30 days prior to election	Yes, but only for president and vice-president	Yes	Yes	

Table 5.2 (*Continued*)

State	Registration Deadline	Same-day Registration	Automatic Registration	Online Registration	Mail-in Voting
South Carolina	30 days prior to election			Yes	
South Dakota	15 days prior to election				
Tennessee	30 days prior to election			Yes	
Texas	30 days prior to election				
Utah	7 days prior to election if in-person or online; must be postmarked 30 days prior to election if mailed	Yes		Yes	Yes[2]
Vermont	Up to and including election day	Yes	Yes	Yes	
Virginia	22 days prior to regular elections			Yes	
Washington	8 days prior to election for in-person registration; 29 days prior to election for mail-in and online registration	Yes	Yes	Yes	Yes[1]
West Virginia	21 days prior to election		Yes	Yes	
Wisconsin	Friday before election for in-person registration; 20 days prior to election for mail-in and online registration	Yes		Yes	
Wyoming	14 days prior to election	Yes			Yes[3]

[1] All mail-in voting.

[2] Permits counties to opt in to conducting all elections by mail.

[3] Permits some elections to be conducted by mail.

[4] Permits certain jurisdictions, based on population, to be designated as all mail-in.

Source: Compiled using data found on National Conference of State Legislatures (NCSL) website; http://ncsl.org.

Documents

The Constitution of the United States (Sections on Voting Rights)

The Constitution addresses, directly or indirectly, voting rights more than any other subject. Excerpted here are provisions from Article I, Sections 2 and 4, and the Fourteenth, Fifteenth, Seventeenth, Nineteenth, Twenty-Third, Twenty-Fourth, and Twenty-Sixth Amendments. Each of the amendments makes the franchise more inclusive or the electoral process more democratic.

Article I

Section 2. The House of Representatives shall be composed of Members chosen every second Year by the People of the several States, and the Electors in each State shall have the Qualifications requisite for Electors of the most numerous Branch of the State Legislature. . . .

Section 4. The Times, Places and Manner of holding Elections for Senators and Representatives, shall be prescribed in each State by the Legislature thereof; but the Congress may at any time by Law make or alter such Regulations, except as to the Places of chusing Senators. . . .

Amendment XIV (1868)

Section 1. All persons born or naturalized in the United States and subject to the jurisdiction thereof, are citizens of the United States and of the State wherein they reside. No State shall make or enforce any law which shall abridge the privileges or immunities of citizens of the United States; nor shall any State deprive any person of life, liberty, or property, without due process of law; nor deny to any person within its jurisdiction the equal protection of the laws.

Section 2. . . . But when the right to vote at any election for the choice of electors for President and Vice President of the United States, Representatives in Congress, the Executive and Judicial officers of a State, or the members of the Legislature thereof, is denied to any of the male inhabitants of such State, being twenty-one years of age, and citizens of the United States, or in any way abridged, except for participation in rebellion, or other crime, the basis of representation therein shall be reduced in the proportion which the number of such male citizens shall bear to the whole number of male citizens twenty-one years of age in such State. . . .

Section 5. The Congress shall have power to enforce, by appropriate legislation, the provisions of this article.

Amendment XV (1870)

Section 1. The right of citizens of the United States to vote shall not be denied or abridged by the United States or by any State on account of race, color, or previous condition of servitude.

Section 2. The Congress shall have power to enforce this article by appropriate legislation.

Amendment XVII (1913)

The Senate of the United States shall be composed of two Senators from each State, elected by the people thereof, for six years; and each Senator shall have one vote. The electors in each State shall have the qualifications requisite for electors of the most numerous branch of the State legislatures. . . .

Amendment XIX (1920)

The right of citizens of the United States to vote shall not be denied or abridged by the United States or by any State on account of sex.

Congress shall have power to enforce this article by appropriate legislation.

Amendment XXIII (1961)

Section 1. The District constituting the seat of Government of the United States shall appoint in such manner as the Congress may direct:

A number of electors of President and Vice President equal to the whole number of Senators and Representatives in Congress to which the District would be entitled if it were a State, but in no event more than the least populous State; they shall be in addition to those appointed by the States, but they shall be considered, for the purposes of the election of President and Vice President, to be electors appointed by a State; . . . .

Section 2. The Congress shall have power to enforce this article by appropriate legislation.

Amendment XXIV (1964)

Section 1. The right of citizens of the United States to vote in any primary or other election for President or Vice President, for electors for President or Vice President, or for Senator or Representative in Congress, shall not be denied or abridged by the United States or any State by reason of failure to pay any poll tax or other tax.

Section 2. The Congress shall have power to enforce this article by appropriate legislation.

Amendment XXVI (1971)

Section 1. The right of citizens of the United States, who are eighteen years of age or older, to vote shall not be denied or abridged by the United States or by any State on account of age.

Section 2. The Congress shall have power to enforce this article by appropriate legislation.

Source: Charters of Freedom, National Archives.

Declaration of Sentiments (1848)

Adopted by the first women's rights convention in Seneca Falls, New York, this Declaration provided evidence of discrimination against women, including denial of the right to vote, and requested "immediate admission" for women to the rights and privileges of citizenship.

When, in the course of human events, it becomes necessary for one portion of the family of man to assume among the people of the earth a position different from that which they have hitherto occupied, but one to which the laws of nature and of nature's God entitle them, a decent respect to the opinions of mankind requires that they should declare the causes that impel them to such a course.

We hold these truths to be self-evident; that all men and women are created equal; that they are endowed by their Creator with certain inalienable rights; that among these are life, liberty, and the pursuit of happiness; that to secure these rights governments are instituted, deriving their just powers from the consent of the governed. Whenever any form of Government becomes destructive of these ends, it is the right of those who suffer from it to refuse allegiance to it, and to insist upon the institution of a new government, laying its foundation on such principles, and organizing its powers in such form as to them shall seem most likely to effect their safety and happiness. Prudence, indeed, will dictate that governments long established should not be changed for light and transient causes; and accordingly, all experience hath shown that mankind are more disposed to suffer, while evils are sufferable, than to right themselves, by abolishing the forms to which they are accustomed. But when a long train of abuses and usurpations, pursuing invariably the same object, evinces a design to reduce them under absolute despotism, it is their duty to throw off such government, and to provide new guards for their future security. Such has been the patient sufferance of the women under this government, and such is now the necessity which constrains them to demand the equal station to which they are entitled.

The history of mankind is a history of repeated injuries and usurpations on the part of man toward woman, having in direct object the establishment of an absolute tyranny over her. To prove this, let facts be submitted to a candid world.

He has never permitted her to exercise her inalienable right to the elective franchise.

He has compelled her to submit to laws, in the formation of which she had no voice.

He has withheld from her rights which are given to the most ignorant and degraded men—both natives and foreigners.

Having deprived her of this first right of a citizen, the elective franchise, thereby leaving her without representation in the halls of legislation, he has oppressed her on all sides.

He has made her, if married, in the eye of the law, civilly dead.

He has taken from her all right in property, even to the wages she earns.

He has made her, morally, an irresponsible being, as she can commit many crimes, with impunity, provided they be done in the presence of her husband. In the covenant of marriage, she is compelled to promise obedience to her husband, he becoming, to all intents and purposes, her master—the law giving him power to deprive her of her liberty, and to administer chastisement.

He has so framed the laws of divorce, as to what shall be the proper causes of divorce; in case of separation, to whom the guardianship of the children shall be given, as to be wholly regardless of the happiness of women—the law, in all cases, going upon the false supposition of the supremacy of man, and giving all power into his hands.

After depriving her of all rights as a married woman, if single and the owner of property, he has taxed her to support a government which recognizes her only when her property can be made profitable to it.

He has monopolized nearly all the profitable employments, and from those she is permitted to follow, she receives but a scanty remuneration.

He closes against her all the avenues to wealth and distinction, which he considers most honorable to himself. As a teacher of theology, medicine, or law, she is not known.

He has denied her the facilities for obtaining a thorough education—all colleges being closed against her.

He allows her in Church as well as State, but a subordinate position, claiming Apostolic authority for her exclusion from the ministry, and with some exceptions, from any public participation in the affairs of the Church.

He has created a false public sentiment, by giving to the world a different code of morals for men and women, by which moral delinquencies which exclude women from society, are not only tolerated but deemed of little account in man.

He has usurped the prerogative of Jehovah himself, claiming it as his right to assign for her a sphere of action, when that belongs to her conscience and her God.

He has endeavored, in every way that he could to destroy her confidence in her own powers, to lessen her self-respect, and to make her willing to lead a dependent and abject life.

Now, in view of this entire disfranchisement of one-half the people of this country, their social and religious degradation, in view of the unjust laws above mentioned, and because women do feel themselves aggrieved, oppressed, and fraudulently deprived of their most sacred rights, we insist that they have immediate admission to all the rights and privileges which belong to them as citizens of these United States.

In entering upon the great work before us, we anticipate no small amount of misconception, misrepresentation, and ridicule; but we shall use every instrumentality within our power to effect our object. We shall employ agents, circulate tracts, petition the State and national Legislatures, and endeavor to enlist the pulpit and the press in our behalf. We hope this Convention will be followed by a series of Conventions, embracing every part of the country.

Source: Elizabeth Cady Stanton, 1889. *A History of Woman Suffrage*. Vol. 1. Rochester, NY: Fowler and Wells, 70–71.

Smith v. Allwright (1944)

This landmark decision of the Supreme Court invalidated the "white primary," the most effective post–Fifteenth Amendment method devised by Southern legislatures to deny blacks meaningful political participation. In 1932, the Texas Democratic Party

resolved that "all white citizens of the State of Texas who are quali-
fied to vote under the Constitution and laws of the State shall
be eligible to membership in the Democratic Party and, as such,
entitled to participate in its deliberations." It was by virtue of this
resolution that the Democratic Party refused to permit Lonnie
Smith to vote in its primary. The vote was 8–1.

Mr. Justice REED delivered the opinion of the Court.

. . . Texas is free to conduct her elections and limit her electorate as she may deem wise, save only as her action may be
affected by the prohibitions of the United States Constitution
or in conflict with powers delegated to and exercised by the
National Government. The Fourteenth Amendment forbids
a state from making or enforcing any law which abridges the
privileges or immunities of citizens of the United States and
the Fifteenth Amendment specifically interdicts any denial or
abridgement by a state of the right of citizens to vote on account
of color. Respondents . . . defended on the ground that the Democratic party of Texas is a voluntary organization with members
banded together for the purpose of selecting individuals of the
group representing the common political beliefs as candidates
in the general election. As such a voluntary organization, it was
claimed, the Democratic party is free to select its own membership and limit to whites participation in the party primary. Such
action, the answer asserted, does not violate the Fourteenth, Fifteenth or Seventeenth Amendment as officers of government
cannot be chosen at primaries and the Amendments are applicable only to general elections where governmental officers are
actually elected. Primaries, it is said, are political party affairs,
handled by party not governmental officers. . . .

Since *Grovey* v. *Townsend* [1935] . . . [w]e did decide *United
States* v. *Classic* [1941]. . . . We held there that Section 4 of
Article I of the Constitution authorized Congress to regulate
primary as well as general elections "where the primary is by
law made an integral part of the election machinery." . . . *Classic* bears upon *Grovey* . . . not because exclusion of Negroes

from primaries is any more or less state action by reason of the unitary character of the electoral process but because the recognition of the place of the primary in the electoral scheme makes clear that state delegation to a party of the power to fix the qualifications of primary elections is delegation of a state function that may make the party's action the action of the state. When *Grovey* . . . was written, the Court looked upon the denial of a vote in a primary as a mere refusal by a party of party membership. . . . [O]ur ruling in *Classic* as to the unitary character of the electoral process calls for a reexamination as to whether or not the exclusion of Negroes from a Texas party primary was state action. . . .

It may now be taken as a postulate that the right to vote in such a primary for the nomination of candidates without discrimination by the State, like the right to vote in a general election, is a right secured by the Constitution. By the terms of the Fifteenth Amendment that right may not be abridged by any state on account of race. Under our Constitution the great privilege of the ballot may not be denied a man by the State because of his color.

We are thus brought to an examination of the qualifications for Democratic primary electors in Texas, to determine whether state action or private action has excluded Negroes from participation. . . .

Primary elections are conducted by the party under state statutory authority. The county executive committee selects precinct election officials and the county, district or state executive committees, respectively, canvass the returns. These party committees or the state convention certify the party's candidates to the appropriate officers for inclusion on the official ballot for the general election. No name which has not been so certified may appear upon the ballot for the general election as a candidate of a political party. No other name may be printed on the ballot which has not been placed in nomination by qualified voters who must take oath that they did not participate in a primary for the selection of a candidate for the office for which the nomination is made. . . .

We think that this statutory system for the selection of party nominees for inclusion on the general election ballot makes the party which is required to follow these legislative directions an agency of the state in so far as it determines the participants in a primary election. The party takes its character as a state agency from the duties imposed upon it by state statutes; the duties do not become matters of private law because they are performed by a political party. . . . When primaries become a part of the machinery for choosing officials, state and national, as they have here, the same tests to determine the character of discrimination or abridgement should be applied to the primary as are applied to the general election. If the state requires a certain electoral procedure, prescribes a general election ballot made up of party nominees so chosen and limits the choice of the electorate in general elections for state offices, practically speaking, to those whose names appear on such a ballot, it endorses, adopts and enforces the discrimination against Negroes, practiced by a party entrusted by Texas law with the determination of the qualifications of participants in the primary. This is state action within the meaning of the Fifteenth Amendment.

The United States is a constitutional democracy. Its organic law grants to all citizens a right to participate in the choice of elected officials without restriction by any state because of race. This grant to the people of the opportunity for choice is not to be nullified by a state through casting its electoral process in a form which permits a private organization to practice racial discrimination in the election. Constitutional rights would be of little value if they could be thus indirectly denied. . . .

Source: *Smith* v. *Allwright*, 321 U.S. 649 (1944).

Lyndon B. Johnson's "We Shall Overcome" Speech (1965)

This speech was delivered by President Lyndon B. Johnson to a joint session of Congress on March 15, 1965, eight days after the nation witnessed the racial violence in Selma, Alabama. Less than five months later, the president signed the Voting Rights Act, the most comprehensive and consequential voting rights legislation in American history.

I speak tonight for the dignity of man and the destiny of democracy.

I urge every member of both parties, Americans of all religions and of all colors, from every section of this country, to join me in that cause.

At times history and fate meet at a single time in a single place to shape a turning point in man's unending search for freedom. So it was at Lexington and Concord. So it was a century ago at Appomattox. So it was last week in Selma, Alabama.

There, long-suffering men and women peacefully protested the denial of their rights as Americans. Many were brutally assaulted. One good man, a man of God, was killed.

There is no cause for pride in what has happened in Selma. There is no cause for self-satisfaction in the long denial of equal rights of millions of Americans. But there is cause for hope and for faith in our democracy in what is happening here tonight.

For the cries of pain and the hymns and protests of oppressed people have summoned into convocation all the majesty of this great Government—the Government of the greatest Nation on earth.

Our mission is at once the oldest and the most basic of this country: to right wrong, to do justice, to serve man.

In our time we have come to live with moments of great crisis. Our lives have been marked with debate about great issues; issues of war and peace, issues of prosperity and depression. But rarely in any time does an issue lay bare the secret heart of America itself. Rarely are we met with a challenge, not to our growth or abundance, our welfare or our security, but rather to the values and the purposes and the meaning of our beloved Nation.

The issue of equal rights for American Negroes is such an issue. And should we defeat every enemy, should we double our wealth and conquer the stars, and still be unequal to this issue, then we will have failed as a people and as a nation.

For with a country as with a person, "What is a man profited, if he shall gain the whole world, and lose his own soul?"

There is no Negro problem. There is no Southern problem. There is no Northern problem. There is only an American problem. And we are met here tonight as Americans—not as Democrats or Republicans—we are met here as Americans to solve that problem.

This was the first nation in the history of the world to be founded with a purpose. The great phrases of that purpose still sound in every American heart, North and South: "All men are created equal"—"government by consent of the governed"—"give me liberty or give me death." Well, those are not just clever words, or those are not just empty theories. In their name Americans have fought and died for two centuries, and tonight around the world they stand there as guardians of our liberty, risking their lives.

Those words are a promise to every citizen that he shall share in the dignity of man. This dignity cannot be found in a man's possessions; it cannot be found in his power, or in his position. It really rests on his right to be treated as a man equal in opportunity to all others. It says that he shall share in freedom, he shall choose his leaders, educate his children, and provide for his family according to his ability and his merits as a human being.

To apply any other test—to deny a man his hopes because of his color or race, his religion or the place of his birth—is not only to do injustice, it is to deny America and to dishonor the dead who gave their lives for American freedom.

The Right to Vote

Our fathers believed that if this noble view of the rights of man was to flourish, it must be rooted in democracy. The most basic right of all was the right to choose your own leaders. The history of this country, in large measure, is the history of the expansion of that right to all of our people.

Many of the issues of civil rights are very complex and most difficult. But about this there can and should be no argument. Every American citizen must have an equal right to vote. There is no reason which can excuse the denial of that right. There is no duty which weighs more heavily on us than the duty we have to ensure that right.

Yet the harsh fact is that in many places in this country men and women are kept from voting simply because they are Negroes.

Every device of which human ingenuity is capable has been used to deny this right. The Negro citizen may go to register only to be told that the day is wrong, or the hour is late, or the official in charge is absent. And if he persists, and if he manages to present himself to the registrar, he may be disqualified because he did not spell out his middle name or because he abbreviated a word on the application.

And if he manages to fill out an application he is given a test. The registrar is the sole judge of whether he passes this test. He may be asked to recite the entire Constitution, or explain the most complex provisions of State law. And even a college degree cannot be used to prove that he can read and write.

For the fact is that the only way to pass these barriers is to show a white skin.

Experience has clearly shown that the existing process of law cannot overcome systematic and ingenious discrimination. No law that we now have on the books—and I have helped to put three of them there—can ensure the right to vote when local officials are determined to deny it.

In such a case our duty must be clear to all of us. The Constitution says that no person shall be kept from voting because of his race or his color. We have all sworn an oath before God to support and to defend that Constitution. We must now act in obedience to that oath.

Guaranteeing the Right to Vote

Wednesday I will send to Congress a law designed to eliminate illegal barriers to the right to vote.

The broad principles of that bill will be in the hands of the Democratic and Republican leaders tomorrow. After they have reviewed it, it will come here formally as a bill. I am grateful for this opportunity to come here tonight at the invitation of the leadership to reason with my friends, to give them my views, and to visit with my former colleagues.

I have had prepared a more comprehensive analysis of the legislation which I had intended to transmit to the clerk tomorrow but which I will submit to the clerks tonight. But I want to really discuss with you now briefly the main proposals of this legislation.

This bill will strike down restrictions to voting in all elections—Federal, State, and local—which have been used to deny Negroes the right to vote.

This bill will establish a simple, uniform standard which cannot be used, however ingenious the effort, to flout our Constitution.

It will provide for citizens to be registered by officials of the United States Government if the State officials refuse to register them.

It will eliminate tedious, unnecessary lawsuits which delay the right to vote.

Finally, this legislation will ensure that properly registered individuals are not prohibited from voting.

I will welcome the suggestions from all of the Members of Congress—I have no doubt that I will get some—on ways and means to strengthen this law and to make it effective. But experience has plainly shown that this is the only path to carry out the command of the Constitution.

To those who seek to avoid action by their National Government in their own communities; who want to and who seek to maintain purely local control over elections, the answer is simple:

Open your polling places to all your people.

Allow men and women to register and vote whatever the color of their skin.

Extend the rights of citizenship to every citizen of this land.

The Need for Action

There is no constitutional issue here. The command of the Constitution is plain.

There is no moral issue. It is wrong—deadly wrong—to deny any of your fellow Americans the right to vote in this country.

There is no issue of States rights or national rights. There is only the struggle for human rights. I have not the slightest doubt what will be your answer.

The last time a President sent a civil rights bill to the Congress it contained a provision to protect voting rights in Federal elections. That civil rights bill was passed after 8 long months of debate. And when that bill came to my desk from the Congress for my signature, the heart of the voting provision had been eliminated.

This time, on this issue, there must be no delay, no hesitation and no compromise with our purpose.

We cannot, we must not, refuse to protect the right of every American to vote in every election that he may desire to participate in. And we ought not and we cannot and we must not wait another 8 months before we get a bill. We have already waited a hundred years and more, and the time for waiting is gone.

So I ask you to join me in working long hours—nights and weekends, if necessary—to pass this bill. And I don't make that request lightly. For from the window where I sit with the problems of our country I recognize that outside this chamber is the outraged conscience of a nation, the grave concern of many nations, and the harsh judgment of history on our acts.

We Shall Overcome

But even if we pass this bill, the battle will not be over. What happened in Selma is part of a far larger movement which reaches into every section and State of America. It is the effort of American Negroes to secure for themselves the full blessings of American life.

Their cause must be our cause too. Because it is not just Negroes, but really it is all of us, who must overcome the crippling legacy of bigotry and injustice.

And we shall overcome.

As a man whose roots go deeply into Southern soil I know how agonizing racial feelings are. I know how difficult it is to reshape the attitudes and the structure of our society.

But a century has passed, more than a hundred years, since the Negro was freed. And he is not fully free tonight.

It was more than a hundred years ago that Abraham Lincoln, a great President of another party, signed the Emancipation Proclamation, but emancipation is a proclamation and not a fact.

A century has passed, more than a hundred years, since equality was promised. And yet the Negro is not equal.

A century has passed since the day of promise. And the promise is unkept.

The time of justice has now come. I tell you that I believe sincerely that no force can hold it back. It is right in the eyes of man and God that it should come. And when it does, I think that day will brighten the lives of every American.

For Negroes are not the only victims. How many white children have gone uneducated, how many white families have lived in stark poverty, how many white lives have been scarred by fear, because we have wasted our energy and our substance to maintain the barriers of hatred and terror?

So I say to all of you here, and to all in the Nation tonight, that those who appeal to you to hold on to the past do so at the cost of denying you your future.

This great, rich, restless country can offer opportunity and education and hope to all: black and white, North and South, sharecropper and city dweller. These are the enemies: poverty, ignorance, disease. They are the enemies and not our fellow man, not our neighbor. And these enemies too, poverty, disease and ignorance, we shall overcome.

An American Problem

Now let none of us in any sections look with prideful righteousness on the troubles in another section, or on the problems of our neighbors. There is really no part of America where the promise of equality has been fully kept. In Buffalo as well as in Birmingham, in Philadelphia as well as in Selma, Americans are struggling for the fruits of freedom.

This is one Nation. What happens in Selma or in Cincinnati is a matter of legitimate concern to every American. But let each of us look within our own hearts and our own communities, and let each of us put our shoulder to the wheel to root out injustice wherever it exists.

As we meet here in this peaceful, historic chamber tonight, men from the South, some of whom were at Iwo Jima, men from the North who have carried Old Glory to far corners of the world and brought it back without a stain on it, men from the East and from the West, are all fighting together without regard to religion, or color, or region, in Viet-Nam. Men from every region fought for us across the world 20 years ago.

And in these common dangers and these common sacrifices the South made its contribution of honor and gallantry no less than any other region of the great Republic—and in some instances, a great many of them, more.

And I have not the slightest doubt that good men from everywhere in this country, from the Great Lakes to the Gulf of Mexico, from the Golden Gate to the harbors along the Atlantic, will rally together now in this cause to vindicate the freedom of all Americans. For all of us owe this duty; and I believe that all of us will respond to it.

Your President makes that request of every American.

Progress through the Democratic Process

The real hero of this struggle is the American Negro. His actions and protests, his courage to risk safety and even to risk his life, have awakened the conscience of this Nation. His demonstrations have been designed to call attention to injustice, designed to provoke change, designed to stir reform.

He has called upon us to make good the promise of America. And who among us can say that we would have made the same progress were it not for his persistent bravery, and his faith in American democracy.

For at the real heart of battle for equality is a deep-seated belief in the democratic process.

Equality depends not on the force of arms or tear gas but upon the force of moral right; not on recourse to violence but on respect for law and order.

There have been many pressures upon your President and there will be others as the days come and go. But I pledge you tonight that we intend to fight this battle where it should be fought: in the courts, and in the Congress, and in the hearts of men.

We must preserve the right of free speech and the right of free assembly. But the right of free speech does not carry with it, as has been said, the right to holler fire in a crowded theater. We must preserve the right to free assembly, but free assembly does not carry with it the right to block public thoroughfares to traffic.

We do have a right to protest, and a right to march under conditions that do not infringe the constitutional rights of our neighbors. And I intend to protect all those rights as long as I am permitted to serve in this office.

We will guard against violence, knowing it strikes from our hands the very weapons which we seek—progress, obedience to law, and belief in American values.

In Selma as elsewhere we seek and pray for peace. We seek order. We seek unity. But we will not accept the peace of stifled rights, or the order imposed by fear, or the unity that stifles protest. For peace cannot be purchased at the cost of liberty.

In Selma tonight, as in every—and we had a good day there—as in every city, we are working for just and peaceful settlement. We must all remember that after this speech I am making tonight, after the police and the FBI and the Marshals have all gone, and after you have promptly passed this bill, the people of Selma and the other cities of the Nation must still live and work together. And when the attention of the Nation has gone elsewhere they must try to heal the wounds and to build a new community.

This cannot be easily done on a battleground of violence, as the history of the South itself shows. It is in recognition of this that men of both races have shown such an outstandingly impressive responsibility in recent days—last Tuesday, again today.

Rights Must Be Opportunities

The bill that I am presenting to you will be known as a civil rights bill. But, in a larger sense, most of the program I am recommending is a civil rights program. Its object is to open the city of hope to all people of all races.

Because all Americans just must have the right to vote. And we are going to give them that right.

All Americans must have the privileges of citizenship regardless of race. And they are going to have those privileges of citizenship regardless of race.

But I would like to caution you and remind you that to exercise these privileges takes much more than just legal right. It requires a trained mind and a healthy body. It requires a decent home, and the chance to find a job, and the opportunity to escape from the clutches of poverty.

Of course, people cannot contribute to the Nation if they are never taught to read or write, if their bodies are stunted from hunger, if their sickness goes untended, if their life is spent in hopeless poverty just drawing a welfare check.

So we want to open the gates to opportunity. But we are also going to give all our people, black and white, the help that they need to walk through those gates.

The Purpose of This Government

My first job after college was as a teacher in Cotulla, Texas, in a small Mexican-American school. Few of them could speak English, and I couldn't speak much Spanish. My students were poor and they often came to class without breakfast, hungry. They knew even in their youth the pain of prejudice. They never seemed to know why people disliked them. But they knew it was so, because I saw it in their eyes. I often walked home late in the afternoon, after the classes were finished, wishing there was more that I could do. But all I knew was to teach them the little that I knew, hoping that it might help them against the hardships that lay ahead.

Somehow you never forget what poverty and hatred can do when you see its scars on the hopeful face of a young child.

I never thought then, in 1928, that I would be standing here in 1965. It never even occurred to me in my fondest dreams that I might have the chance to help the sons and daughters of those students and to help people like them all over this country.

But now I do have that chance—and I'll let you in on a secret—I mean to use it. And I hope that you will use it with me.

This is the richest and most powerful country which ever occupied the globe. The might of past empires is little compared to ours. But I do not want to be the President who built empires, or sought grandeur, or extended dominion.

I want to be the President who educated young children to the wonders of their world. I want to be the President who helped to feed the hungry and to prepare them to be taxpayers instead of taxeaters.

I want to be the President who helped the poor to find their own way and who protected the right of every citizen to vote in every election.

I want to be the President who helped to end hatred among his fellow men and who promoted love among the people of all races and all regions and all parties.

I want to be the President who helped to end war among the brothers of this earth.

And so at the request of your beloved Speaker and the Senator from Montana; the majority leader, the Senator from Illinois; the minority leader, Mr. McCulloch, and other Members of both parties, I came here tonight—not as President Roosevelt came down one time in person to veto a bonus bill, not as President Truman came down one time to urge the passage of a railroad bill—but I came down here to ask you to share this task with me and to share it with the people that we both work for. I want this to be the Congress, Republicans and Democrats alike, which did all these things for all these people.

Beyond this great chamber, out yonder in 50 States, are the people that we serve. Who can tell what deep and unspoken hopes are in their hearts tonight as they sit there and listen. We all can guess, from our own lives, how difficult they often find their own pursuit of happiness, how many problems each little family has. They look most of all to themselves for their futures. But I think that they also look to each of us.

Above the pyramid on the great seal of the United States it says—in Latin—"God has favored our undertaking."

God will not favor everything that we do. It is rather our duty to divine His will. But I cannot help believing that He truly understands and that He really favors the undertaking that we begin here tonight.

Source: *Public Papers of the Presidents of the United States. Lyndon B. Johnson, 1965, Book 1*. Washington, DC: Government Printing Office, 1966, 281–287.

Shelby County v. *Holder* (2013)

Shelby County, Tennessee, brought action against the attorney general of the United States, challenging Sections 4 and 5 of the Voting Rights Act. Section 4 established a "coverage formula" to determine which states and local governments fell under Section 5, which required covered jurisdictions to demonstrate that proposed voting law changes were not discriminatory. The Supreme Court struck down Section 4. The vote was 5–4.

Chief Justice ROBERTS delivered the opinion of the Court.

The Voting Rights Act of 1965 employed extraordinary measures to address an extraordinary problem. . . . This was strong medicine, but Congress determined it was needed to address entrenched racial discrimination in voting, "an insidious and pervasive evil which had been perpetuated in certain parts of our country through unremitting and ingenious defiance of the Constitution." . . . There is no denying, however, that the conditions that originally justified these measures no longer characterize voting in the covered jurisdictions. By 2009, "the racial gap in voter registration and turnout [was] lower in the States originally covered by §5 than it [was] nationwide." Since that time, Census Bureau data indicate that African-American voter turnout has come to exceed white voter turnout in five of the six States originally covered by §5, with a gap in the sixth State of less than one half of one percent.

At the same time, voting discrimination still exists; no one doubts that. The question is whether the Act's extraordinary measures, including its disparate treatment of the States, continue to satisfy constitutional requirements.

The Constitution and laws of the United States are "the supreme Law of the Land." State legislation may not contravene federal law. The Federal Government does not, however, have a general right to review and veto state enactments before they go into effect. A proposal to grant such authority to "negative" state laws was considered at the Constitutional Convention, but rejected in favor of allowing state laws to take effect, subject to later challenge under the Supremacy Clause.

Outside the strictures of the Supremacy Clause, States retain broad autonomy in structuring their governments and pursuing legislative objectives. Indeed, the Constitution provides that all powers not specifically granted to the Federal Government are reserved to the States or citizens. . . .

Not only do States retain sovereignty under the Constitution, there is also a "fundamental principle of *equal* sovereignty" among the States. . . .

The Voting Rights Act sharply departs from these basic principles. It suspends "*all* changes to state election law—however innocuous—until they have been precleared by federal authorities in Washington, D.C." States must beseech the Federal Government for permission to implement laws that they would otherwise have the right to enact and execute on their own, subject of course to any injunction. . . .

And despite the tradition of equal sovereignty, the Act applies to only nine States (and several additional counties). . . .

In 1966, we found these departures from the basic features of our system of government justified. The "blight of racial discrimination in voting" had "infected the electoral process in parts of our country for nearly a century." Several States had enacted a variety of requirements and tests "specifically designed to prevent" African-Americans from voting. Case-by-case litigation had proved inadequate to prevent such racial discrimination in voting, in part because States "merely switched to discriminatory devices not covered by the federal decrees," "enacted difficult new tests," or simply "defied and evaded court orders." Shortly before enactment of the Voting Rights Act, only 19.4 percent of African-Americans of voting age were registered to vote in Alabama, only 31.8 percent in Louisiana, and only 6.4 percent in Mississippi. Those figures were roughly 50 percentage points or more below the figures for whites. . . .

Nearly 50 years later, things have changed dramatically. . . . In the covered jurisdictions, "[v]oter turnout and registration rates now approach parity. Blatantly discriminatory evasions of federal decrees are rare. And minority candidates hold office at unprecedented levels." The tests and devices that blocked access to the ballot have been forbidden nationwide for over 40 years. Those conclusions are not ours alone. Congress said the same when it reauthorized the Act in 2006. . . .

There is no doubt that these improvements are in large part *because of* the Voting Rights Act. The Act has proved immensely successful at redressing racial discrimination and integrating the voting process. . . . Yet the Act has not eased the restrictions in §5 or narrowed the scope of the coverage formula in §4(b) along the way. . . .

Respondents do not deny that there have been improvements on the ground, but argue that much of this can be attributed to the deterrent effect of §5, which dissuades covered jurisdictions from engaging in discrimination that they would resume should §5 be struck down. Under this theory, however, §5 would be effectively immune from scrutiny; no matter how "clean" the record of covered jurisdictions, the argument could always be made that it was deterrence that accounted for the good behavior.

The provisions of §5 apply only to those jurisdictions singled out by §4. We now consider whether that coverage formula is constitutional in light of current conditions. . . .

Coverage today is based on decades-old data and eradicated practices. The formula captures States by reference to literacy tests and low voter registration and turnout in the 1960s and early 1970s. But such tests have been banned nationwide for over 40 years. And voter registration and turnout numbers in the covered States have risen dramatically in the years since. Racial disparity in those numbers was compelling evidence justifying the preclearance remedy and the coverage formula. There is no longer such a disparity.

In 1965, the States could be divided into two groups: those with a recent history of voting tests and low voter registration and turnout, and those without those characteristics. Congress based its coverage formula on that distinction. Today the Nation is no longer divided along those lines, yet the Voting Rights Act continues to treat it as if it were.

The Government falls back to the argument that because the formula was relevant in 1965, its continued use is permissible so long as any discrimination remains in the States Congress identified back then—regardless of how that discrimination compares to discrimination in States unburdened by coverage. . . . But history did not end in 1965. By the time the Act was reauthorized in 2006, there had been 40 more years of it. In assessing the "current need [ ]" for a preclearance system that treats States differently from one another today, that history cannot be ignored. During that time, largely because of the Voting Rights Act, voting tests were abolished, disparities in voter registration and turnout due to race were erased, and African–Americans attained political office in record numbers. And yet the coverage formula that Congress reauthorized in 2006 ignores these developments, keeping the focus on decades-old data relevant to decades-old problems, rather than current data reflecting current needs.

The Fifteenth Amendment commands that the right to vote shall not be denied or abridged on account of race or color, and it gives Congress the power to enforce that command. The Amendment is not designed to punish for the past; its purpose is to ensure a better future. . . . To serve that purpose, Congress— if it is to divide the States—must identify those jurisdictions to be singled out on a basis that makes sense in light of current conditions. It cannot rely simply on the past. . . .

There is no valid reason to insulate the coverage formula from review merely because it was previously enacted 40 years ago. If Congress had started from scratch in 2006, it plainly could not have enacted the present coverage formula. It would have been irrational for Congress to distinguish between States in such a fundamental way based on 40-year-old data, when today's statistics tell an entirely different story. And it would have been irrational to base coverage on the use of voting tests

40 years ago, when such tests have been illegal since that time. But that is exactly what Congress has done. . . .

Our decision in no way affects the permanent, nationwide ban on racial discrimination in voting found in §2. We issue no holding on §5 itself, only on the coverage formula. Congress may draft another formula based on current conditions. Such a formula is an initial prerequisite to a determination that exceptional conditions still exist justifying such an "extraordinary departure from the traditional course of relations between the States and the Federal Government." Our country has changed, and while any racial discrimination in voting is too much, Congress must ensure that the legislation it passes to remedy that problem speaks to current conditions.

Justice GINSBURG, dissenting.

In the Court's view, the very success of §5 of the Voting Rights Act demands its dormancy. Congress was of another mind. Recognizing that large progress has been made, Congress determined, based on a voluminous record, that the scourge of discrimination was not yet extirpated. The question this case presents is who decides whether, as currently operative, §5 remains justifiable, this Court, or a Congress charged with the obligation to enforce the post–Civil War Amendments "by appropriate legislation." With overwhelming support in both Houses, Congress concluded that, for two prime reasons, §5 should continue in force, unabated. First, continuance would facilitate completion of the impressive gains thus far made; and second, continuance would guard against back sliding. Those assessments were well within Congress' province to make and should elicit this Court's unstinting approbation.

"[V]oting discrimination still exists; no one doubts that." But the Court today terminates the remedy that proved to be best suited to block that discrimination. The Voting Rights Act of 1965 (VRA) has worked to combat voting discrimination where other remedies had been tried and failed. Particularly effective is the VRA's requirement of federal preclearance for all changes to voting laws in the regions of the country with the most aggravated records of rank discrimination against minority voting rights.

A century after the Fourteenth and Fifteenth Amendments guaranteed citizens the right to vote free of discrimination on the basis of race, the "blight of racial discrimination in voting" continued to "infec[t] the electoral process in parts of our country." Early attempts to cope with this vile infection resembled battling the Hydra. Whenever one form of voting discrimination was identified and prohibited, others sprang up in its place. This Court repeatedly encountered the remarkable "variety and persistence" of laws disenfranchising minority citizens. . . .

Congress learned from experience that laws targeting particular electoral practices or enabling case-by-case litigation were inadequate to the task. In the Civil Rights Acts of 1957, 1960, and 1964, Congress authorized and then expanded the power of "the Attorney General to seek injunctions against public and private interference with the right to vote on racial grounds." But circumstances reduced the ameliorative potential of these legislative Acts:

Voting suits are unusually onerous to prepare, some times requiring as many as 6,000 man-hours spent combing through registration records in preparation for trial. Litigation has been exceedingly slow, in part because of the ample opportunities for delay afforded voting officials and others involved in the proceedings. Even when favorable decisions have finally been obtained, some of the States affected have merely switched to discriminatory devices not covered by the federal decrees or have enacted difficult new tests designed to prolong the existing disparity between white and Negro registration. Alternatively, certain local officials have defied and evaded court orders or have simply closed their registration offices to freeze the voting rolls.

Patently, a new approach was needed. . . .

After a century's failure to fulfill the promise of the Fourteenth and Fifteenth Amendments, passage of the VRA finally led to signal improvement on this front. . . . [I]n assessing the overall effects of the VRA in 2006, Congress found that "[s]ignificant progress has been made in eliminating first generation barriers experienced by minority voters, including increased numbers of registered minority voters, minority voter turnout, and minority representation in Congress, State legislatures, and local elected offices. This progress is the direct result of the Voting Rights Act of 1965." On that matter of cause and effects there can be no genuine doubt. . . .

. . . Congress reauthorized preclearance for another 25 years, while also undertaking to reconsider the extension after 15 years to ensure that the provision was still necessary and effective. The question before the Court is whether Congress had the authority under the Constitution to act as it did.

In answering this question, the Court does not write on a clean slate. It is well established that Congress' judgment regarding exercise of its power to enforce the Fourteenth and Fifteenth Amendments warrants substantial deference. The VRA addresses the combination of race discrimination and the right to vote, which is "preservative of all rights." When confronting the most constitutionally invidious form of discrimination, and the most fundamental right in our democratic system, Congress' power to act is at its height. . . .

It cannot tenably be maintained that the VRA, an Act of Congress adopted to shield the right to vote from racial discrimination, is inconsistent with the letter or spirit of the Fifteenth Amendment, or any provision of the Constitution read in light of the Civil War Amendments. Nowhere in today's opinion . . . is there clear recognition of the transformative effect the Fifteenth Amendment aimed to achieve. Notably, "the Founders' first successful amendment told Congress that it could 'make no law' over a certain domain"; in contrast, the Civil War Amendments used "language [that] authorized transformative new federal statutes to uproot all vestiges of unfreedom and inequality" and provided "sweeping enforcement powers . . . to enact 'appropriate' legislation targeting state abuses."

The stated purpose of the Civil War Amendments was to arm Congress with the power and authority to protect all persons within the Nation from violations of their rights by the States. In exercising that power, then, Congress may use "all means which are appropriate, which are plainly adapted" to the constitutional ends declared by these Amendments. So when Congress acts to enforce the right to vote free from racial discrimination, we ask not whether Congress has chosen the means most wise, but whether Congress has rationally selected means appropriate to a legitimate end. . . .

Until today, in considering the constitutionality of the VRA, the Court has accorded Congress the full measure of respect its judgments in this domain should garner. . . .

[T]he Constitution vests broad power in Congress to protect the right to vote, and in particular to combat racial discrimination in voting. This Court has repeatedly reaffirmed Congress' prerogative to use any rational means in exercise of its power in this area. . . .

Congress approached the 2006 reauthorization of the VRA with great care and seriousness. The same cannot be said of the Court's opinion today. The Court makes no genuine attempt to engage with the massive legislative record that Congress assembled. Instead, it relies on increases in voter registration and turnout as if that were the whole story. . . . [T]he Court dismissively brushes off arguments based on "data from the record," and declines to enter the "debat[e about] what [the] record shows" One would expect more from an opinion striking at the heart of the Nation's signal piece of civil-rights legislation. . . .

Given a record replete with examples of denial or abridgment of a paramount federal right, the Court should have left the matter where it belongs: in Congress' bailiwick. Instead, the Court strikes §4(b)'s coverage provision because, in its view, the provision is not based on "current conditions." It discounts, however, that one such condition was the preclearance remedy in place in the covered jurisdictions, a remedy Congress designed both to catch discrimination before it causes harm, and to guard against return to old ways. Volumes of evidence supported Congress' determination that the prospect of retrogression was real. Throwing out preclearance when it has worked and is continuing to work to stop discriminatory changes is like throwing away your umbrella in a rainstorm because you are not getting wet. . . .

The Court holds §4(b) invalid on the ground that it is "irrational to base coverage on the use of voting tests 40 years ago, when such tests have been illegal since that time." But the Court disregards what Congress set about to do in enacting the VRA. That extraordinary legislation scarcely stopped at the particular tests and devices that happened to exist in 1965. The grand aim of the Act is to secure to all in our polity equal citizenship stature, a voice in our democracy undiluted by race. As the record for the 2006 reauthorization makes abundantly clear, second-generation barriers to minority voting rights have emerged in the covered jurisdictions as attempted *substitutes* for the first-generation barriers that originally triggered preclearance in those jurisdictions.

The sad irony of today's decision lies in its utter failure to grasp why the VRA has proven effective. The Court appears to believe that the VRA's success in eliminating the specific devices extant in 1965 means that preclearance is no longer needed. With that belief, and the argument derived from it, history repeats itself. . . .

Source: *Shelby County v. Holder*, 570 U.S. 2 (2013).

6 Resources

This chapter begins with an annotated bibliography of print resources related to voting rights. It also includes a table of all cases referenced in the text, with full citations, and an explanatory note on legal citations and accessing judicial decisions. The chapter concludes with internet resources on voting and elections, a brief description of forty alphabetically listed public and private organizations with an interest in voting or elections and their website addresses.

Annotated Bibliography

Alexander, Robert M. 2019. *Representation and the Electoral College*. New York: Oxford University Press.
>   Examines how the Electoral College has evolved from its founding through the 2016 election through the lens of representation and federalism.

Alvarez, R. Michael, Delia Bailey, and Jonathan N. Katz. 2008. "The Effect of Voter Identification Laws on Turnout." *California Institute of Technology Social Science Working Paper 1267R.* January. https://papers.ssrn.com/sol3/papers.cfm?abstract_id=1084598

With the punchcard voting system, voters use a special pen to punch holes in the ballot next to the names of their preferred candidates. States updated their voting technology after the 2000 disputed presidential election, when two key Florida counties used poorly designed punchcard ballots, resulting in electoral uncertainty in that state, and thus the nation. (iStockPhoto.com)

Using data from the 2000 and 2004 presidential elections and the 2002 and 2006 midterm elections, this paper concludes that state voter ID laws had no effect on voter participation.

Amar, Akhil Reed. 2005. *America's Constitution: A Biography*. New York: Random House.
The "life story" of the U.S. Constitution, explaining what it says and why it says it.

Anderson, Carol. 2018. *One Person, No Vote: How Voter Suppression Is Destroying Our Democracy*. New York: Bloomsbury Publishing.
Examines modern efforts to disenfranchise racial and ethnic minorities, including voter ID laws, purging of voter rolls, and gerrymandering.

Annbinder, Tyler G. 1992. *Nativism and Slavery: The Northern Know Nothings and the Politics of the 1850s*. New York: Oxford University Press.
The rise, tenure, and fall of the Know-Nothings, the most prominent anti-immigrant movement in American history. Suggests the movement's success was partly due to its antislavery sentiment, and credits the infusion of the Know-Nothings into the Republican Party as transforming the Republicans into the dominant political party.

Baldino, Thomas J., and Kyle L. Kreider. 2010. *Of the People, By the People, for the People: A Documentary History of Voting Rights and Electoral Reform*. 2 vols. Santa Barbara, CA: Greenwood Press.
Presents the evolution of U.S. election law through historical documents, including colonial charters, state laws, municipal ordinances, party rules, constitutional amendments, and Supreme Court decisions.

Bardolph, Richard, ed. 1970. *The Civil Rights Record: Black Americans and the Law, 1849–1970.* New York: Thomas Y. Crowell.
 A collection of laws, cases, and other documents on civil rights, many of which deal with the struggle of blacks to earn the franchise.

Beard, Charles. 1913. *An Economic Interpretation of the Constitution.* New York: The Macmillan Company.
 Argues that the framers of the U.S. Constitution were motivated primarily by their economic interests and sought to protect their personal property and financial standing.

Beeman, Richard. 2009. *Plain, Honest Men: The Making of the American Constitution.* New York: Random House.
 An engaging and authoritative narrative of the Constitutional Convention, among the best ever written.

Bennett, David H. 1988. *The Party of Fear: From Nativist Movements to the New Right in American History.* Chapel Hill, NC: The University of North Carolina Press.
 Looks at anti-immigrant movements in U.S. history, including the rise and influence of the Know-Nothing political party of the 1850s.

Berman, Ari. 2015. *Give Us the Ballot: The Modern Struggle for Voting Rights in America.* New York: Picador.
 Discusses the importance of the Voting Rights Act, twenty-first-century attempts to deny suffrage, and the fragility of the right to vote.

Berman, Ari. 2016. "The GOP's War on Voting Is Working." *The Nation,* 29 June. https://www.thenation.com/article/archive/the-gops-war-on-voting-is-working/
 Inspects how Wisconsin and Minnesota, despite their cultural and political similarities, diverged with respect to voter ID laws and voting rights legislation.

Binnall, James. 2017. "Summonsing Criminal Desistance: Convicted Felons' Perspectives on Jury Service." *Law and Social Inquiry*, Vol. 43 (1): 4–27.

> Using interviews from ex-felon jurors in Maine, the only state that allows ex-felons to serve on juries, argues that jury service provides ex-felons an enhanced sense of self-worth, democratic commitment, and encourages prosocial behavior.

Blackstone, Sir William. [1765–1769] 1872. *Commentaries on the Laws of England*. 4 vols. Chicago, IL: Callaghan and Company.

> The most influential law book and primary legal authority for eighteenth- and nineteenth-century lawyers in the United States.

Bowen, Catherine Drinker. 1966. *Miracle at Philadelphia: The Story of the Constitutional Convention, May to September 1787*. Boston, MA: Little, Brown and Company.

> A hagiographic narrative of the Constitutional Convention taken from newspapers, diaries, and letters and utterances of delegates.

Buhle, Mari Jo, and Paul Buhle, eds. 1978. *The Concise History of Woman Suffrage: Selections from the Classic Work of Stanton, Anthony, Gage, and Harper*. Urbana, IL: University of Illinois Press.

> A collection of materials relevant to the campaign for female suffrage, with selections drawn for the six-volume *History of Woman Suffrage*, compiled by Elizabeth Cady Stanton, Susan B. Anthony, and others.

"Building Confidence in U.S. Elections: Report of the Commission on Federal Election Reform." 2005. https://www.legislationline.org/download/id/1472/file/3b50795b2d0374cbef5c29766256.pdf

Provides recommendations on modernizing American elections and instilling confidence in the American electoral system.

Burden, Barry C., David T. Canon, Kenneth R. Mayer, and Donald P. Moynihan. 2014. "Election Laws, Mobilization, and Turnout: The Unanticipated Consequences of Election Reform." *American Journal of Political Science*, Vol. 58 (1): 95–109.
Evaluates electoral reforms and their effects on voter mobilization, concluding that in-person early voting does not increase voter turnout by itself, while attributing same-day voter registration to more significant voter turnout.

Cashin, Maria Hoyt. 2012. *Sustaining the League of Women Voters in America*. Washington, DC: New Academia Publishing.
Examines the history and role of the League of Women Voters.

Catt, Carrie C., and Nettie R. Shuler. 1923. *Woman Suffrage and Politics: The Inner Story of the Suffrage Movement*. New York: Charles Scribner's Sons.
Written just after the ratification of the Nineteenth Amendment, the two second-generation suffragists provide a contemporary history of the campaign "to the gates of political enfranchisement."

Chute, Marchette. 1969. *The First Liberty: A History of the Right to Vote in America, 1619–1850*. New York: E. P. Dutton.
Considers voting rights from the colonial period to the mid-nineteenth century, including the rise and fall of property requirements.

Clegg, Roger, George T. Conway, III, and Kenneth K. Lee. 2006. "The Bullet and the Ballot—The Case for Felon

Disenfranchisement Statutes." *American University Journal of Gender Social Policy and the Law*, Vol. 14: 1–26.
> Argues that state felon disenfranchisement laws are constitutional and have significant historical support.

Cooper, John Milton, Jr. 2007. *Woodrow Wilson: A Biography*. New York: Alfred Knopf.
> A biography of the twenty-eighth president, including a discussion of his role in pushing for the Nineteenth Amendment.

Cottrell, David, Michael C. Herron, and Sean J. Westwood. 2018. "A Rigged Election? Evaluating Donald Trump's Claims of Massive Voter Fraud in the 2016 Presidential Election." *Electoral Studies*, Vol. 51: 123–142.
> Using aggregate election statistics, concludes that massive voter fraud, as alleged by President Donald Trump, did not occur.

Crotty, William J. 1977. *Political Reform and the American Experiment*. New York: Thomas Y. Crowell.
> The first chapter provides a concise look at the evolution of the franchise, concluding that reform efforts should press for the broadest electorate possible.

Cruikshank, Alfred B. 1920. *Popular Misgovernment in the United States*. New York: Moffat, Yard.
> Discusses the failures and dangers of universal suffrage, claiming that the oldest and best of American traditions favor restricted suffrage.

Cushman, Claire, ed. 2013. *The Supreme Court Justices: Illustrated Biographies, 1789–2012*. Washington, DC: CQ Press.
> A useful resource on justices of the Supreme Court.

Daley, David. 2016. *Ratf**ked: The True Story behind the Secret Plan to Steal America's Democracy*. New York: Liveright.

Story of the 2010 Republican scheme—called REDMAP, for Redistricting Majority Project—to use the provisions of the Voting Rights Act governing majority–minority districts to pack as many Democratic voters as possible in a single congressional district, and bleach the surrounding districts whiter and more Republican.

Davidson, Chandler, and Bernard Grofman, eds. 1994. *Quiet Revolution in the South: The Impact of the 1965 Voting Rights Act, 1965–1990*. Princeton, NJ: Princeton University Press.
A compilation of essays on the effect of the Voting Rights Act in its first quarter century.

de Alth, Shelley. 2008. "ID at the Polls: Assessing the Impact of Recent State Voter ID Laws on Voter Turnout." *Harvard Law & Policy Review*, Vol. 3: 185–202.
Examines the impact that voter ID laws had on nationwide voter turnout between 2002 and 2006, concluding that photo and nonphoto ID laws decreased voter turnout between 1.6 percent and 2.2 percent.

DeClerico, Robert E. 2004. *Voting in America: A Reference Handbook*. Santa Barbara, CA: ABC-CLIO.
A solid reference work on voting rights, voting practices, and voting controversies.

DeCrescenzo, Michael G., and Kenneth R. Mayer. 2019. "Supporting Information: Estimating the Effect of Voter ID on Nonvoters in Wisconsin in the 2016 Presidential Election." *Election Law Journal*. https://doi.org/10.1089/elj.2018.0536.
Analyzes the effect of Wisconsin's voter ID law in the 2016 presidential election.

Donald, David Herbert. 1995. *Lincoln*. New York: Simon and Schuster.
The modern-day definitive and highly readable biography of the sixteenth president.

Doughty, Howard. 1962. *Francis Parkman*. New York: Macmillan.
> Biography of the American historian, political reformer, critic of democracy, and outspoken opponent of universal suffrage.

Dubois, Ellen Carol. 1978. *Feminism and Suffrage: The Emergence of an Independent Women's Movement in America*. Ithaca, NY: Cornell University Press.
> A modern account of the women's suffrage movement, written by a self-professed feminist.

Elliot, Jonathan. 1859. *Debates on the Adoption of the Federal Constitution, in the Convention held at Philadelphia, in 1787, with a diary of the debate of the Congress of the Confederacy; as reported by James Madison, a member, and deputy from Virginia*. 5 vols. Philadelphia, PA: J. B. Lippincott and Company.
> A massive compilation of the documentary records of the Constitutional Convention.

Elliott, Ward E. Y. 1974. *The Rise of Guardian Democracy: The Supreme Court's Role in Voting Rights Disputes, 1845–1969*. Cambridge, MA: Harvard University Press.
> Chronicles the Supreme Court's intervention in voting right cases, especially after 1937, and the effect of that involvement on American democracy.

Fager, Charles F. 1974. *Selma, 1965*. New York: Charles Scribner's Sons.
> Retelling of the event that led to the Voting Rights Act of 1965.

Fairman, Charles. 1971. *Reconstruction and Reunion 1864–88, Part One—History of the Supreme Court of the United States*. Vol. 6. New York: Macmillan.
> Explores the role and significance of the Supreme Court during the chief justiceship of Morrison R. Waite, in which

the Court grappled with the new liberties proclaimed by the Reconstruction Amendments and the federal structure bequeathed by the Constitution. Part of the Oliver Wendell Holmes Devise History of the Supreme Court.

Fairman, Charles. 1988. *Five Justices and the Electoral Commission of 1877—History of the Supreme Court of the United States: Supplement to Volume VII*. New York: Macmillan.
Part of the Oliver Wendell Holmes Devise History of the Supreme Court, this volume chronicles the role of five Supreme Court justices, with particular emphasis on Justice Joseph Bradley, in resolving the disputed presidential election of 1876.

Farrand, Max, ed. 1966. *The Records of the Federal Convention of 1787*. 4 vols. New Haven, CT: Yale University Press.
Collections of speeches as reported by the delegates to the Constitutional Convention, together with elaborately footnoted letters and remarks made later.

Fellner, Jamie, and Marc Mauer. 1998. *Losing the Vote: The Impact of Felony Disenfranchisement Laws in the United States*. Washington, DC: The Sentencing Project.
Analysis of the effect of laws that denied the ballot to persons convicted of serious crimes.

Firth, C. H., ed. 1891. *The Clarke Papers*. New Series XLIX, Vol. 1. London: The Camden Society.
Full transcripts of the consequential debates at Putney, near London, in 1647.

Fletcher, George. 2001. *Our Secret Constitution: How Lincoln Redefined American Democracy*. New York: Oxford University Press.
Examines how Abraham Lincoln used the Civil War to recast the central meaning of the Constitution, from liberty to equality.

Flexnor, Eleanor, and Ellen Fitzpatrick. 1996. *Century of Struggle: The Women's Rights Movement in the United States*. Cambridge, MA: Harvard University Press.
>   A well-documented history of woman suffrage.

Fogel, Robert William. 1994. *Without Consent or Contract: The Rise and Fall of American Slavery*. New York: W. W. Norton.
>   Recounts the rise of slavery and the transformation of the abolitionist movement into a politically powerful force.

Foner, Eric. 2000. "Reconstruction: Change or Stasis?" *Interpretations of American History: Patterns and Perspectives*. 7 vols. Edited by Francis G. Couvares, Martha Saxton, Gerald N. Grob, and George Athon Billias. New York: Free Press, vol. 1: 381–416.
>   Summarizes the three competing historical schools of thought about Reconstruction.

Foner, Eric. 2014. *Reconstruction: America's Unfinished Revolution, 1863–1877*. New York: Harper Collins.
>   The definitive history of the post–Civil War era, from the Emancipation Proclamation to the Compromise of 1877, in which the federal government attempted to protect the civil rights of the former slaves.

Foner, Eric. 2019. *The Second Founding: How the Civil War and Reconstruction Remade the Constitution*. New York: W. W. Norton.
>   Traces the history of the Thirteenth, Fourteenth, and Fifteenth Amendments from their origins to their virtual nullification in the late nineteenth century as a result of Supreme Court decisions.

Fridlington, Robert. 1987. *The Reconstruction Court, 1864–1888*. Millwood, NY: Associated Faculty Press.

A reference work on the events and decisions of the Supreme Court under the chief justiceships of Salmon P. Chase (1864–1873) and Morrison R. Waite (1873–1888).

Fuentes-Rohwer, Luis, and Charles E. Guy-Uriel. 2007. "The Politics of Pre-clearance." *Michigan Journal of Race and Law*, Vol. 12 (4): 514–535.
Studies the degree to which politics has affected Section 5 preclearance process, concluding that politics have not played a significant role in Attorney General enforcement of the Act, at least up until the Clinton Administration.

Garrow, David J. 1978. *Protest at Selma: Martin Luther King, Jr., and the Voting Rights Act of 1965*. New Haven, CT: Yale University Press.
The story of the Selma-to-Montgomery march, the event that resulted in the passage of the most important voting rights bill in U.S. history.

Gienapp, William E. 1987. *Origins of the Republican Party: 1852–1856*. New York: Oxford University Press.
A political history of the 1850s, showing how the anti-slavery movement transformed American political parties.

Gienapp, William E. 2002. *Abraham Lincoln and Civil War America: A Biography*. New York: Oxford University Press.
A concise biography of the sixteenth president.

Goel, Shared, Marc Meredith, Michael Morse, David Rothschild, and Houshmand Shirani-Mehr. 2020. "One Person, One Vote: Estimating the Prevalence of Double Voting in U.S. Presidential Elections." *American Political Science Review*, Vol. 114 (2): 456–469.
Examines the incidences of double-voting in America, finding the problem to be less pervasive than is often reported in the media.

Goldman, Robert. 2001. *Reconstruction and Black Suffrage: Losing the Vote in Reese and Cruikshank*. Lawrence, KS: University Press of Kansas.
> Analysis of two consequential Supreme Court decisions during Reconstruction, giving sufficient attention to the role federalism played in resolving those constitutional disputes.

Graham, Sara Hunter. 1996. *Women's Suffrage and the New Democracy*. New Haven, CT: Yale University Press.
> Chronicles how the National American Woman Suffrage Association (NAWSA) became one of the most effective single-issue interest groups in American history.

Greenberg, Jack. 1994. *Crusaders in the Court: How a Dedicated Band of Lawyers Fought for the Civil Rights Revolution*. New York: Basic Books.
> Memoir of a lawyer with the Legal Defense Fund of the National Association for the Advancement of Colored People (NAACP); the author participated in dozens of lawsuits demanding the nondiscriminatory administration of voting requirements.

Gronke, Paul, Eva Galanes-Rosenbaum, and Peter A. Miller. 2007. "Early Voting and Turnout." *PS: Political Science and Politics*, Vol. 40 (4): 639–645.
> Investigates the effect that various methods of early voting have on voter turnout, concluding that most methods do not increase voter turnout; and that voting-by-mail in Oregon increases voter turnout in presidential elections.

Gurko, Miriam. 1974. *The Ladies of Seneca Falls: The Birth of the Women's Rights Movement*. New York: Schocken Books, Inc.
> A brief history of the early years of the women's rights movement, with particular emphasis on the women responsible for starting the movement.

Hacker, Andrew. 1964. *Congressional Districting*. Washington, DC: Brookings Institute.

> A constitutional and historical background of congressional districting prior to the Supreme Court's intervention in 1964.

Hajnal, Zoltan, Nazita Lajevardi, and Lindsay Nielson. 2017. "Voter Identification Laws and the Suppression of Minority Votes." *The Journal of Politics*, Vol. 79 (2): 363–379.

> Examines the effect of voter ID laws on voter turnout, concluding that they decrease voter turnout of racial and ethnic minorities particularly.

Hamilton, Alexander, James Madison, and John Jay. [1787–1788] 1961. *The Federalist Papers*. Edited by Clinton Rossiter. New York: Mentor.

> Includes the eighty-five essays by Alexander Hamilton, James Madison, and John Jay, written in the 1780s, urging ratification of the proposed Constitution.

Hamilton, Charles V. 1973. *The Bench and the Ballot: Southern Federal Judges and Black Voters*. New York: Oxford University Press.

> Recounts the role of southern federal judges in voting rights cases in the 1950s and 1960s.

Hasen, Richard L. 2003. *The Supreme Court and Election Law: Judging Equality from* Baker *v.* Carr *to* Bush *v.* Gore. New York: New York University Press.

> Shows how the Supreme Court has resolved various types of voting rights cases in the last four decades of the twentieth century.

Hasen, Richard L. 2012. *The Voting Wars: From Florida 2000 to the Next Election Meltdown*. New Haven, CT: Yale University Press.

Investigates the causes and consequences of perpetual partisan disputes over election law and how the growth of social media is likely to make the problem worse moving forward; also addresses various reform ideas designed to de-escalate partisan voting wars.

Hasen, Richard L. 2016. "Softening Voter ID Laws through Litigation? Is It Enough?" *Wisconsin Law Review Forward*, 1: 100–121.
    Looks at the legal landscape, post-*Crawford* v. *Marion County Election Board* (2008) and whether litigation designed to soften, or weaken, voter ID laws is the best legal strategy to protect minority voting rights.

Hasen, Richard L. 2018. "The 2016 U.S. Voting Wars: From Bad to Worse." *William and Mary Bill of Rights Journal*, 26: 629–655.
    Investigates the "voting wars" that occurred during the 2016 election and compares them to the scope of frequency of the voting rights litigation that occurred in the 2012 election cycle.

Hayden, Grant M. 2002. "Voting and Political Participation." In Kermit L. Hall, ed., *The Oxford Companion to American Law*. New York: Oxford University Press.
    Essay in a standard reference work that concisely summarizes the history of the expansion and contraction of the franchise.

Hill, Adams Sherman. 1868. "The Chicago Convention." *The North American Review*, Vol. 107 (220): 167–186.
    Essay on the politics and passage of (what became) the Fifteenth Amendment, written during that period.

Hill, David, and Seth McKee. 2005. "The Electoral College, Mobilization, and Turnout in the 2000 Presidential Election." *American Politics Research*, Vol. 33 (5): 700–725.

Empirically tests the impact that the Electoral College has on candidate visits, media buys, and voter turnout.

Holt, Michael F. 1978. *The Political Crisis of the 1850s*. New York: W. W. Norton.
Discusses the factors that gave rise to the Know-Nothing Party, its brief tenure, and its rapid dissolution.

Holt, Michael F. 1999. *The Rise and Fall of the American Whig Party: Jacksonian Politics and the Onset of the Civil War*. New York: Oxford University Press.
A comprehensive account of American politics between the 1820s and 1860.

Holzer, Harold. 1993. *The Lincoln-Douglas Debates: The First Complete, Unexpurgated Text*. New York: Harper Collins.
Reproduction of the transcripts, as reported in the press, of this series of debates, in which Lincoln revealed his views of racial equality and black suffrage.

Howe, Julia Ward, Lucy Stone, Thomas Wentworth Higginson, Elizabeth Cady Stanton, and Wendell Phillips. 1879. "The Other Side of the Woman Question." *The North American Review*, Vol. 129 (276): 413–446.
A point-by-point response to Francis Parkman's critique of women's suffrage.

Johnson, Lyndon B. 1966. *Public Papers of the Presidents of the United States: Lyndon B. Johnson, 1965*. 2 vols. Washington, DC: Government Printing Office.
Papers of the thirty-sixth president of the United States, including documents related to his support for the Voting Rights Act of 1965.

Kellogg, Charles Flint. 1967. *NAACP: A History of the National Association for the Advancement of Colored People, 1909–1920*. Vol. 1. Baltimore, MD: Johns Hopkins Press.

The story of the early years of the National Association for the Advancement of Colored People (NAACP); the intended second volume of this history was never published.

Key, V. O., Jr. 1949. *Southern Politics in State and Nation*. New York: Alfred A. Knopf.
Influential book on southern politics, written prior to the civil rights movement, highlighting the pervasive role of race.

Keyssar, Alexander. 2000. *The Right to Vote: The Contested History of Democracy in the United States*. New York: Basic Books.
The most comprehensive book on the history of voting rights published in the last generation; includes a sixty-three-page appendix of state suffrage laws that provides a factual skeleton of the evolution of the franchise in the United States.

Keyssar, Alexander. 2006. Written Testimony of Alexander Keyssar Submitted to the Subcommittee on the Constitution, Civil Rights, and Property Rights of the Senate Committee on the Judiciary. *Reauthorizing the Voting Rights Act's Temporary Provisions: Policy Perspectives and Views from the Field*. 109th Cong., 2nd sess., 21 June 2006.
Congressional testimony of a voting rights scholar on the necessity and desirability of renewing Section 5 of the Voting Rights Act of 1965, urging the subcommittee to safeguard the right to vote with "great energy and ongoing zeal."

Kimberling, William. 1992. *The Electoral College*. Washington, DC: National Clearinghouse of Election Administration, Federal Election Commission.
A short but incredibly informative history of the development of the Electoral College and its advantages and disadvantages.

King, Anthony. 2012. *The Founding Fathers v. The People: Paradoxes of American Democracy*. Cambridge, MA: Harvard University Press.

> Invites readers to consider how the United States' commitment to democratic principles exists in tension with its federal structure.

Klarman, Michael J. 2004. *From Jim Crow to Civil Rights: The Supreme Court and the Struggle for Racial Equality*. New York: Oxford University Press.

> A comprehensive account of the civil rights movement from the late nineteenth century through the 1960s, including the role of the Supreme Court in the movement.

Kleppner, Paul. 1992. "Defining Citizenship: Immigration and the Struggle for Voting Rights in Antebellum America." In Donald W. Rogers, ed., *Voting and the Spirit of American Democracy: Essays on the History of Voting and Voting Rights in America*. Urbana, IL: University of Illinois Press.

> A chapter on voting rights for immigrants prior to the Civil War.

Kousser, J. Morgan. 1974. *The Shaping of Southern Politics: Suffrage Restriction and the Establishment of the One-Party South*. New Haven, CT: Yale University Press.

> A story of how race-based voting restrictions helped the Democratic Party dominate southern politics in the late nineteenth and early twentieth centuries.

Kousser, J. Morgan. 1984. "Suffrage." In Jack P. Greene, ed., *Encyclopedia of American Political History*. New York: Charles Scribner's Sons, 1236–1258.

> A brief essay on the franchise in a standard reference work.

Kousser, J. Morgan. 1999. *Colorblind Injustice: Minority Voting Rights and the Undoing of the Second Reconstruction*. Chapel Hill, NC: University of North Carolina Press.

Compares the Supreme Court's role in the first Reconstruction (1863–1877) to its role in the second (post–World War II); highly critical of the Court's Equal Protection Clause jurisprudence.

Kousser, J. Morgan. 2008. "The Strange, Ironic Career of Section 5 of the Voting Rights Act, 1965–2007." *Texas Law Review*, Vol. 86: 667–775.
Traces the history of the Voting Rights Act's most controversial provision—Section 5's preclearance requirement—and examines what can be learned from this history in trying to protect minority voting rights.

Kraditor, Aileen. 1981. *Ideas of the Woman Suffrage Movement, 1890–1920*. New York: W. W. Norton.
Explores the ideas and tactics of the second-generation suffragists in the decades preceding the Nineteenth Amendment.

Kreider, Kyle L., and Thomas J. Baldino, eds. 2016. *Minority Voting in the United States*. 2 vols. Santa Barbara, CA: Praeger.
Analyzes the voting behaviors of significant minority voting blocs, including Arab-Americans, Asians, blacks, Filipinos, Jewish-Americans, Latinos, the LGBT community, Muslim-Americans, Native Americans, Pacific Islanders, and women; prescient commentary given anticipated demographic shifts over the next quarter century.

Lane, Charles. 2008. *The Day Freedom Died: The Colfax Massacre, the Supreme Court, and the Betrayal of Reconstruction*. New York: Henry Holt.
An engaging, moment-by-moment retelling of the events that led to the Supreme Court's decision in *United States v. Cruikshank*, which helped shape the Supreme Court's attitude toward civil rights for several generations.

Levine, Bruce. 1992. *Half Slave and Half Free: The Roots of the Civil War*. New York: Hill and Wang.

A succinct look at the issue that precipitated the Civil War.

Levinson, Paul. 1963. *Race, Class, and Party: A History of Negro Suffrage and White Politics in the South*. New York: Russell and Russell.

Examines the role of race (and class) in southern politics in the late nineteenth and early twentieth centuries.

Levitt, Justin. 2007. "The Truth about Voter Fraud." Brennan Center for Justice. https://www.brennancenter.org/our-work/research-reports/truth-about-voter-fraud

An early systematic study of voter fraud claims that argues that voter ID laws will not address the types of irregularities that are considered by many to be voter fraud.

Lichtman, Allen J. 2018. *The Embattled Vote in America: From the Founding to the Present*. Cambridge, MA: Harvard University Press.

Chronicles the history of suffrage restrictions, concluding that voter suppression efforts today are neither new nor surprising.

Lincoln, Abraham. 1953. *The Collected Works of Abraham Lincoln*. 9 vols. Edited by Roy P. Basler. New Brunswick, NJ: Rutgers University Press.

A comprehensive collection of the sixteenth president's correspondences, speeches, and other writings.

Lipsitz, Keena. 2009. "The Consequences of Battleground and Spectator State Residency for Political Participation." *Political Behavior*, Vol. 31 (2): 187–209.

Analyzes participation gaps between battleground and safe-state voters in presidential elections.

Litwack, Leon. 1963. *North of Slavery: The Negro in the Free States, 1790–1860.* Chicago, IL: University of Chicago Press.
A study of the civil rights and social status of free blacks outside of the South from the founding to the Civil War.

Litwack, Leon. 1998. *Trouble in Mind: Black Southerners in the Age of Jim Crow.* New York: Knopf.
A vivid account of life in the Jim Crow South.

Locke, John. [1690] 1960. *Two Treatises of Government.* New York: Cambridge University Press.
Widely read in the American colonies, this work of political philosophy was as influential on the political leaders of the 1770s as any other. The principles found within were cited in the Declaration of Independence as justification for the American Revolution.

Madison, James. 1865. *Letters and Other Writings of James Madison, Fourth President of the United States.* 4 vols. Philadelphia, PA: J. B. Lippincott and Company.
The collected works of the fourth president of the United States.

Madison, James. [1787] 2005. *The Debates in the Federal Convention of 1787: Which Framed the Constitution of the United States.* Edited by Galliard Hunt and James Brown Scott. Clark, NJ: The Lawbook Exchange, Ltd.
Madison's notes on the Constitutional Convention; much of what historians know today about the Convention derives from this meticulous commentary.

Manza, Jeff, Clem Brooks, and Christopher Uggen. 2004. "Public Attitudes toward Felon Disenfranchisement in the United States." *Public Opinion Quarterly*, Vol. 68 (2): 275–286.
Using survey data, investigates Americans' attitudes concerning different types of felon disenfranchisement practices.

Mason, Alpheus Thomas. 1965. *Free Government in the Making: Readings in American Political Thought.* 3rd ed. New York: Oxford University Press.
A classic work on American political thought, including excerpts from suffrage debates from the 1640s to the early 1960s.

Mason, Alpheus Thomas, and Richard H. Leach. 1959. *In Quest of Freedom: American Political Thought and Practice.* Englewood Cliffs, NJ: Prentice-Hall.
A classic work on American political thought, emphasizing the link between property rights and suffrage; includes lengthy excerpts on the subject from the state constitutional conventions of early nineteenth century.

Mayer, Henry. 1998. *All on Fire: William Lloyd Garrison and the Abolition of Slavery.* New York: St. Martin's Press.
A seminal biography of perhaps the most significant abolitionist in American history.

Minnite, Lorraine C. 2010. *The Myth of Voter Fraud.* New York: Cornell University Press.
Investigates empirical reality of voter fraud, the political motivations behind voter fraud claims, as well as the effect that discourse has had on electoral reform.

Morrison, Samuel Eliot. 1965. *The Oxford History of the American People.* New York: Oxford University Press.
An encyclopedic account of American history, from the early seventeenth century to the mid-1960s.

Mycoff, Jason D., Michael W. Wagner, and David C. Wilson. 2009. "The Empirical Effects of Voter ID Laws: Present or Absent?" *PS: Political Science and Politics,* Vol. 42 (1): 121–126.
Studies the effect of voter ID laws on voter turnout at the state and individual level, finding that the burdens of

voter ID laws do not override the interest or motivations for voting.

Nedelsky, Jennifer. 1990. *Private Property and the Limits of American Constitutionalism: The Madisonian Framework and its Legacy*. Chicago, IL: The University of Chicago Press.
    A dense explication of James Madison's views of the importance of private property and its relationship to voting rights.

Oakes, James. 2007. *The Radical and the Republican: Frederick Douglass, Abraham Lincoln, and the Triumph of Antislavery Politics*. New York: W. W. Norton.
    Explores the relationship between the nineteenth-century black statesman (and noted orator) and the sixteenth president of the United States; the former was influential in persuading the latter to support black civil rights and, eventually, black suffrage for some.

Padover, Saul K. 1962. *To Secure These Blessings: The Great Debates of the Constitutional Convention of 1787*. New York: Washington Square Press.
    A topical arrangement of the debates at the Constitutional Convention.

Palast, Greg. 2016. "The GOP's Stealth War against Voters." *Rolling Stone*, August 24, 2016. https://www.rollingstone.com/politics/politics-features/the-gops-stealth-war-against-voters-247905/
    A journalistic investigation into the Interstate Voter Registration Crosscheck Program that states use to purge voter registration rolls.

Parkman, Francis. 1878. "The Failure of Universal Suffrage." *The North American Review*, Vol. 127 (263): 1–20.
    Written by an American historian and nineteenth-century reformer, this brief essay cautions against universal suffrage.

Parkman, Francis. 1879. "The Woman Question." *The North American Review*, Vol. 129 (275): 303–321.

A brief article that succinctly presents the case against women's suffrage; this essay merited a response from five noted suffragists.

Parkman, Francis. 1880. "The Woman Question Again." *The North American Review*, Vol. 130 (278): 16–30.

A response by the noted political reformer to those suffragists who questioned his opposition to voting rights for women.

Parkman, Francis. [1849] 2008. *The Oregon Trail.* New York: Oxford University Press.

A memoir of an historian's westward journey; includes his dehumanizing views on Native Americans, which were later repeated by states to deny the franchise to Native Americans.

Patterson, Thomas E. 2002. *The Vanishing Voter: Public Involvement in an Age of Uncertainty.* New York: Knopf.

Tackles the various reasons for low voter turnout and suggests some ways to increase Americans' interest in electoral politics.

Peterson, Merrill D., ed. 1966. *Democracy, Liberty, and Property: The State Constitutional Conventions of the 1820s.* Indianapolis, IN: Bobbs-Merrill.

A detailed study of the numerous state constitutional conventions in the 1820s, in which people throughout the country debated the links between property and suffrage.

Piott, Steven L. 2003. *Giving Voters a Voice: The Origins of the Initiative and Referendum in America.* Columbia, MO: University of Missouri Press.

Investigates the original purposes of the initiative and referendum, part of the populist movement of the late nineteenth and early twentieth centuries.

Piven, Francis Fox and Richard A. Cloward. 2000. *Why Americans Still Don't Vote, and Why Politicians Want It That Way*. Boston, MA: Beacon Press.

An analysis of voter registration and its implications on elections, politics, and governance; suggests why neither party is particularly interested in serious voter registration reform; written by two advocates for voter registration reform.

"Policy Brief on Voter Identification." 2006. Brennan Center for Justice, 12 September. https://www.brennancenter.org/our-work/research-reports/policy-brief-voter-identification

Analyzes voter ID practices across the states, concluding that their use disproportionately harms racial and ethnic minorities, among other groups, and that voter turnout will decrease as a result.

Porter, Kirk Harold. 1918. *A History of Suffrage in the United States*. Chicago, IL: The University of Chicago Press.

An essential source for understanding suffrage in the colonial and early national periods, especially the importance of property ownership to voting rights; published when most blacks were effectively prevented from voting and two years before the ratification of the Nineteenth Amendment.

"Restricted Voting." 1940. *The New Republic*, Vol. 103 (9): 260.

A quick synthesis of a survey of state restrictions of the franchise in 1940, concluding, "the wonder is that anyone is left to go to the polls."

Rhodes, Jesse H. 2017. *Ballot Blocked: The Political Erosion of the Voting Rights Act*. Stanford, CA: Stanford University Press.

Examines the passage and evolution of the Voting Rights Act of 1965, with particular attention given to the Department of Justice's enforcement and Supreme Court's interpretation at various time periods.

Rogers, Donald W., ed. 1992. *Voting and the Spirit of American Democracy: Essays on the History of Voting and Voting Rights in America*. Urbana, IL: University of Illinois Press.
A collection of essays on voting rights in American history.

Rogers, Michael. 2010. "A Mere Deception—A Mere *Ignis Fatuus* on the People of America: Lifting the Veil on the Electoral College." In Gary Bugh, ed., *Electoral College Reform: Challenges and Possibilities*. Burlington, VT: Ashgate Publishing.
Examines the criticisms of the Electoral College at the Constitutional Convention and in the post-Convention debates. Argues that while the Antifederalists had significant reservations and concerns with the Electoral College, they focused their energy on other provisions of the Constitution.

Scher, Richard K. 2010. *The Politics of Disenfranchisement: Why Is It So Hard to Vote in America?* New York: Routledge.
Examines the myriad ways in which citizens are formally or effectively disenfranchised in the United States.

Schwartz, Bernard. 1980. *The Roots of the Bill of Rights*. New York: Chelsea House.
An informative and readable history of the Bill of Rights, tracing its development from English antecedents through most of the twentieth century.

Schwartz, Bernard. 1983. *Super Chief: Earl Warren and His Supreme Court*. New York: New York University Press.
A biography of the fourteenth chief justice of the United States, including discussions about the Supreme Court's consequential reapportionment revolution.

Seymour, Charles. 2017. *Electoral Reform in England and Wales: The Development and Operation of the Parliamentary Franchise, 1832–1885*. London, England: Forgotten Books.
    A study of the extraordinary transformation in English political conditions during the nineteenth century, summarizing the state of electoral reforms and the democratic developments resulting from them.

Seymour, Charles, and Donald Paige Frary. 1918. *How the World Votes: The Story of Democratic Development in Elections*. 2 vols. Springfield, MA: C. A. Nichols Company.
    Though now dated, a collection of facts concerning the state of the world's progress toward democracy as expressed though the ballot.

Shaw, Daron R. 2006. *The Race to 270: The Electoral College and the Campaign Strategies of 2000 and 2004*. Chicago, IL: University of Chicago Press.
    Examines the state-by-state campaign strategies of presidential candidates.

Stanton, Elizabeth Cady. 1898. *Eighty Years and More: Reminiscences, 1815–1897*. New York: T. Fisher Unwin.
    A memoir of the cofounder and long-time president of the National Woman Suffrage Association (NWSA); and the first president of its successor, the NAWSA.

Stanton, Elizabeth Cady, Susan Brownell Anthony, Matilda Joslyn Gage, and Ida Husted Harper. 1881–1922. *History of Woman Suffrage*. 6 vols. Rochester, NY: Charles Mann.
    More than 5,000 pages of primary documentation about the women's suffrage movement; written by the leaders of the NWSA, its coverage of the rival group, the American Woman Suffrage Association (AWSA), is limited.

Stein, Robert M., Christopher Mann, Charles Stewart, Zachary Birenbaum, Anson Fung, Jed Greenberg, Farhan Kawsar,

et al. 2019. "Waiting to Vote in the 2016 Presidential Election: Evidence from a Multi-County Study." *Political Research Quarterly*. https://doi.org/10.1177/1065912919832374
Investigates the effect of voter ID laws on voting wait times in both white and non-white polling places.

Stephenson, D. Grier, Jr. 1988. "The Supreme Court, The Franchise, and the Fifteenth Amendment: The First Sixty Years." *UMKC Law Review*, Vol. 57: 47–65.
A concise review of the constitutional history of the Fifteenth Amendment from its ratification (1870) through the early 1930s, demonstrating the difficulty of making its protections a reality; the author's 2004 book includes the constitutional history of the Fifteenth Amendment throughout the rest of the twentieth century.

Stephenson, Donald Grier, Jr. 2003. *The Waite Court: Justices, Rulings, and Legacy*. Santa Barbara, CA: ABC-CLIO.
A probing analysis of the important decisions of the Waite Court, including many dealings with the civil rights of blacks.

Stephenson, Donald Grier, Jr. 2004. *The Right to Vote: Rights and Liberties under the Law*. Santa Barbara, CA: ABC-CLIO.
A highly readable account of voting rights in American history; explains well the interplay of the elements, forces, and factors that directed its development.

Stewart, Charles H., III, and Stephen A. Ansolabehere. 2013. "Waiting in Line to Vote." Report, Election Assistance Commission, Washington, DC.
Examines voter wait lines across the states, with recommendations for how states can decrease voting wait times.

Sugrue, Thomas J. 2008. *Sweet Land of Liberty: The Forgotten Struggle for Civil Rights in the North*. New York: Random House.

A broad history of the civil rights movement outside of the Southern United States; one of only a few books that addresses this lesser known chapter in civil rights history.

Sydnor, Charles S. 1962. *American Revolutionaries in the Making: Political Practices in Washington's Virginia.* New York: Collier.

Examines political structures and processes in colonial Virginia; includes material on voting and elections.

Thompson, Dennis F. 2002. *Just Elections: Creating a Fair Electoral Process in the United States.* Chicago, IL: University of Chicago Press.

Discusses the building blocks of fair and just elections— equal respect, free choice, and popular sovereignty; and what can be done to improve the electoral process.

Turner, Frederick Jackson. 1920. *The Frontier in American History.* New York: Henry Holt.

Argues that American democracy was formed not out of the British or revolutionary experiences, but by the American frontier; offered as a partial justification for the expansion of the franchise in the early nineteenth century in Western states.

Uggen, Christopher, Ryan Larson, and Sarah Shannon. 2016. "6 Million Lost Voters: State-Level Estimates of Felon Disenfranchisement, 2016." https://www.sentencingproject.org/publications/6-million-lost-voters-state-level-estimates-felony-disenfranchisement-2016/

A comprehensive report on the felon disenfranchisement laws and the criminal justice system, concluding that approximately 6.1 million Americans are disenfranchised due to felony convictions.

"Voting and Registration in the Election of November 2016." 2017. U.S. Census Bureau.

Official vote and registration data from the 2016 presidential election

Waldman, Michael. 2016. *The Fight to Vote*. New York: Simon and Schuster.
Traces the evolution of voting rights in the United States, from the Constitutional Convention to the early twenty-first century.

Wattenberg, Martin P. 2002. *Where Have All the Voters Gone?* Cambridge, MA: Harvard University Press.
Argues that the weakening of political parties, the rise of candidate-centered politics, and the complexity of elections depresses voter turnout; offers suggestions to make elections more user-friendly.

White, G. Edward. 1982. *Earl Warren: A Public Life*. New York: Oxford University Press.
A judicial biography of the fourteenth chief justice of the United States; important among the Warren Court's decisions were those on racial gerrymandering, congressional and state malapportionment, and the "one person, one vote" principle.

White, Ronald C., Jr. 2009. *A. Lincoln: A Biography*. New York: Random House.
A deeply personal account of the sixteenth president's public life; includes material on Lincoln's views on black and women's suffrage.

Wilentz, Sean. 1992. "Property and Power: Suffrage Reform in the United States, 1787–1860." In Donald W. Rogers, ed., *Voting and the Spirit of American Democracy: Essays on the History of Voting and Voting Rights in America*. Urbana, IL: University of Illinois Press.
Chronicles the demise of property and taxpaying tests for voting in the first half of the eighteenth century.

Williamson, Chilton. 1960. *American Suffrage from Property to Democracy, 1760–1860*. Princeton, NJ: Princeton University Press.

> An exhaustive look at property and taxpaying qualifications for voting in the colonial and early national period.

Woodward, C. Vann. 1957. *The Strange Career of Jim Crow*. New York: Oxford University Press.

> One of the classic works of Southern history; argues that racial segregation was not rooted in American history, but rather a product of the late nineteenth century; Martin Luther King, Jr., proclaimed this book "the historical Bible of the civil rights movement."

Yarbrough, Tinsley E. 2002. *Race and Redistricting: The* Shaw-Cromartie *Cases*. Lawrence, KS: University Press of Kansas.

> Examines the Supreme Court's pronouncements on the majority–minority districting controversies in North Carolina.

Zelden, Charles L. 2002. *Voting Rights on Trial: A Handbook with Cases, Laws, and Documents*. Santa Barbara, CA: ABC-CLIO.

> A survey of voting rights in American history; includes essays, statutes, case excerpts, and other materials on various dimensions of voting rights.

Table of Cases

Abbott v. *Perez*, 585 U.S. ___ (2018)
Baker v. *Carr*, 369 U.S. 186 (1962)
Bradwell v. *Illinois*, 86 U.S. 130 (1873)
Breedlove v. *Suttles*, 302 U.S. 277 (1937)
Brown v. *Board of Education*, 347 U.S. 483 (1954)
The Civil Rights Cases, 109 U.S. 3 (1883)
Colegrove v. *Green*, 328 U.S. 549 (1946)
Crawford v. *Marion County Election Board*, 553 U.S. 181 (2008)

Davis v. *Bandemer*, 478 U.S. 109 (1986)

Davis v. *Beason*, 133 U.S. 333 (1890)

Dred Scott v. *Sandford*, 60 U.S. 393 (1857)

Dunn v. *Blumstein*, 405 U.S. 330 (1972)

Elk v. *Watkins*, 112 U.S. 94 (1884)

Ex parte Yarbrough, 110 U.S. 651 (1884)

Fish v. *Kobach*, 309 F. Supp. 3d 1048 (D. Kansas, June 18, 2018)

Giles v. *Harris*, 189 U.S. 475 (1903)

Gill v. *Whitford*, 585 U.S. ___ (2018)

Gomillion v. *Lightfoot*, 364 U.S. 339 (1960)

Gray v. *Sanders*, 372 U.S. 368 (1963)

Grovey v. *Townsend*, 295 U.S. 45 (1935)

Guinn v. *United States*, 238 U.S. 347 (1915)

Harman v. *Forssenius*, 380 U.S. 528 (1965)

Harper v. *Virginia State Board of Elections*, 383 U.S. 663 (1966)

Hunt v. *Cromartie*, 532 U.S. 234 (2001)

Hunter v. *Underwood*, 471 U.S. 222 (1985)

Husted v. *A. Randolph Institute*, 584 U.S. ___ (2018)

Johnson v. *Governor of Florida*, 405 F.3d 1214 (2003)

Lane v. *Wilson*, 307 U.S. 268 (1939)

Lassiter v. *Northampton County Board of Elections*, 360 U.S. 45 (1959)

Miller v. *Johnson*, 515 U.S. 900 (1995)

Minor v. *Happersett*, 88 U.S. 162 (1875)

Mobile v. *Bolden*, 446 U.S. 55 (1980)

Murphy v. *Ramsey*, 114 U.S. 15 (1885)

Myers v. *Anderson*, 238 U.S. 368 (1915)

Newberry v. *United States*, 256 U.S. 232 (1921)

Nixon v. *Condon*, 286 U.S. 83 (1932)

Nixon v. *Herndon*, 273 U.S. 536 (1927)

Northwest Austin Municipal Utility District No. One v. *Holder*, 557 U.S. 193 (2009)

Oregon v. *Mitchell*, 400 U.S. 112 (1970)

Pope v. *Williams*, 193 U.S. 621 (1904)

Reynolds v. *Sims*, 377 U.S. 533 (1964)

Richardson v. *Ramirez*, 418 U.S. 24 (1974)

Rucho v. *Common Cause*, 588 U.S. ___ (2019)
Schnell v. *Davis*, 336 U.S. 933 (1949)
Shaw v. *Reno*, 509 U.S. 630 (1993)
Shelby County v. *Holder*, 570 U.S. 529 (2013)
Smith v. *Allwright*, 321 U.S. 649 (1944)
South Carolina v. *Katzenbach*, 383 U.S. 301 (1966)
Terry v. *Adams*, 345 U.S. 461 (1953)
United States v. *Classic*, 313 U.S. 299 (1941)
United States v. *Cruikshank*, 92 U.S. 524 (1876)
United States v. *Reese*, 92 U.S. 214 (1876)
Vieth v. *Jubelirer*, 541 U.S. 267 (2004)
Virginia v. *Tennessee*, 148 U.S. 503 (1893)
Wesberry v. *Sanders*, 376 U.S. 1 (1964)
Williams v. *Mississippi*, 170 U.S. 213 (1898)

An Explanatory Note on Legal Citations and Accessing Judicial Decisions

U.S. Supreme Court: Decisions of the U.S. Supreme Court are available in printed form in several publications and widely accessible on the internet.

(1) *United States Reports.* The *official* edition of all decisions of the U.S. Supreme Court is the *United States Reports*, published by the Government Printing Office in permanent bound volumes. Each decision is usually referred to by the names of the petitioner (or appellant) and respondent (or appellee): hence, *Marbury* v. *Madison*. After the name of the case is the volume number in the *U.S. Reports* and the page number on which the case begins, followed by the year of the decision. *Marbury* v. *Madison*, 5 U.S. 137 (1803), thus may be found in volume 5 of the *U.S. Reports* beginning on page 137. When citing a case, it is common practice to provide the full name, citation, and year in the first instance, with all subsequent citations abbreviated. Example: *Marbury* v. *Madison*, 5 U.S. 137 (1803); then

later, simply *Marbury*. (In this book, the full citations do not appear in the text, but are reproduced above.) Early decisions of the Court were identified by the name of the Reporter of Decisions, the official charged with publishing the opinions. So, for example, *Marbury* was originally cited as 1 Cranch 137, William Cranch being the Reporter of Decision. Since 1875, however, the reports have been cited only by the designation "U.S." and all Reporter of Decisions designations have been folded into the *U.S. Reports*. Many college and university libraries have the bound volumes of the *U.S. Reports*.

(2) *United States Supreme Court Reports, Lawyers' Edition.* An *unofficial* reporter of Supreme Court decisions is the *United States Supreme Court Reports, Lawyers' Edition*. Now published by Lexis-Nexis and well in advance of the official reports, these reports include headnotes, case summaries, and annotations. A comparable citation method is employed: *Marbury v. Madison*, 2 L. Ed. 60 (1803) may be found in volume 2 of the *Lawyers' Edition*, beginning on page 60. Decisions since 1956 can be found in a second series, identified as "L. Ed. 2d."

(3) *Supreme Court Reporter.* Another *unofficial* reporter of decisions is the *Supreme Court Reporter*. Similar conceptually to the *Lawyers' Edition*, these reports, published by West, have headnotes and synopses prepared by attorney editors. The *Supreme Court Reporter* employs the standard volume-page citation method, with the designation "S. Ct."

Lower Federal Courts: Decisions of lower federal courts are also available in printed form and are accessible on the internet.

(1) *Federal Reporter:* Since 1880, federal appellate courts have published their opinions in the *Federal Reporter*. "F.," "F.2d," or "F.3d" refers to the *Federal Reporter*, first (or second or third) series, containing decisions by the U.S. courts

of appeals. (Prior to 1880, these decisions were published in *Federal Cases* and abbreviated "Fed. Cas.")

(2) *Federal Supplement*: Since 1932, federal trial courts have published their opinions in the *Federal Supplement*. "F. Supp." or "F. Supp. 2d." refers to the *Federal Supplement*, first (or second) series, which includes decisions of the U.S. district courts. (Prior to 1880, these decisions were published in *Federal Cases*. Between 1880 and 1932, these decisions appeared in the *Federal Reporter*.)

Internet Accessibility: Supreme Court and lower federal court (and state court) decisions are available on the internet.

(1) Westlaw and Lexis-Nexis: The two leaders in online legal research are Westlaw and Lexis-Nexis. Both have proprietary databases that offer legal research service to subscribers, including access to treatises, statutes, codes, cases, public records, law reviews, law journals, and legal forms. As for judicial decisions, Westlaw and Lexis-Nexis have the most comprehensive databases available: Just about every judicial decision in U.S. history can be accessed. Many institutions of higher learning have university subscriptions, thus providing access to their students, faculty, and staff.

(2) Legal Information Institute: The Legal Information Institute (LII) of Cornell Law School (https://www.law.cornell.edu) offers free access to legal research sources online, including decisions of the U.S. Supreme Court since 1990 and more than six hundred pre-1990 decisions. At no charge, interested persons can sign up for LII's bulletins, which provide previews of upcoming cases and timely notification of decisions with links to the opinions.

(3) SCOTUSblog: Short for "Supreme Court of the United States Blog," SCOTUSblog (https://www.scotusblog.com) is an online gathering place for lawyers, law professors, and law students to talk about all things related to the

Supreme Court. The site also tracks cases on the Court's docket, from the petitions for certiorari through the opinions, and provides links to all Court decisions since the October 2007 Term.

(4) The U.S. Supreme Court: The official site (https://www.supremecourt.gov) provides access to the Court's docket, calendar, and (as of December 2019) links to all cases decided since the October 1991 Term. Regular access of this site leads the authors to conclude that links to additional (earlier cases) are slowly forthcoming.

(5) GOVINFO: Short for "Government Information," GOVINFO (https://www.govinfo.gov/app/collection/uscourts), a collaborative effort between the U.S. Government Printing Office (GPO) and the Administrative Office of the United States Courts (AOUSC), provides free public access to opinions from federal district, bankruptcy, and appellate courts. The collection, in a text searchable format, dates back to April 2004.

Other Internet Resources on Voting and Elections

The internet is a remarkable tool for disseminating information, some of which may even be accurate. One must be thus very careful with the internet: Material found on it may or may not be reputable. Regardless, the internet has become a commonly accessed "real-time" source for students and others to gather and evaluate information on voting and elections. The "real-time" aspect is important for voting rights and election laws are constantly changing. Any standard text with factual information about voting rights and election laws has a limited shelf life. That is part of the draw of the internet; it has the capacity to connect the reader with the information with ease and immediacy. That said, readers should proceed with caution, for, especially with the internet, rumor can travel around the globe before truth has its boots on. As Abraham Lincoln once said—at least according to the internet he did—"Just because it is on the internet does not mean that it is true."

The following websites, listed alphabetically, belong to and are maintained by organizations, associations, and agencies—public and private—with an interest in voting or elections. Some have as their primary goal the dissemination of information; they seek to report, explain, and educate citizens about voting or elections, publishing or making available data and documents on these topics. Others seek to persuade the viewer to support or oppose a reform or reforms in these areas. And still others campaign to increase the number of persons who participate in electoral politics, irrespective of partisanship or politics. All universal resource locators (URL) are accurate as of early 2020. Additionally, every state and many county election commissions maintain websites where one can gather information about state or local elections, voter restrictions, and voting procedures and protocols.

ACE Electoral Knowledge Network (https://www.aceproject .org) claims to be the world's largest online community and repository of electoral knowledge, providing comparative data on election-related matters in more than two hundred countries. Founded under the auspices of the United Nations, ACE seeks to foster the integrity of elections and to promote inclusive electoral processes across the globe. Its partner organizations include the Carter Center, the International Institute for Democracy and Electoral Assistance, and the International Foundation for Electoral Systems.

The *American Civil Liberties Union* (ACLU), through its Voting Rights Section (https://www.aclu.org/voting-rights), opposes (and litigates against) attempts to curtail the right to vote; it supports the expansion of same-day and online voter registration.

American National Election Studies (ANES) (https://www .electionstudies.org) strives to provide high-quality data on voting, public opinion, and political participation and to inform explanations of election outcomes.

Ballot Access News (https://www.ballot-access.org) reports on legislative and legal developments about access of candidates and parties to the ballot in the United States and compares that access to access in other democratic nations.

Founded as a project of People for the American Way, the *Ballot Initiative Strategy Center* (BISC) (https://www.ballot .org) supports ballot measures as the most desirable avenue for thwarting

Republican governance and promoting progressive policy change.

Inspired by former associate justice of the U.S. Supreme Court William Brennan's devotion to core democratic principles, the *Brennan Center for Justice* (https://www.brennancenter.org) at the New York University School of Law seeks to ensure that every eligible person can vote, supports independent redistricting commissions, offers a plan to upgrade voting technology to protect election integrity, and recommends small donor public financing in elections to remove the role of big money in political campaigns.

California Clean Money Campaign (http://www.caclean.org) educates citizens on the problems of big money in elections and advocates public funding of political campaigns

Perhaps the world's most well-known elections monitoring organization, the *Carter Center*, (https://www.cartercenter .org), named for former president Jimmy Carter, sends teams of observers to countries to analyze election laws, assess registration procedures, and evaluate voter education, all for the purpose of determining the legitimacy of elections.

The *Center for Public Integrity* (https://www.publicintegrity .org) uses investigative reporting to expose betrayals of the public trust by powerful interest, including the role of money in elections.

The *Center for Responsive Politics* (https://www.opensecrets .org) tracks financial contributions in politics.

The *Coalition for Free and Open Elections* (http://www.cofoe .org) promotes full and fair access to the electoral process.

Often referred to as a "watchdog group," *Common Cause* (https://www.commoncause.org) supports public financing of elections, voter-verified paper audit trails in elections, and a national popular vote for electing presidents; and opposes partisan gerrymandering.

The *Democracy 21 Project* (https://www.democracy21.org) supports stricter campaign finance limits and opposes independent expenditures by corporations in political campaigns.

Demos (https://www.demos.org) advocates making real the promise of American democracy by ensuring that political participation is available and accessible to all regardless of economic or social status and to hold states accountable in court when they subvert voting rights. The organization's research, advocacy, and litigation work seek to reduce the role of money in politics.

The *Early Voting Information Center* (https://blogs.reed.edu /earlyvoting) at Reed College seeks solutions to problems in the administration of elections, which may include the administration of early voting.

This election law blog by Professor Richard Hasen of the University of California, Irvine School of Law (https:// electionlawblog.org), compiles and disseminates information related to campaign finance, redistricting, voting rights, and electoral reform.

Election Data Services (https://www.electiondataservices .com) is a political consulting firm that specializes in redistricting, election administration, and the analysis and presentation of census and political data. The website includes a "2018 Apportionment Study."

The *Election Law Journal* (https://home.liebertpub.com /publications/election-law-journal/101/), published online by Mary Ann Liebert, Inc., covers voting rights, campaign regulations, and elections.

Fair Vote (https://www.fairvote.org) champions electoral reforms at the local, state, and national levels that provide voters with greater choice and a stronger voice. The organization supports advanced ranked-choice voting and multimember legislative districts.

One of the more important official sites related to voting rights and elections is the *Federal Election Commission* (FEC) (https://www.fec.gov). This independent regulatory agency administers and enforces federal campaign finance law, with jurisdiction over all federal elections. This site contains numerous databases on campaign funding, voting, and elections and recommendations for uniform voting system standards.

The *Federal Voting Assistance Program* (https://www.fvap .gov) provides voting information and assistance to U.S. military personnel and their families stationed overseas and to other citizens living abroad.

A nonpartisan educational organization at the University of Southern California, the *Initiative and Referendum Institute* (http://www.iandrinstitute.org) dedicates itself to the study of the two important processes of direct democracy. It collects and distributes information on various aspects of direct democracy, including a state-by-state guide to the initiative and referendum processes.

The *International Republican Institute* (https://www.iri.org) assists citizens in participating in government planning and seeks to increase the role of marginalized groups in the political process. Its online resource center includes election observation assessment reports from around the world.

Through coordinated and integrated programs of litigation, voter protection, advocacy, and education, the Voting Rights Project of the *Lawyers' Committee for Civil Rights under Law* (https://lawyerscommittee.org/project/voting-rights-project/) seeks to ensure that the right to vote is afforded equally to all.

The Voting Rights Section of the *Leadership Conference on Civil Rights* (https://civilrights.org/value/voting-rights/) strives to secure the right to vote and dismantle barriers to the ballot box.

The *League of Women Voters* (https://www.lwv.org) encourages informed participation in electoral politics. Nonpartisan, the League neither supports nor opposes candidates or political parties at any level, but offers voter information on public policy issues.

The oldest and largest civil rights organization in the United States, the *National Association for the Advancement of Colored People* (NAACP) (https://www.naacp.org), has a long history of combating racial discrimination in elections. Its current strategic plan calls for greater protection and enhancement of voting rights and fair representation; and for more blacks to be elected to political office.

The *National Conference of State Legislatures* (NCSL) (https://www.ncsl.org) seeks to support, defend, and strengthen state legislatures. The NCSL's Elections and Campaigns page has extensive resources on election laws and procedures, with links to popular resources on campaign finance and instruments of direct democracy.

With members who are election directors, commissioners, and supervisors from across the country, the *National Association of State Election Directors* (https://www.nased.org) disseminates election administration best practices to those responsible for implementing election laws and practices.

The *National Democratic Institute* (https://www.ndi.org) works to promote transparency and accountability in governments around the globe by, among things, safeguarding elections.

Selma, Alabama—the location of the bloody voter registration march that led to the Voting Rights Act of 1965—is home to the *National Voting Rights Museum and Institute*. Its website (http://www.nvrmi.com) displays a collection of material that honors those who participated in those events. As an institute, the organization seeks to identify, acquire, organize, preserve, and administer records and information of enduring value to remind individuals of the lessons of the long march to suffrage.

Project Vote Smart (https://www.votesmart.org) provides carefully researched data on elected officials at the national, state, and local levels, including biographies, issue positions, voting records, public statements, and campaign funding sources.

"The Informed Voter's Guide to Making Sure Your Vote Counts," published by *Pro Publica* (https://projects .propublica.org/graphics/election-day-voting-guide) identifies the most common issues voters face—from malfunctioning machines to registration purges to ominous tweets about voter fraud—and suggests ways to make sure that none happens to you.

Founded to motivate young people to participate in elections, *Rock the Vote* (https://www.rockthevote.org) provides an amalgamation of voting and election materials, including voter registration information.

The voter registration and voter data—tables, publications, and visualizations—presented by the *U.S. Census Bureau* (https://www.census.gov/topics/public-sector/voting.html) is a treasure trove of historical and current information.

The Civil Rights Division of the *U.S. Department of Justice* (DOJ) (https://www.justice.gov/crt/voting-section) enforces the civil provisions of the federal laws that protect the right to vote, including the Voting Rights Act, the Uniformed and Overseas Citizens Absentee Voting Act, the National Voter Registration Act, the Help America Vote Act, and the Civil Rights Acts.

Established by the Help America Vote Act of 2002, the *U.S. Election Assistance Commission* (EAC) (https://www.eac.gov) recommends voting system guidelines and serves as a national clearinghouse of information on election administration.

Votem (https://www.votem.com) advocates online voting and provides mobile election services to business and government entities. Its founder and chief executive officer, Pete Martin, wrote a perspectives essay in chapter 3 of this book.

Through voter registration campaigns, strategic partnerships, and get-out-the-vote initiative, *Voto Latino* (https://www.votolatino.org) encourages its members to make their voices heard in national, state, and local elections.

Your Vote Matters (https://www.yourvotematters.org) promotes voter education and awareness and participation and facilitates online voter registration. Its website has a section devoted to student engagement in electoral politics.

1430   The English Parliament limits the franchise in elections for the House of Commons to "forty-shilling freeholders."

1619   The first representative assembly in America convenes in Jamestown in the colony of Virginia. Members of its lower house are elected by the free, white, male property-owning inhabitants of the colony.

1647   Following England's first Civil War, debates take place at Putney, England; much of the discussion is about whether suffrage should be limited to property holders.

1715   Connecticut imposes a property qualification for voting.

1734   Delaware limits the franchise to property owners.

1762   Rhode Island establishes a property qualification for voting.

1776   By the eve of the American Revolution, each of the thirteen colonies has a property requirement for voting. Some extend suffrage based on acreage, others on value, and still others on the income the property produces or tax payments.

A citizen exercises his right to vote. To increase voter turnout, many states have adopted alternative methods of voting, including mail-in voting, no excuse absentee ballots, and even online voting. (PhotoDisc, Inc.)

Maryland and North Carolina widen the franchise to freemen (white and free black males) who own property of a certain acreage or value.

Pennsylvania extends suffrage to freemen who meet the one-year residency and taxpaying requirements.

Virginia limits the franchise to white males and adopts a property qualification.

1777   Georgia restricts the franchise to white males who possess property and are liable to pay taxes.

1778   South Carolina confines suffrage to white males who own property or pay taxes.

1780   Massachusetts permits freemen who possess property of a particular income or value to vote.

1781   The Articles of Confederation is ratified. Suffrage under the Articles is exclusively a state prerogative.

1784   New Hampshire adopts a poll tax.

1787   Congress under the Articles of Confederation passes the Northwest Ordinance, which provides for the governance of the Northwest Territory, the land north and west of the Ohio River to the Mississippi River that today includes Ohio, Indiana, Illinois, Michigan, and Wisconsin. In the largest piece of land under federal control, the confederal Congress limits the franchise to citizens and aliens who own fifty acres of land. (The U.S. Congress reaffirms the Ordinance in 1789.)

The Constitutional Convention convenes in Philadelphia, Pennsylvania. After considerable debate, the delegates opt to defer to the states on establishing voter qualifications. The lone reference to voter qualifications in the proposed Constitution is in Article I, Section 2: "The House of Representatives shall be composed of Members chosen by the People of the several States, and the Electors in each State shall have the Qualifications requisite for Electors of the most numerous Branch of the State Legislature." By its neutrality on suffrage, the Convention disarms some who might otherwise have opposed the proposed

Constitution, for in the hands of states alone remains the critical question of who could vote.

1788 The U.S. Constitution is ratified.

1789 Government under the U.S. Constitution begins.

1790 New Jersey clarifies that its constitution, which grants suffrage to "all inhabitants" worth fifty pounds, permits property-owning women to vote. (Because married women cannot own property in New Jersey, however, this right exists only for unmarried women. Married women remain voteless.)

Most states retain a property requirement for voting, although in some property other than real estate suffices. In a few states, tax payment replaces property ownership.

1791 Vermont joins the United States, permitting all free adult white males to vote. No property or taxpaying requirement ever prevails in Vermont, even prior to statehood.

1792 Kentucky enters the union, without a property requirement for voting, but specifically excluding black, mulattoes, and Native Americans from the franchise.

1796 Tennessee becomes the sixteenth state. Though it has a freehold requirement, it exempts free males who are inhabitants of any county in the state for six months.

1800 Only nine of the sixteen states have a property qualification.

The electors for president and vice-president vote in the first disputed presidential election, between John Adams (Federalist) and Thomas Jefferson (Democratic-Republican). Each elector has two votes. The Democratic-Republican electors each cast one vote for Jefferson and one vote for his running mate, Aaron Burr. Because Jefferson and Burr receive the same number of electoral votes, the election is decided in early 1801 by the House of Representatives.

1801 Massachusetts becomes the first state to adopt a voter registration system.

1803 Ohio joins the union, with a taxpaying qualification for voting.

1804 The Twelfth Amendment, adopted in response to the election of 1800, is ratified. Under its terms, presidential electors cast separate ballots for president and vice-president.

1807 New Jersey limits franchise to "free, white male citizens," thus ending a practice, dating back to 1776, that permitted some women to vote.

1810 Maryland abandons its property qualification for voting.

1812 Louisiana, with a taxpaying requirement for voting, becomes the eighteenth state.

The War of 1812 commences. This war stimulates the movement for suffrage extension: Soldiers asked to defend the liberties of others should not themselves be denied the same liberties.

1817 Mississippi earns statehood. After Mississippi's admission, no state enters the union with a property or taxpaying requirement.

1821 New York abolishes its property requirement for whites at a constitutional convention in which Chancellor James Kent and others condemn universal suffrage as dangerous in the extreme.

1829 At a Virginia constitutional convention, Chief Justice of the United States John Marshall calls property requirements a departure from the "fundamental maxims . . . of Republican Government." The conventioners are unpersuaded.

1838 Kentucky permits "school suffrage" to some women. Because of their expertise in rearing children, mothers are allowed to vote in school elections.

1841 Connecticut jettisons its property qualification for voting for native-born males.

1848   The women's rights movement begins in Seneca Falls, New York, with "A Convention to discuss the social, civil, and religious condition and rights of women." The Convention insists that women have "immediate admission" to all the rights and privileges of citizenship, including the right to vote.

1849   The Order of the Star-Spangled Banner is founded in New York. The Order later enters politics as the American Party, but is more commonly known as the "Know-Nothings." This nativist political party was hostile toward immigrants and Catholics and sought to restrict the political power of both groups by championing lengthy residency requirements, tough voter registration laws, and stringent literacy tests. In the 1850s, the Know-Nothings rival the major political parties.

1850   Virginia abandons its property and taxpaying requirements for voting.

1851   Ohio becomes the last state to end taxpaying qualifications for voting.

1855   Michigan grants "school suffrage" to taxpaying women.

1856   North Carolina becomes the last state to discard its property requirement for voting.

1860   By the start of the Civil War, all property and taxpaying qualifications for voting are repealed. Near-universal white male suffrage exists.

1861   Abraham Lincoln becomes the sixteenth president. The Civil War commences. More than 180,000 black soldiers will fight for the Union cause during the four-year war.

The Kansas Territory extends "school suffrage" to women.

1864   Lincoln, in remarks at the battlefield in Gettysburg, Pennsylvania, summons the nation to a "new birth of freedom."

1865   The Civil War concludes. Lincoln is assassinated. Andrew Johnson becomes president. The Thirteenth Amendment abolishes slavery. The task of reconstructing the country begins.

1866   To enforce the Thirteenth Amendment, Congress passes the Civil Rights Act of 1866. It confers citizenship upon individuals born in the United States and criminalizes racial discrimination in contractual rights and rights in the criminal justice system, but it is silent on voting rights.

1868   The Fourteenth Amendment grants citizenship to all persons born or naturalized in the United States and subject to the jurisdiction thereof; prohibits a state from abridging the privileges or immunities of citizens of the United States and denying to any person the equal protection of the law; and threatens to deny equal representation in the House of Representatives to states that refuse suffrage to any of their adult male inhabitants. The amendment does not, however, insist upon black suffrage.

1869   The women's rights movement divides over the proposed Fifteenth Amendment. The American Woman Suffrage Association (AWSA), which supported the amendment, focuses its efforts at the state level. The National Woman Suffrage Association (NWSA), which condemned the amendment as an injustice to women, seeks national reform.

1869   The Wyoming Territory grants full suffrage to women.

1870   The Fifteenth Amendment forbids states from denying the right to vote "on account of race, color, or previous condition of servitude." To implement the amendment, Congress passes the Enforcement Act of 1870, which makes it a federal crime for state officials to discriminate among voters on account of race and for private actors to conspire to hinder any citizen from the exercise and enjoyment of rights and privileges granted by the Constitution.

1873   In *Bradwell* v. *Illinois*, the Supreme Court upholds over a Fourteenth Amendment equal protection challenge, a state law that precludes women from the practice of law.

Susan B. Anthony is fined for casting a ballot in a federal election. She refuses to pay and the judge does not press the issue, thus precluding an appeal.

1875 The Supreme Court upholds a Missouri law that denies the right to vote to women, declaring in *Minor* v. *Happersett* that the Fourteenth Amendment's Equal Protection Clause does not confer the right of suffrage upon anyone.

1876 In two critically important decisions—*United States* v. *Reese* and *United States* v. *Cruikshank*—the Supreme Court narrowly interprets congressional power to enforce the Fourteenth and Fifteenth Amendments, thereby limiting federal authority to protect the civil rights of black citizens.

1877 The "Compromise of 1877" resolves the presidential election of 1876. Rutherford B. Hayes is awarded the contested electoral votes and the presidency, in exchange for his promise to remove federal troops from the South. Reconstruction formally ends.

1884 In upholding the Ku Klux Klan Act of 1871, which criminalizes various forms of voter intimidation, the Supreme Court declares that the Fifteenth Amendment "substantially confer[s] on the negro the right to vote" and grants Congress legislative authority to protect and enforce that right. *Ex parte Yarbrough* is the only case during the nineteenth century in which the justices sustain federal power to punish private obstruction of a citizen's voting rights.

The Supreme Court rules in *Elk* v. *Watkins* that because a Native American was not "subject to the jurisdiction" of the United States at the time of his birth, the Fourteenth Amendment does not confer citizenship upon him and, therefore, his right to vote is not protected by the Fifteenth Amendment.

1885 The Idaho Territory disenfranchises members of the Church of Jesus Christ of the Latter-Day Saints (Mormons) who are active polygamists, advocate polygamy, or belong to any organization that believes in polygamy.

1890   The AWSA and the NWSA merge to form the National American Woman Suffrage Association (NAWSA).

Mississippi adopts a new constitution that imposes poll taxes and literacy tests and excludes individuals for minor criminal offenses.

1900   The Progressive Era formally begins. Frustrated by the "political machines" in Northeastern cities and fearful of what an immigrant class manipulated by those machines might be able to accomplish at the ballot box, Progressives question universal adult male suffrage.

1904   In *Giles* v. *Harris*, the Supreme Court upholds a provision of the Alabama Constitution that in effect requires strict property, literacy, and employment qualifications for voting for blacks but not for whites.

The Supreme Court sustains Maryland's one-year residency requirement for voting in *Pope* v. *Williams*.

1909   The National Association for the Advancement of Colored People (NAACP) is founded in response to anti-black violence. Its first charter lists among the NAACP's goals, "to advance the interests of colored citizens; to secure for them impartial suffrage; and to increase their opportunities for securing justice in the courts, education for their children, employment according to their ability, and complete equality before law."

1913   The Seventeenth Amendment provides for the direct election of U.S. senators. Prior to 1913, senators were chosen by state legislatures.

1915   In *Guinn* v. *United States*, the Supreme Court invalidates Oklahoma's grandfather clause, which effectively allows almost everyone but blacks to avoid a literacy test.

1916   The Democratic and Republican party platforms support women's suffrage, but recognize the right of each state to make this determination. Neither party backs a constitutional amendment.

1917   The United States enters World War I. Women contribute to the war effort in unprecedented ways.

New York becomes the first state east of the Mississippi River to fully enfranchise women.

1920   The largest mass movement for suffrage in the nation's history concludes with ratification of the Nineteenth Amendment, which forbids states from denying voting rights on account of sex. More than eight million women cast ballots in November.

1921   The Supreme Court declares in *Newberry* v. *United States* that primaries are exempt from the Fifteenth Amendment's prohibition on racial discrimination.

1924   The Indian Citizenship Act confers citizenship upon Native Americans born in the United States. The intent of the law is to grant suffrage to Native Americans who were denied the right to vote by states because they were not citizens.

1927   In *Nixon* v. *Herndon*, the Supreme Court strikes down a Texas law that precludes blacks from voting in the Democratic primary.

1932   The Supreme Court decision in *Nixon* v. *Condon* invalidates the Texas Democratic Party's rule against blacks voting in primaries because the party's authority to adopt such a rule stemmed from power conferred upon it by the state legislature.

1935   *Grovey* v. *Townsend* upholds the Texas Democratic Party's decision, adopted in the absence of any state legislation, to limit participation in primaries to white citizens. The Supreme Court reasons that the Democratic Party is a private actor and, therefore, not bound by the Fourteenth and Fifteenth Amendments.

1937   The Supreme Court sustains a Georgia poll tax in *Breedlove* v. *Suttles*.

1939   The Supreme Court in *Lane* v. *Wilson* declares unconstitutional an Oklahoma law that institutes a twelve-day window for disenfranchised blacks to register to vote and effectuates a lifetime ban from voting on those who fail to register during that window.

1941   In *United States* v. *Classic*, the Supreme Court holds that primaries are an integral part of elections, effectively allowing Congress to regulate primaries.

1942   The Soldiers Voting Act guarantees voting rights to American military personnel stationed overseas in a time of war in federal elections and provides the means for them to do so.

1944   The Supreme Court, in *Smith* v. *Allwright*, invalidates the white primary, however adopted.

1945   Georgia sets its minimum voting age at eighteen.

1953   The Supreme Court invalidates a "white preprimary" to the Democratic Party primary in *Terry* v. *Adams*.

1957   The Civil Rights Act of 1957, the first broadly gauged Civil Rights Act since Reconstruction, creates a Civil Rights Commission within the Department of Justice (DOJ) and authorizes the DOJ to intervene on behalf of persons denied the right to vote based on race.

1959   In *Lassiter* v. *Northampton County Board of Elections*, the Supreme Court upholds a North Carolina literacy test that applies to all persons seeking to vote.

1960   The Civil Rights Act of 1960 strengthens the federal government's authority to protect the civil rights of blacks. The Act institutes judicial review of voting interference claims and gives judges the authority to appoint "voting referees" to voting district where voter intimidation occurs.

In *Gomillion* v. *Lightfoot*, the Supreme Court finds a Fifteenth Amendment violation in the redrawing of the boundaries of the city of Tuskegee such that virtually all blacks are outside the city limits.

1961   The Twenty-Third Amendment gives citizens of the District of Columbia the right to vote in presidential elections.

1962   The Supreme Court, in *Baker* v. *Carr*, authorizes federal courts to decide Fourteenth Amendment's Equal Protection Clause challenges to claims of malapportionment.

1963   In *Gray* v. *Sanders*, the Supreme Court announces the "one person, one vote" standard.

1964   The Twenty-Fourth Amendment bans poll taxes as a prerequisite to voting in all federal elections.

The Civil Rights Act of 1964 prohibits discriminatory practices in federal elections by requiring states to apply the same standards and rules in determining the eligibility of a person to vote, regardless of race and sex.

1965   The Voting Rights Act (VRA) authorizes federal examiners to register voters in any jurisdiction where the attorney general deems that it is necessary to enforce the Fifteenth Amendment; outlaws any "voting qualification or prerequisite to voting" that denies the right to vote based on race, including literacy tests, tests for educational achievement and understanding, and proofs of good moral character; and requires that states and localities with histories of racial discrimination obtain approval (or "preclearance") from the U.S. attorney general or a federal court prior to any changes to voting laws taking effect.

Calling suffrage a fundamental right, the Supreme Court declares poll taxes unconstitutional in all elections in *Harper* v. *Virginia School Board of Elections*.

1966   Over a Tenth Amendment challenge, the Supreme Court upholds the constitutionality of the VRA in *South Carolina* v. *Katzenbach*.

1970   Congress renews the VRA, which sets a minimum age of eighteen for voting in federal and state elections.

The Supreme Court decision in *Oregon* v. *Mitchell* strikes down Congress's attempt to lower the voting age in state elections.

1971   The Twenty-Sixth Amendment lowers the voting age to eighteen for federal and state elections.

1972   In *Dunn* v. *Blumstein*, the Supreme Court declares a Tennessee law unconstitutional that requires persons to reside in the state for one year and the county for three months before becoming eligible to vote.

1974   The Supreme Court upholds a California law that prohibits ex-felons from registering to vote in *Richardson* v. *Ramirez*.

1975   Congress renews the VRA, extending its provisions and making permanent the ban on literacy tests.

1982   Congress renews the VRA for twenty-five years, while making clear that the statute bans any voting or election rule or practice that results in a denial or restriction on suffrage.

1984   The Voting Accessibility for the Elderly and Handicapped Act, the first federal law focused exclusively on the voting problems experienced by older and disabled citizens, requires that polling places in federal elections be accessible for elderly and disabled citizens.

1986   The Supreme Court declares partisan gerrymandering to be justiciable under the Fourteenth Amendment's Equal Protection Clause in *Davis* v. *Bandemer*.

The Uniformed and Overseas Citizens Absentee Voting Act (UOCAVA) creates a national, uniform law to govern Americans who are stationed or living abroad who want to vote absentee.

1993   The National Voter Registration Act (NVRA), also known as the "Motor Voter" law, eases the registration process by making forms and assistance more widely available, specifically when and where people register their cars, at welfare agencies, and by mail. The Act also governs when states can purge voters from the rolls.

The Supreme Court decision in *Shaw* v. *Reno* announces that the Fourteenth Amendment's Equal Protection Clause forbids racial gerrymandering unless the government demonstrates a "compelling interest" for creating majority-minority districts.

1995 In *Miller* v. *Johnson*, the Supreme Court invalidates a congressional districting plan in which race is the predominant factor.

2001 The Supreme Court in *Hunt* v. *Cromartie* upholds a majority-minority congressional districting plan because there is substantial evidence that the legislature is motivated primarily by political behavior and not race.

2002 The Help America Vote Act (HAVA) mandates that every state create a unified voter registration list and replace outdated voting technology; and provides federal funds to assist states in revamping their voting systems.

2005 The Supreme Court renders partisan gerrymandering claims nonjusticiable, at least in the absence of a judicially enforceable standard, in *Vieth* v. *Jubelirer*.

2008 In *Crawford* v. *Marion County Election Board*, the Supreme Court upholds Indian's voter ID law.

2013 In *Shelby County* v. *Holder*, the Supreme Court strikes down Section 4 of the VRA, which specifies a formula for singling out certain states and counties for pre-clearance review by the DOJ under Section 5, noting that the conditions that originally justified the "coverage formula" adopted in 1965 no longer characterize voting in the covered jurisdictions.

2018 The Supreme Court sustains Ohio's practice of purging registered voters in *Husted* v. *A. Philip Randolph Institute*.

2019 After noting that partisan gerrymandering may be incompatible with democratic principles, the Supreme Court, in *Rucho* v. *Common Cause*, rules that such claims present political questions "beyond the reach" of federal courts. The majority makes clear that Congress and states may prevent partisan gerrymandering.

Alien Declarant Noncitizen who has formally declared intent to seek citizenship; in the mid-nineteenth century, a number of states and territories permitted alien declarants to vote.

Apportionment Process of allotting congressional seats to each state.

Apportionment Act Federal law from 1842 requiring that members of the House of Representatives be chosen from single-member districts.

Articles of Confederation Governing document of the Confederate states between 1781 and 1789; under the Articles, voting rights was exclusively a state prerogative.

Automatic Voter Registration State system that registers eligible voters whenever they interact with government agencies.

Caucus Closed-door meeting of political party chieftains, common in the nineteenth century, in which a political party selects its candidates for office.

Civil Right Privilege conferred selectively upon citizens and others by government; voting is commonly referred to as a civil right.

Constitutional Convention Gathering of delegates assembled in Philadelphia in 1787 that drafted what became the U.S. Constitution.

Declaration of Sentiments   Document adopted in 1848 by the first women's rights convention in Seneca Falls, New York, requesting "immediate admission" for women to the rights and privileges of citizenship.

Early Voting   Permitting voters to cast ballots in advance of election day; typical methods include voting by mail, in-person early voting, and absentee voting.

Electoral College   Body of electors that formally elects the president and vice-president.

Electorate   Individuals who are entitled to vote.

Felon Disenfranchisement   Common state practice of disqualifying those with felony convictions from voting.

Fifteenth Amendment   Provision of the U.S. Constitution prohibiting the United States or any state from denying the right to vote to citizens "on account of race, color, or previous condition of servitude"; adopted in 1870.

Fourteenth Amendment   Provision of the U.S. Constitution that, among other limitations, prevents a state from denying to any person within its jurisdiction the "equal protection of the laws"; adopted in 1868.

Franchise   The right to vote; to be enfranchised is to be authorized to vote; to be disenfranchised is to be deprived of that right.

Freeholder   One who owns real property, free of debt; in 1430, Parliament limited the franchise to "forty-shilling freeholders," those persons who owned property worth forty shillings a year in rental value or income.

Gender Gap   Difference between men and women in voter turnout.

General Election   Electoral contest to select officeholders.

Gerrymandering   Drawing legislative districts to benefit or harm a party, group, or incumbent.

Get-Out-The-Vote (GOTV) Drive Effort of governments, parties, or candidates to increase voter turnout.

"Good Character" Clause State law exempting individuals from voting requirements if they could get a local official to certify their good character; adopted in some Southern states after Reconstruction to keep blacks from voting.

Grandfather Clause State law excusing individuals from certain voting requirements if they or their ancestors had been eligible to vote prior to a certain date; common in Southern states after Reconstruction as a means to prevent blacks from voting.

Help America Vote Act Federal law mandating that states create a unified voter registration list and replace outdated voting technology; the 2002 law also created the Election Assistance Commission as a resource for states in administering elections.

Initiative Procedure that allows citizens to bypass the legislative process by placing proposed laws or constitutional amendments on the ballot for voters to support or oppose.

Jim Crow Laws Laws prevalent in the South requiring public accommodations and facilities to be segregated by race.

Literacy Test State-imposed reading and comprehension requirement as a precondition to voting; used to keep blacks, immigrants, and others from voting.

Mail-In Voting State practice of allowing ballots to be submitted by U.S. mail; also known as "postal voting."

Majority-Minority District Congressional or state legislative district composed of less than 50 percent non-Hispanic whites.

Mid-term Election Election that takes place halfway through a presidential four-year term; always includes congressional, and usually state and local, races.

Multimember District   Electoral district that sends two or more members to a legislative chamber; disallowed for congressional elections by the Apportionment Act of 1842.

National Voter Registration Act   Federal law from 1993 requiring states to register voters in federal elections at public agencies, though the U.S. mail, and by attaching voter registration forms to driver's license applications; also known as "Motor Voter" Law.

Nineteenth Amendment   Provision of the U.S. Constitution prohibiting the United States and any state from denying to right to vote to citizens "on account of sex"; adopted in 1920.

"One Person, One Vote"   Principle adopted by the Supreme Court that as nearly as practicable, one person's vote in a congressional or state legislative district is to be worth as much as another's.

Online Voting   Voting via a mobile device or computer.

Partisan Gerrymandering   Drawing legislative districts to advantage or disadvantage a particular party.

Pauperage Restriction   State law disenfranchising those who receive public aid or live in poorhouses, poor asylums, or charitable institutions.

Political Machine   Urban organization popular in the late nineteenth and early twentieth centuries providing political favors to its followers in exchange for electoral support.

Poll Tax   State-imposed tax on the privilege of voting; used regularly in the South after the Civil War to keep blacks from voting.

Primary Election   Electoral contest to select a party's candidate for the general election.

Property Restriction   State law common in the early national period limiting the franchise to those who owned property.

Proportional Representation   Electoral system in which political parties earn legislative seats in proportion to its percentage of the total vote; only possible with multimember district.

Putney Debates Grand debate held at Putney (near London) in 1647; much of the debate centered around whether suffrage should be limited to property holders.

Racial Gerrymandering Drawing legislative districts to advantage or disadvantage a particular race or ethnicity.

Reapportionment Revolution Term used to describe a series of Supreme Court decisions in the 1960s that resulted in congressional and state legislative districts being relatively equal in population.

Recall Election Procedure available in some states allowing voters to remove an elected official prior to the conclusion of his or her term.

Reconstruction Amendments The Thirteenth, Fourteenth, and Fifteenth Amendments, adopted between 1865 and 1870.

Redistricting Process of redrawing congressional or state legislative district lines; typically happens every ten years after the national census.

Referendum Procedure permitting citizens to hold a popular vote on laws or constitutional amendments passed by legislatures.

Religious Test State law limiting the franchise to those who professed a particular religion.

Residency Requirement State law requiring would-be voters to reside in the state for a specified period of time before becoming eligible to vote.

Runoff Election "Second-round" election between the top two candidates from the first round; required in some states when one candidate does not obtain a majority of the votes in the first round.

Same-Day Registration Option in some states to register at the polling place on the day, rather than in advance, of the election.

Selma-to-Montgomery March Voter registration march between two Alabama cities in 1965; provoked a violent reaction by local police, the televised spectacle of which led to the Voting Rights Act of 1965.

Seventeenth Amendment   Provision of the U.S. Constitution providing for the direct election of U.S. senators; prior to its adoption in 1913, senators were elected by state legislatures.

Single-Member District   Electoral district that sends only one member to the legislative chamber.

Suffrage   The right to vote.

Suffragettes   The female advocates of the right to vote for women; most notable are Lucretia Mott, Elizabeth Cady Stanton, Lucy Stone, Susan B. Anthony, and Carrie Chapman Catt.

Taxpayer Restriction   State law limiting the franchise to those who paid taxes; common in the middle of the nineteenth century.

Twenty-Fourth Amendment   Provision of the U.S. Constitution abolishing the use of poll or other taxes in federal elections; adopted in 1964.

Twenty-Sixth Amendment   Provision of the U.S. Constitution prohibiting the United States or any state from denying to any citizen, eighteen years of age or older, the right to vote "on account of age"; adopted in 1971.

Twenty-Third Amendment   Provision of the U.S. Constitution conferring upon the District of Columbia the number of electoral votes it would be entitled if it were a state, but not exceeding those allocated to the smallest state; adopted in 1961.

U.S. Constitution   Document that has governed the United States since 1789.

U.S. Department of Justice   Cabinet-level executive department responsible for the implementation of federal laws, including voting rights laws.

Voter ID Law   Requirement in some states that prospective voters show positive identification to election officials prior to casting a ballot.

Voter Registration   State law mandating that would-be voters register to vote prior to voting, thus making the act of voting a two-step process.

Voter Roll Purging   Removal of registered voters from the list of eligible voters, often done under the auspices of preventing voter fraud.

Voter Turnout   Percentage of eligible persons who vote in any given election.

Voting Rights Act   Single most important voting law in American history, prohibiting any "voting qualification or prerequisite to voting" that denied the right to vote based on race; passed in 1965.

"White Primary"   Southern practice between 1870 and 1944 of restricting participation in the Democratic primary to whites.

Winner-Take-All System   Electoral system in which the candidate with the most votes wins the election; in the Electoral College, this means that presidential and vice-presidential candidates who win the most popular votes in a state receive all of that state's electoral votes.

Index

Page numbers followed by *t* indicate tables and *f* indicate figures.

About the Authors

Richard A. Glenn (PhD, University of Tennessee, 1995) is professor of government and political affairs at Millersville University. He is the author of *The Right to Privacy* (ABC-CLIO, 2003) and *Unreasonable Searches and Seizures* (ABC-CLIO, 2006) and numerous articles, chapters, essays, and reviews appearing in many journals, books, and other publications on a variety of U.S. political subjects. He lives with his wife, Lorena, and their sons, Ryan and Andrew, in Lancaster, Pennsylvania.

Kyle L. Kreider (PhD, Temple University, 2004) is professor of political science at Wilkes University. With Thomas J. Baldino, he has coauthored *Of the People, by the People, for the People: A Documentary Record of Voting Rights and Electoral Reform* (Greenwood, 2010) and *U.S. Election Campaigns: A Documentary and Reference Guide* (Greenwood, 2011) and coedited *Minority Voting in the United States* (Praeger, 2016). He lives with his wife, Susanne, and their children, Kathryn and Ben, in Mountain Top, Pennsylvania.